Though it was never designed to accommodate musical performance, the Crystal Palace at Sydenham (which was opened in 1854 and was an enlarged rebuilding of the famous glass and iron structure first erected in Hyde Park for the Great Exhibition of 1851) quickly established itself as the most important single location for public music-making in the United Kingdom. For almost fifty years the orchestral concerts conducted by August Manns provided weekly performances which set new standards and introduced a range of new repertory (not least British) unparalleled anywhere in its time. The giant choral festivals offered performers and listeners a musical experience of an entirely new kind, as well as opening up the choral literature (especially of Handel) to vast new audiences. Numerous other activities served a range of musical, social and educational functions well into the twentieth century, which the unique physical context of the Palace itself often helped to shape.

Since its spectacular destruction by fire in 1936, the once familiar patterns of music-making have been long forgotten. This is the first book to reconstruct the musical history of the Crystal Palace. In doing so, Michael Musgrave also offers a unique survey of British musical life stretching from the Victorian period to the eve of the Second World War. Fully illustrated and with valuable catalogues of performers and repertory, the book will be of interest to students and scholars of nineteenth- and twentieth-century music, British social history and architecture, as well as to the general music enthusiast.

THE MUSICAL LIFE OF THE CRYSTAL PALACE

THE MUSICAL LIFE
OF THE
CRYSTAL PALACE

MICHAEL MUSGRAVE

CAMBRIDGE
UNIVERSITY PRESS

Published by the Press Syndicate of the University of Cambridge
The Pitt Building, Trumpington Street, Cambridge CB2 IRP
40 West 20th Street, New York, NY 10011–4211, USA
10 Stamford Road, Oakleigh, Melbourne 3166, Australia

First published 1995

Printed in Great Britain at the University Press, Cambridge

A catalogue record for this book is available from the British Library

Library of Congress cataloguing in publication data
Musgrave, Michael.
The musical life of the Crystal Palace / Michael Musgrave.
p.   cm.
Includes bibliographical references and index.
ISBN 0 521 37562 2 (hardback)
1. Music – England – London –19th century – History and criticism.
2. Music – England – London – 20th century – History and criticism.
3. Crystal Palace (London, England)   I. Title.
ML286.8.L5M87   1995
780.78′42163 – dc20   93–49053 CIP MN

ISBN 0 521 37562 2 hardback

CE

For Liza

Contents

Illustrations

Preface

I first became interested in the music of the Crystal Palace whilst researching the first performances of Brahms's orchestral music in England: I had no idea of the true extent of its importance. I soon discovered that Brahms formed only a very small part of its musical story: that a considerable slice of what was soon to be regarded as the standard orchestral repertory had first been heard in Britain at the Crystal Palace. And when reading the programmes to find out more, a whole world of music-making of all kinds, decade on decade, began to emerge. Moreover, the literature concerning the musicians of the later nineteenth century revealed that, for them, the Crystal Palace was one of the central venues: they all knew its musical life intimately and looked to it for a musical lead, and more than musicians, the lives of countless people were touched by the role of music in other public contexts over the eighty years or so of its existence from 1854–1936. Yet none of this accorded with the status given the music of the Palace in the modern historical literature: apart from a few brief dictionary entries, it was for the modern reader a non-subject. Thus the reconstruction of the musical life as a whole became an imperative: not just the music performed, but how it came to be performed in this extraordinary building which so captured the Victorian imagination, though it had never been designed for music. Hence the scope and character of the present book. No such study can ever be wholly comprehensive, since it rests on the blessing and the curse of all work of the kind: the availability and non-availability of programmes in providing the essential detail of what took place or was planned to take place. Crystal Palace programmes are never to be found in complete runs of more than a few years without significant omissions, and the programmes for the early years are very rare indeed. Of several projects which have

xiii

emerged from this work, the provision of a union catalogue of sources in different libraries is one of the most pressing.

The importance of the programmes signals my special debt of gratitude to three libraries which have been particularly helpful to my work: to the staff of the Library and of the Portraits Gallery of the Royal College of Music, for access to their unique holdings in this period of British music and for their response to numerous enquiries; to the staff of the Music Library of the British Library, who kept their extensive runs of programmes on what seemed like permanent standby for me for months on end; and to the Local History Library of Bromley Central Library. Other libraries I have consulted have included the University of London Library; Goldsmith's College Library; the Bodleian Library, Oxford; the Local History Library of Lewisham; West Norwood Library; Lower Norwood Library; Upper Norwood Library; the Local History Library of Croydon; the Greater London Record Office; the Public Record Office; the Guildhall Library; the Minet Library, Lambeth; the Coke Collection; the Heritage Centre of the Salvation Army. I acknowledge the permission of the following libraries to reproduce illustrations from materials in their collections; the Guildhall Library (Nos. 1, 3, 4, 5, 6, 8, 9, 12, 18, 19); the Portraits Gallery of the Royal College of Music (Nos. 13, 15), the British Architectural Library, RIBA, London (No. 2), the Local History Library of Bromley Library (No. 20); the Salvation Army (No. 21); the Greater London Record Office (Nos. 8, 19). I am grateful for the supportive interest of many friends. I particularly wish to acknowledge the benefit of conversations with Professor Cyril Ehrlich, who freely shared his unique understanding of the period with me. Quotations from *Shaw's Music* are by permission of the Society of Authors on behalf of the Bernard Shaw Estate. Finally I wish to thank Miss Mary Cullwick to whom I was introduced through Celia Clarke of the Royal College of Music Library, and who has a special connection with the Palace as a close friend of many years standing of Louise Bonten, the granddaughter of August Manns: not only did Miss Cullwick provide me with some valuable materials, but above all with a real sense of a continuity from the great days of the Palace down to my own attempts to capture something of its achievements. I am only sorry that it has taken so long for her to see the results.

Michael Musgrave
London

PART I

The beginnings

Introduction

There are many Londoners who still vividly recall the night of 30 November 1936: the night the Crystal Palace burnt down. The destruction of such a familiar landmark could hardly go unnoticed. Strategically placed on the Sydenham Hills in South London, it was inevitable that any fire would be quickly visible to inner London or the southern suburbs and countryside beyond, over which it commanded alike superb views. There had been disasters before[1]: the supervision of such a vast building, vulnerable in its contents and power systems, quite apart from its exposed position, was almost impossible; but this time, aided by the fanning effect of a strong wind, the outcome was finally to prove fatal. Coming as it did in a period of international and domestic upheaval – with ominous developments in mainland Europe and constitutional crisis at home – the disappearance of such a famous building was widely interpreted as portending some kind of disaster. 'This is the end of an age'[2] was the pointed comment of Winston Churchill when he stopped to survey the scene en route for his home at Westerham from Westminster: and so it was. Within three years Britain would be involved in a War which would finally signal its imperial decline, the Palace site be requisitioned by the government, and its famous water towers razed to the ground to discourage German bombers. Yet throughout the post-war rebuilding of London, which included the creation of an international athletics stadium in the grounds, characteristic remnants of the site and landscape have remained stubbornly resistant to change, as though to remind new generations of what was once there.[3] For at its founding, the 'Crystal Palace'[4] at Sydenham, like its previous incarnation as the building for the Great Exhibition of 1851 in Hyde Park, was widely regarded as the greatest single symbol of Victorian technical prowess and cultural expression. Through the events that took place there we

3

observe the opening up of a whole new world of knowledge and experience to vast new audiences. And in its decline, when the spheres of activity associated with it had shifted away to better-situated and purpose-built venues, the Palace continued, if fitfully, to host important events and provide a home for unusual activities: there seems, for example, something wholly appropriate in its having been the home of Baird's early experiments with television up to the time of the fire, bringing the original spirit of the place right into the modern age.[5]

Nostalgia for such an extraordinary building certainly has its place – not least in a district of London that still retains so many vistas of its elegant past. But there is a more important reality to be sought behind the romance, here in connection with one of the Palace's greatest preoccupations, the subject of this book: to give proper acknowledgement to the vital role of the Crystal Palace in the unfolding of British musical life in the second half of the nine-teenth century and beyond, activities which (as well as reflecting Victorian society in its high period) left indelible marks on the infinitely richer musical world of the twentieth century. Though the Palace has retained a tentative musical association through passing reference to the works first performed there, the broader context of its musical life, to say nothing of cultural life more broadly defined, has never been presented. There are obvious explanations of this. The Palace was never built for any one role alone, beyond its first permanent exhibitions, but as an enabling location, designed to be filled with temporary exhibits and to host events, rather than to serve any larger institutional function. Most of the events came through outside organizations, and their activities have to be traced as much through reference to their own backgrounds as to their role at the Palace; moreover, any (presumably extensive) records which would have given a more consistent internal view of its affairs were apparently destroyed in the fire.[6] Nor should it be forgotten that the Palace as a place of recreation was so well known to generations of visitors, that, after the publications that accompanied the opening in 1854, the innumerable details of its daily life were taken for granted and the many subsequent internal structural changes and additions never systematically recorded. The record of the music-making is profoundly influenced by these considerations, given its remarkable range – from symphonic music of the highest quality to popular religious or competitive festivals with vast numbers of participants. And seen in historical perspective – for in the middle of the nineteenth century, public concerts such as we understand them today hardly existed – it takes on a special significance in showing the creation of a public venue: the way in which the vast new building attracted, influenced and was in turn influenced by, the music-making that found a place there.

In the present age, which offers at the press of a button access to cultural materials that only slowly became available through the nineteenth century (even to the better placed of the populace), it is difficult to overestimate the focal status the Palace quickly assumed. But it is equally difficult to characterize its achievement: whether in the simple physical sense of comparing its concert and educational provision with that of the modern London cultural complexes of the South Bank or the Barbican Centre, or the more elusive sense of adjudging what was a response to emerging musical needs, or a stimulus to them. Its achievements are better sensed in the record of the various activities as they appeared and developed, thus illuminating the individual nature as well as the generality of the achievement. This approach inevitably divides the musical history into two parts: roughly the first fifty years from the opening in 1854 to the turn of the century, and the remaining period. The first fifty years saw the heyday of the Palace's 'quality' music-making, especially of choral and orchestral music, and, consequently, of its social status. Later observers always stressed the dramatic change in the character of the building as between the beginning of these eras: the brilliance, colour and elegance of the new building and its grounds, and the run-down state it had reached towards the First World War, when plans were laid for its radical restoration.[7] But though its role had changed irrevocably, it continued to occupy a special position in musical life, which is a necessary part of its story. Changed as it became, it never really had a rival, though the building of an analogous structure on a hill position in North London, named Alexandra Palace, paralleled its functions in a limited way.[8]

The special character of the building provides the natural starting point, as it did for its first musical users, as they explored the vast potential and also the attendant problems of the building. The first musical interaction was with choral activity, leading to the massive Handel Festivals. In total contrast to the ethos of these meetings was the specialist orchestral tradition which was carefully nurtured by the pioneering August Manns and George Grove; many more

popular kinds of concerts provide links of various kinds between
these two most famous activities. Developing later were the great
celebratory festivals of the movements for educational and social
reform, and imperial assertion, which moved confidently into the
twentieth century, though rapidly changing character after the
War. And apart from these great public events, there also existed the
quieter, daily educational provision which gave added focus to the
building as a cultural centre.

The musical life of the Crystal Palace touches on every aspect of
British music during its period, both in the types of music performed
and the kinds of issues emerging from them: issues of repertory,
performance, reception and the sociology of music. Any one would
be the subject of an individual study in relation to the music of the
Palace alone. The aim of the present book is necessarily more
general, in offering a reconstruction of the musical life which can
give perspective not only on these factors, but on the broader
emergence of music as a public activity, so as to do justice to the
remarkable achievements of the Palace and those of the individuals
associated with it. But the story begins before the Palace at Sydenham, in the origins of the very first conception of the building of a
'Crystal Palace' in Hyde Park.

CHAPTER I

The Crystal Palace at Hyde Park

The idea of a British Exhibition of National Design and Manufacture went back to 27 June 1849, when Prince Albert, president of the Royal Society of Arts since 1847, met with Henry Cole, Assistant Keeper of the Public Record Office and active member of the Society.[1] Cole had long been involved in imaginative public ventures and had already worked with the Consort on exhibitions of 'Art Manufacture' held in London in successive years from 1847 to 1849; the growing popularity of these exhibitions, which expanded from a mere 20,000 visitors in the first year to 100,000 in the third, naturally led Cole to suggest a more all-encompassing event, and his familiarity with exhibitions already well established in Paris was an important stimulus in planning for 1851. Its aim was to be the display to the public of examples of scientific and industrial achievement, inventions and works of art, not merely of British but also of international origin. But this splendid goal was by no means without opposition as the potential scale of the project began to sink in to public consciousness. The offer by the government of rooms in Somerset House had caused no stir; but once the inadequacy of this provision for the vast number of exhibits expected became apparent and suggestions were made for a special centre in Hyde Park, the columns of *The Times* began to picture a kind of disorder the like of which London had never seen before. Although Parliament eventually approved the scheme in July 1850, valuable time had been wasted and none of the 245 plans submitted for competition to design the exhibition building was thought worthy of implementation by the Executive Committee appointed by the Royal Commission, chaired by the engineer Robert Stephenson. When they published their own design, public reaction was harsh: the building was seen as not only too ugly, but, crucially, too solid to be taken down and leave no scar when, in a matter of only a few months, the Exhibition was over.[2]

The omens were that the plan would come to nothing when, on 6 July 1850, a spectacularly different design appeared in the *Illustrated London News*. It was by Joseph Paxton,[3] head gardener at the Duke of Devonshire's home, Chatsworth House, since 1826 and an expert on greenhouses, one of which, the Great Conservatory built in 1836–40, was the biggest in the world. But it was a much smaller example, that designed to house the giant water lily 'Victoria Regia' and enable it to grow to its full size, which offered the model for the Hyde Park scheme. While very strong from its iron and glass construction, the new design had a lightness and delicacy of appearance which completely captured the public imagination and which – as Paxton had obviously intended – more or less coerced the committee to the view that, at the last hour, this was the answer to their problems. Despite lingering opposition elsewhere, they decided on 15 July 1850 to abandon their existing plans with a mere nine months to go before the preparations for the scheduled opening on 1 May 1851. In fact the building went up in seven months despite its vast size and weight: a ground size of 1,848 feet long by 408 feet wide; a transept of 72 feet wide by 108 feet high; a total of 293,655 panes of glass weighing over 400 tons and iron-work of no less than 4,500 tons – a building of unique shape and size.[4]

The Great Exhibition of the Works of Industry of all Nations was duly opened on time and ran for six months until 15 October 1851. During this period there were over six million visitors from all over the world, making an average of around 43,000 per day, though variable prices created popular days, which were cheaper and even better attended, at one shilling admission. One hundred thousand exhibits were on display, about half from Britain and the Empire, and each country's exhibits were divided into four categories: raw materials, machinery, manufactures and sculpture and the fine arts.[5] Consistent with the emphasis on technology and raw materials, aesthetic matters were incidental and though sculpture was present there were no paintings. Likewise, music's role was restricted to the mechanical. Over 1,800 musical instruments were on display, chosen for their technical interest. Although the Official Illustrated Catalogue and its supplementary volume contain detailed descriptions of the exhibits and many plates, the display according to country and specific technology makes it difficult to trace the entire picture since no one type of instrument appears in a single section.[6] Given the emphasis of the undertaking, it is natural that greatest attention should have been attracted by the largest and most power- ful musical instruments, the organs and pianos, though the range was in fact vast. The instruments attracted great interest among musicians, not least from Berlioz,[7] who, as a recognized authority on instruments, was a member of the jury required to judge the many submissions and conceived a great enthusiasm for the building.

Although many of the instruments were demonstrated – the biggest used for recitals – musical performance on a broader scale had no place as such in the Exhibition.[8] The only connection that exists between the Exhibition and the world of performance is in reference to the opening ceremony, which was a major event for the onlookers as well as the participants. There were around a million people in Hyde Park and 30,000 invited guests and ticket holders inside the building when the Queen arrived to a fanfare of trumpets at twelve noon on 1 May 1851, and moved into position for the ceremony.[9] The musical arrangements were in the hands of the Sacred Harmonic Society and its conductor Sir Michael Costa, at that time the biggest choral organization in the capital. It provided the choir for the National Anthem, which was sung by 600 voices accompanied by an organ and 200 instrumentalists. But in fact this grand provision, which so well matched the importance of the Exhibition, was planned on this scale only at the last minute. Paxton's original intention was for a choir of 100 at most drawn from the metropolitan cathedral choirs. Following the Prince Consort's speech, the Queen's reply and the Archbishop of Canterbury's prayers, the choir sang the 'Halleluia Chorus' and the royal party set off to inspect part of the vast Exhibition.[10] More fanfares accom- panied the Queen's return to the dais, where she declared the Exhibition open, then left for the journey back to Buckingham Palace. The closing ceremony, if less elaborate, was similar in essence: a short speech by Prince Albert and a performance of the 'Halleluia Chorus'.[11]

Despite the uncertainties of its planning, the Great Exhibition of 1851 was a spectacular success, making a profit of £180,000, which was doubled by a government grant. The money was used to buy twenty-two acres of land in Brompton, land which now constitutes the biggest focus of educational display in the country, housing some of the major collections and colleges as well: for many of the exhibits became the nucleus of the vast exhibitions that now became increasingly a part of cultural life. But if the Exhibition laid new foundations in one sense, the physical foundations of the Crystal Palace itself were guaranteed no such future. All the dormant objections to the original siting of the building re-emerged and, despite many suggestions for new uses elsewhere, Parliament determined that it must all come down again. But Joseph Paxton, ever alive to business matters as to those of engineering, had anticipated this outcome and had no intention of letting his unique structure disappear. He formed the Crystal Palace Company and, by selling shares in it, raised enough money to buy the building and to purchase a new site for its re-erection: Penge Place, near the hamlets of Sydenham, Penge and Norwood, to the south of London.

CHAPTER 2

The Crystal Palace at Sydenham

The first column of the new Crystal Palace[1] was planted on 5 August 1852. The building took some two years to complete and involved significant extension of the original design, which now seemed modest in size by comparison. Since the new site sloped down steeply (to the east), it was necessary to add a new basement storey. Then, at the suggestion of Charles Barry, Paxton had the flat roof vaulted from end to end. So that this arch did not detract from the prominence of the transept, the latter was greatly enlarged and doubled in width. This involved the addition of two more storeys which in turn entailed considerable (increase in the width of the nave. The transept was now so large that Paxton decided that two end transepts were necessary to balance it and these required the addition of two wings. Thus the simple three-storied building grew into a complex five-storied one with a total floor area, including galleries, of nearly half as much again as the original, now with 1,650,000 square feet of glass. Then there were the gardens. The sloping site, covering an area of no less than 200 acres, offered opportunities for landscaping, including the provision of terraces (including those in English and Italian style), and, especially, of water fountains without parallel in Hyde Park. These seem to have been intended to outshine those of Versailles: although the original water towers at the high Palace level quickly proved inadequate for the vast pressure placed upon them (as part of the complex water system which also provided a reservoir and lake at the north end), the problem was eventually solved (at vast expense) with towers newly designed by the great engineer Brunel, facilitating the provision of cascades, waterfalls and water temples in classical Greek style, as well as lavish fountains, of which the chief ones soared to a height of no less than 250 feet when they were finally opened on 18 June 1856.

1 The Building for the Great Exhibition in Hyde Park, as pictured in the year of the Exhibition, 1851.

2 'Bird's Eye View' of the Crystal Palace at Sydenham by James Duffield Harding.

3 An aerial photograph of the Crystal Palace in 1934.

4 The nave from the south transept, with Osler's crystal fountain in the foreground. The Court of Musical Instruments was close to this location, out of sight to the right.

Both inside and out, the Crystal Palace at Sydenham offered an environment of an entirely new kind. In its totality it was vastly greater than London's traditional pleasure park with facilities for music, the Vauxhall Gardens, which offered the only vaguely relevant example for comparison: 'the Crystal Palace of its day, to compare small things with great', as the Palace loftily reminded its concert patrons in the early years. A cultural facility of such scope had never existed before. Moreover, without the pressure of competitive exhibiting, a much more relaxed atmosphere prevailed, mixing the educational with the recreative. Rather than providing a

5 The garden frontage from the south east; photograph *c.* 1860.

microcosm of Victorian industry, the new Palace offered one of
Victorian leisure. Inside the Palace, there was a new lavishness of
decor, with the interior set out like a Winter Garden, making the
most of the extraordinary quantity of light which flooded into the
delicately arched structure; it did, however, incorporate the one
most distinctive feature of the original interior, now repositioned in
a comparable focal position under the south transept of the new
building: Osler's Crystal Fountain, twenty-seven feet high and
made of four tons of pure crystal glass. The concept of a series of
Courts was also taken over from the earlier building. Thus, the Fine
Art Courts running down the central nave, each illustrating a
different period in the history of art. Pugin's Medieval Court had

been transferred bodily from the Hyde Park building; it was now joined by Grecian, Roman, Byzantine, Romanesque, Pompeian, Chinese, Alhambra, Renaissance and Egyptian Courts, illustrating the development of architecture, sculpture and mural decoration from the earliest times to the sixteenth century, so that the visitor might 'trace the course of art from centuries long anterior to Christianity, down to the very moment in which he lives, and obtain by this means an idea of the successive stages of civilization which from time to time have arisen in the world, flourished for a greater or less period, until overturned by the aggression of barbarians or the no less destructive agency of a sensual and degraded luxury'.[2] Vast reproductions of all manner of objects were a feature of the Courts, indeed to be observed throughout, as, for example, the giant sphinxes in the Egyptian Court and on the terraces, and the huge prehistoric monsters in the park. In time new permanent exhibits were added, including Italian galleries and an art gallery.

But there were also industrial courts, illustrating the activities of particular cities, such as Birmingham or Sheffield, or particular types of industry. The Courts flanked the sides of the rectangular contour of the building, leaving space in the middle for temporary exhibitions and shows. For example, as early as 2 June 1855, the Royal Horticultural fete and show were held there and attended by 30,000 people; almost fifty years later, in 1903, the first show organized by the Society of Motor Manufacturers and Traders with over 180 exhibitors took place there as well, a sign of changing times. In addition to the Courts and exhibitions, there were entire departments on other floors devoted to specific subjects: natural history, machinery and carriages, a Hall of Fame, a Court of Kings and Queens. In time many more facilities were added. An Aquarium was opened in 1872;[3] a Theatre catered for everything from pantomime to Greek tragedy; a Concert Room would eventually be made to hold 4,000. The educational dimension was further stressed by the provision of a Reading Room and of Schools of Engineering and of Arts, Science and Literature, arising from the interest generated by the exhibitions and performances. With the passing of time, the rather high moral tone that informed the undertaking, as it had the Great Exhibition itself, tended to be mollified, and the entertainment character to develop: the ease with which visitors could move inside and out certainly helped this. The grounds in particular were exploited, featuring balloon ascents (a great feature in Hyde

Park as well), high-wire walks by the famous Blondin and, most popular of all (ironically so in retrospect), massive firework displays by the Brock Company. In the present century, speedway racing, football (including two Cup Finals during the First War)[4] and, anticipating post-war developments, athletics meetings, became important, all contributing to a unique atmosphere which brought together at one location many activities which would today be regarded as quite separate, and occupied a very special place in the amenities of the metropolis. The Crystal Palace was one of the most frequently visited and quoted of London's sights, and patronized for much of its life by royalty.

ORGANIZATION AND ETHOS

Despite the general enthusiasm for the building and the popular support, the Palace was never free of money worries. Although applications for shares in the Company had initially been well oversubscribed, Paxton's expanding plans soon drained resources. Even before the opening, the total cost had soared to the extraordinary figure of £1,350,000, a striking increase from the projected capital of £500,000 in 1852. Much of the loss arose from the difficulties with the complex water system, and the problems with the water towers compounded the financial problems. Then there was the vexed problem of Sunday opening: the Palace could not open on the Lord's Day, and, since this was the working man's only free day, it could generate income only on Bank Holidays, where admission was made favourable: 1 shilling as opposed to 2s. 6d. Only children under twelve represented the 'shilling public' in the earlier years of the Palace. Doors opened at 10 a.m. and closed at 6 p.m. It was open the year round, closed only for four traditional holidays.

In planning its economic viability, which was always to be a problem, Paxton had ensured one major facility for attracting support to his original plans: the availability of rail transport for visitors. The grounds of Penge Place had been skirted by the London, Brighton and South Coast Railway, of which the owner, Leo Schuster, was a director. A spur was built from this so that trains could actually go into the grounds and a new station of imposing grandeur built and linked to the main building by a long glass corridor. Such was the business to be done that a second station was opened in the early 1860s, terminating opposite the Palace and linked to it by an underground passage, ornately decorated with Italian brickwork; henceforth this was known as the 'High Level Station' and the original station as the 'Low Level Station'.[5] The High Level line, of the London, Chatham and Dover Railway, connected to Ludgate Hill or Victoria, with other connections from the former, including to King's Cross, thus bringing the Palace into direct communication with the Great Northern and Midland Lines. Trains ran at roughly fifty-minute intervals throughout the day. The London and Brighton Railway ran the Low Level link to London Bridge, Victoria, Kensington, and West Croydon in the country direction. Trains were again roughly hourly, though intersecting, so that a train to London departed from one or other station twice an hour. This was the minimum provision; special concerts and festivals prompted additional arrangements.

Mention of the railway appropriately introduces the name of George Grove, who became Secretary of the Crystal Palace Company in May 1852, after having been Secretary to the Royal Society of Arts. He embodied the educational ethos of the Palace and undoubtedly influenced its favourable cultural development. Grove had worked in earlier years as an Inspector of the permanent way for the Great Northern and East Indian Railway Companies and assisted Brunel with the building of the Clifton Suspension Bridge. But he was also a scholar, a distinguished Biblical authority.[6] He combined high aspirations and a great love of learning with a love of people and the desire to communicate with them. Though an amateur in music, his passion for it combined with these qualities to give him a crucial influence in the musical life of the Crystal Palace, which later extended beneficially from the Palace years to his most famous role, that of Director of the newly created Royal College of Music from 1883. His musical ambitions for the Palace knew no bounds as he approached the planning of the opening ceremony on 10 June 1854. He wanted to persuade the poet laureate, Lord Tennyson, to write an ode for the occasion, and Berlioz to compose a musical setting (a natural wish in view of his interest in the Hyde Park building).[7] Tennyson, however, had no interest whatever, and the resulting ceremony was actually just a repeat of that held three years earlier. Though Grove's role was soon to become very much more fruitful, at first music had but a small function in the life of the Palace.

THE PLACE OF MUSIC

The exhibition function offered little opportunity for the promotion of music at the Crystal Palace at Sydenham. Only one court was devoted to it. Although termed an industrial court, the Musical Instruments Court clearly balanced the technological with the aesthetic in its decor. An early commentator noted that 'the aim of the architect here has been, not so much to build a mere Court for the exhibition of musical intruments, as to produce a temple dedicated to music, and to render the architectural detail and ornament typical of the high and beautiful art, as well as of the subservient mechanical craft'.[8] To this end the courts included many relief figures and statues of biblical and mythological subjects relating to music, and three-quarter columns made to represent organ pipes. The interior part of the court was more highly decorated than the exterior. 'Over the entrances are figures of St Cecilia and Erato, under which lines from Dryden and Collins. Around the other portion of the court are ranged the busts of the most celebrated English and foreign composers, and on the frieze are figures of boys playing upon various instruments. In fact the whole court, externally and internally is descriptive of the music of all ages and all countries; whilst the pleasant subdued colouring harmonises charmingly with the pervading spirit.'[9] The windows of the court also provided the facility for exhibiting printed music.

But, unlike the exhibition in Hyde Park, there was to be no performance function at Sydenham, for the musical instruments (which included, as well as harps, drums, wind and stringed instruments both ancient and modern, many varieties of pianos) were for display, not for performance and sale. The only performance function that the Palace offered at its opening was that of its brass band,[10] for outdoor as well as indoor entertainment. The resources of the great opening ceremony would not be drawn from the Palace, but, again, from outside.

THE OPENING CEREMONY

Though of little purely musical interest, the musical arrangements for the opening are important in telling the first part of the musical story of the Palace; for they required a measure of transformation of the building for musical purposes. The facilities provided at Sydenham were essentially just extensions of those for the Great

Exhibition: there was no designed musical location. The intended grandeur of the opening ceremony instantly made new demands.[11] It was natural that the Sacred Harmonic Society under Costa should again be invited to take the responsibility for the music, in view of their role at Hyde Park. But Costa had obviously learnt some lessons from that very unusual experience and its mismanaged planning. Before replying to the Directors' invitation, which was now issued in May (10 June had only just been agreed as the day of the opening), he insisted on a private meeting with Paxton, Grove and several others to clarify the details.[12] Bowley, the Secretary to the Company, recalls that he wanted sole control, insisting that it was 'unwise that any musical performance should be entered into unless upon a very grand scale: say, 200 instrumentalists, 1,000 chorist[er]s and two military and the Crystal Palace bands'. Although Costa intended that 'an amateur spirit' should prevail, he wanted all the principal instrumentalists to be professionals, incurring a total cost of about £150. It was also estimated that nearly 6,000 feet of orchestral flooring in a rising semicircle would be required. The Sacred Harmonic would loan 'a large number of desks, stools, orchestral fittings and the use of music' and provide the use of Exeter Hall, its own concert hall, for rehearsals, the Directors of the Palace 'defraying expenses and also paying for the printing and stationery, and providing all who attended with railway passes to and from London and the Crystal Palace'. This was agreed. But, as shown, Paxton had no great sensitivity to the musical practicalities and soon objected to the planning of the orchestral platform so that 'everyone could see the conductor clearly' – also for its projecting too far into the transept. But Costa insisted and the platform came to within twelve or fifteen feet of the dais for the royal party. The location for this – hence to be called 'Orchestra' – was the west end of the Centre Transept. It was finally 150 feet wide by 50–60 feet deep, rising in an amphitheatre to a height of 42 feet, with each performer's seat defined and numbered. Bowley recalled of the performance 'so firm and stable was it under the might of the vast mass of performers that not the slightest crack or deflection was apparent, and it will remain long in the recollection of all connected with the musical arrangements for the opening of the Crystal Palace how much the exertions of Mr Cochrane (the chief superintendent) contributed to their successful issue...' (the work had eventually been completed in one week and at the last minute).

Hardly less of a challenge was the requisitioning of the orchestra and choir. Beginning with the regular members of the Sacred Harmonic Society's orchestra, invitations were issued throughout London, finally producing a much larger orchestra than formerly. For the choir, invitations were issued to all the main provincial choral societies, offering specific numbers of places to augment the choir of the Sacred Harmonic: at largest, forty-eight were offered to the combined choirs of Bradford, Leeds, Halifax, Huddersfield and York, thirty-two to Birmingham, sixteen to Liverpool, twelve to Manchester, right down to four for smaller cities, including those of the Three Choirs Festival. The orchestral disposition allowed for the orchestra to be 'flanked by 60 cellos and double basses followed by 12 rows of seats for the choir above which, "fringing as it were", will be the Bands of the Coldstream and Grenadier Guards (about 85 performers) and 60 Brass Instrument players of the Crystal Palace Company.' The general ensemble included leading singers of the Italian Opera which also included 'Mesdames Clara Novello and Dolby, with Mr Sims Reeves' and others who had requested to participate, perhaps most notably Pauline Viardot Garcia. Clara Novello was soloist in the National Anthem and the 100th Psalm in arrangements by Costa himself. The music for the occasion was printed for all performers by Novello.

The ceremony was predictably magnificent in effect, in the presence of 40,000 people who were raised to an even greater pitch of anticipation by the time it inevitably took for the royal party to progress from Westminster to Sydenham. *The Times* reported as follows:

Soon after one o'clock the majority of the visitors had assembled, and the vast interior of the building presented a sublime spectacle. The area of the centre transept, filled with a grand representation of English Society, and having the throne in the midst, was in itself a remarkable sight. On the north side the semi-circular orchestra swarmed with the celebrities of our musical world, the instrumental forces below, the vocalists on upper benches, a military band on the crest of the harmonious 'mountain', and, below, Costa, with Miss Clara Novello by his side ... Scarcely had the illustrious party taken their places, and the cheers with which their arrival was welcomed subsided, when the music of the National Anthem was rolling in rich volumes of sound over the length and breadth of the Palace. The solo parts were sung by Clara Novello with most thrilling effect, while the reverberation of a Royal salute fired from the park served to mark with additional grandeur the powers of the great orchestra and chorus.

After addresses by Samuel Laing (the builder) and several heads of departments, the royalty and distinguished dignitaries formed themselves into a procession which then progressed around the building, the Queen subsequently returning to the main transept where the 'Hundreth Psalm was sung, the Archbishop of Canterbury offered a prayer, followed by the Halleluiah Chorus, and the Queen declared the Palace open'.[13]

But impressive as it all was, the ceremony had nothing directly to do with the formal musical activity of the Palace itself. This is vividly illustrated in the fact that many of the performers, to say nothing of the instruments, had to get back to the Royal Opera House in time for the evening performance, the ceremony only having ended around 4.30 pm.[14] With the great occasion over, the Palace was left with its meagre musical provision. More remarkable still, even Grove seems never to have envisaged larger performance.[15] But events were soon to change his mind. A start had been made with large-scale choral performance and soon expansion was to appear in the orchestral field as well, setting in motion a groundswell for music-making which would soon begin to add a new, unsuspected dimension of activity to the exciting new building.

PART 2

The choral life

CHAPTER 3

The Handel Festivals, 1857–1926

FROM OPENING CEREMONY TO TRIAL FESTIVAL

If it can fairly be said that the network of choral societies was the one unifying feature of English musical life in the first half of the nineteenth century, it was the music of Handel which embodied its spirit. Handel performance had never died out in England since his death in 1759 and the attraction of large-scale metropolitan performance had already manifested itself in the Westminster Abbey performance of *Messiah* in 1784, involving 526 performers; this was followed by a sequence of performances, of which that of 1834, for the 150th anniversary of Handel's assumed birth, was the last of this type.[1] Such events kept Handel in the popular choral imagination even before the burgeoning choral movements (not least in the developing industrial centres of the midlands and north of England) began to provide very different public venues and audiences.[2] The opening of the Crystal Palace presented a venue of a scope unimagined before, and it soon came to epitomize the sense of Victorian expansion in music making as in technology: in its vast spaces, progress would be rendered as sound. A visit to the Crystal Palace for a major performance or competitive festival would become a major ambition of an aspiring regional or metropolitan chorister: a very special event.

But at the time of its opening, the only large-scale choral performances to be experienced in London focusing on the most popular oratorios of Handel, were firmly in the hands of the Sacred Harmonic Society and its dynamic conductor, Michael Costa. Appointed in 1848 to revive this society's flagging impetus, Costa had already increased its total choral and orchestral forces to 700 and it was in the period of its highest success, destined to last over thirty years. Founded in 1836,[3] much of the Society's musical significance had rested on its devotion to single works in concert performance, rather than the selections from different works which had constituted 'Oratorio' performance before, not least in its own preliminary years (with the sole exception of *Messiah*, always given 'complete').[4] Haydn's oratorios *The Creation* and *The Seasons* were also given, as were those of the greatest young composer known to England, Mendelssohn's *St Paul* and *Elijah*, though none of these works came anywhere near rivalling the popularity of Handel. For the 1836 performance of *Messiah*, the orchestra had comprised 300, and Mendelssohn had been overwhelmed when he heard his *St Paul* given by them in the same year.[5] At the time of his appointment, Costa was the dominant figure of London music-making: conductor of the orchestra of the Philharmonic Society since 1846, he was effectively the founder of modern orchestral conducting in Britain, possessing above all 'the secret of command. Under Costa's rule the orchestra became a model of punctuality and serious work.'[6]

But the significance of the performances of the Sacred Harmonic Society went beyond purely musical factors. It represented a new social force in British music, markedly prompted by the strong reaction to the establishment patronage of the Handel Commemoration Festival of 1834. As a consequence of the exclusion of many religious Nonconformists from the 1834 performance, many more members had joined the Society, founded two years before in 1832. Involvement in public performances was therefore significantly tied to the public demonstration of status by Nonconformists.[7] The large numbers soon involved intensified this aspect as well as ensuring a broad social mix; performers who would formerly have had less natural opportunity to play a public role in London's musical life could now participate in large-scale and increasingly prestigious musical events. The patronage of royalty, arising as much for political as musical reasons, contributed to this sense.[8] The new social and musical character of the Sacred Harmonic Society influenced its attitude towards performance venue. Rather than in a church or cathedral, it soon found its permanent home in a public hall: from 1836, the Large Hall of the Exeter Hall complex in the Strand.[9] And the opportunity to use any new, especially larger, performance venue was naturally seized on: thus the attraction of the new Crystal Palace in Hyde Park, and, in turn, its successor at Sydenham.

To the Society's new era of confidence, the vast audiences drawn

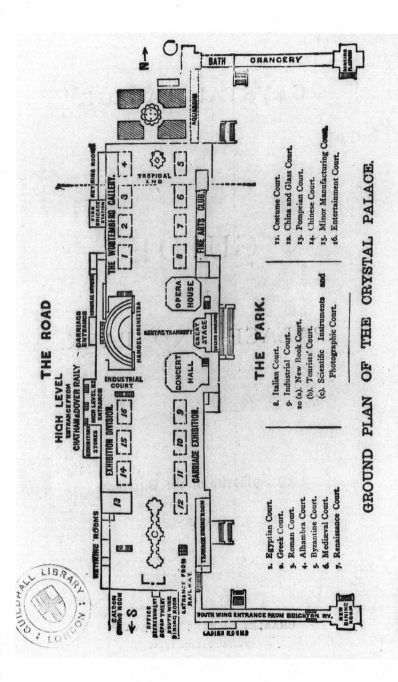

GROUND PLAN OF THE CRYSTAL PALACE.

THE ROAD

HIGH LEVEL

ENTRANCE FROM
CHATHAM & DOVER RAILY.

HIGH LEVEL R2.
EXHIBITORS' ENTRANCE
STORES

EXHIBITION DIVISION.

RETIRING ROOMS

SALOON
DINING ROOM

OFFICE
REFRESHMENT
DEPARTMENT
SOUTH WING
DINING ROOM

S

ENTRANCE FROM
RAILWAY.

SOUTH WING ENTRANCE FROM BRIGHTON RY.

LADIES ROOMS

NEW
DINING
ROOM

TERRACE DINING ROOM

CARRIAGE EXHIBITION.

INDUSTRIAL COURT

CARRIAGE ENTRANCE

CENTRAL OFFICE

FIRE
BRIGADE
STATION

THE WURTEMBERG GALLERY.

TROPICAL END

HANDEL ORCHESTRA

CENTRE TRANSEPT.

CONCERT HALL

OPERA HOUSE

GREAT STAGE

FINE ARTS CLUB.

N

BATH   ORANGERY

AQUARIUM

DANCING PLATFORM

THE PARK.

1. Egyptian Court.
2. Greek Court.
3. Roman Court.
4. Alhambra Court.
5. Byzantine Court.
6. Medieval Court.
7. Renaissance Court.

8. Italian Court.
9. Industrial Court.
10 (a). New Book Court.
   (b). Tourists' Court.
   (c). Scientific Instruments and
       Photographic Court.

11. Costume Court.
12. China and Glass Court.
13. Pompeian Court.
14. Chinese Court.
15. Minor Manufacturing Court.
16. Entertainment Court.

6 The ground plan of the Palace after the addition of the Concert Room and Theatre to the centre transept.
By this time the north transept had been destroyed and replaced with gardens and a lake.

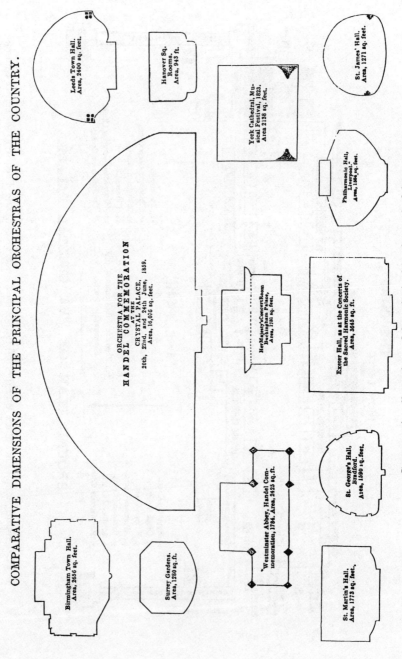

COMPARATIVE DIMENSIONS OF THE PRINCIPAL ORCHESTRAS OF THE COUNTRY.

Leeds Town Hall. Area, 2400 sq. feet.

Hanover Sq. Rooms. Area, 943 ft.

St. James' Hall. Area, 1271 sq. feet.

York Cathedral, Musical Festival, 1823. Area 2138 sq. feet.

Philharmonic Hall, Liverpool. Area, 1664 sq. feet.

ORCHESTRA FOR THE HANDEL COMMEMORATION AT THE CRYSTAL PALACE, 20th, 22nd, and 24th June, 1859. Area, 16,076 sq. feet.

Her Majesty's Concert Room Buckingham Palace, Area, 1731 sq. feet.

Exeter Hall, as at the Concerts of the Sacred Harmonic Society. Area, 3645 sq. ft.

St. George's Hall, Bradford. Area, 1590 sq. feet.

Birmingham Town Hall. Area, 2656 sq. feet.

Surrey Gardens. Area, 1280 sq. ft.

"Westminster Abbey, Handel Commemoration, 1784. Area, 2425 sq.ft.

St. Martin's Hall, Area, 1773 sq. feet.

7 Comparative dimensions of the principal 'orchestras' of the country.

THE GREAT HANDEL FESTIVAL AT THE CRYSTAL PALACE—FROM A PHOTOGRAPH BY NEGRETTI AND ZAMBRA.

8 The 'Handel Orchestra' for the 1857 Festival.

THE GREAT HANDEL FESTIVAL AT THE CRYSTAL PALACE.—SEE NEXT PAGE.

9 The 'Handel Orchestra' for the 1859 Festival, showing the addition of the canvas awning.

A SKETCH AT THE HANDEL FESTIVAL IN THE CRYSTAL PALACE.—SEE PAGE 15.

10 The 1865 Handel Festival (Third Triennial Festival), showing Sir Michael Costa as conductor and Sims Reeves as tenor soloist with other soloists seated. Distin's bass drum and giant timpani are situated on the raised dais at the centre of the orchestra.

to the capital for the six months of the Great Exhibition in 1851 offered even greater opportunities for self-promotion. It gave weekly oratorio performances – *Messiah*, *Elijah* and *The Creation* in turn – for the whole summer from May to September. And, having been invited to execute the impressive musical formalities for the opening ceremony of the Sydenham Crystal Palace, it hardly took the Society long to grasp the possibilities of the new building for more extended performance: in particular, its central transept, now the largest enclosed public area not only in London but in the United Kingdom, and the subject of constant advantageous comparisons with other buildings; it could clearly hold all the musicians envisaged as well as an audience of hitherto undreamed-of size – ten to twelve thousand at least. But its capabilities had never been tried. The stimulus to do so came with the approaching centenary of

MENDELSSOHN FESTIVAL AT THE CRYSTAL PALACE.—THE TORCHLIGHT PROCESSION.—SEE PAGE 486.

11 The torchlight procession to the Mendelssohn statue, 1860.

Handel's death, 1859, for which the Society had begun to envisage a celebration on a larger scale than ever before to 'produce the broadest, grandest effects' only to be obtained by 'a very great number of musicians'.[10] But such a venture required preparation: indeed a 'trial festival'. The original idea had been that of Robert Bowley, who was both Secretary of the Sacred Harmonic Society and the Manager of the Crystal Palace; with Grove, as Secretary of the Palace (who already knew Costa) as the other key figure, it was decided to organize a festival to be known as 'The Great Handel Festival' at the Crystal Palace in 1857.[11] As ever, the financial benefits implicit in so large a gathering could never have been far from the minds of the Directors of the Company in envisaging such a giant event, a fact confirmed in the emphasis placed on the 'pecuniary aspect' in later assessments.[12]

Further to Bowley's initiative, the Sacred Harmonic Society had made its intentions clear in a public statement in *The Musical Times* of 1 December 1856, detailing the striking attractions of the building. But no special facilities existed. Work therefore began to enlarge the west end staging which had been used for the official opening over three years before to accommodate 700 people, and to redesign it for the new forces; to create from the former 'Grand Orchestra' what was now to be known as the 'Handel Auditorium' through the addition of a complete stage rather than the original dais.[13] The great musical addition was a new organ at the centre top of the staging, suitably to be known as the Handel Organ, a four-manual instrument of seventy-four speaking stops and 4,568 pipes by Gray and Davidson, and weighing twenty tons; at its completion it was the largest in Britain.[14] Although there was naturally some scepticism by members of the well-drilled Society towards this vast cavernous new location, the response of the public to the impending festival was highly enthusiastic and the ticket sales were beyond the expectations of 'even the most sanguine'. The choral recruitment followed the lines adopted for the opening ceremony, though now with much larger forces: the Sacred Harmonic provided a nucleus of 1200 singers 'picked from the leading professionals and amateurs in London' to which were added 800 singers from the principal towns in the UK.

It was an entirely new musical and organizational phenomenon. As one commentator observed, 'from every large town in England came numbers of intelligent young persons of the highest respectability, carefully trained under the new system of choral singing, and having an intellectual and personal enjoyment of the sublime strains they were to render'.[15] The solo singers were those of the opening ceremony, Clara Novello, Charlotte Dolby and Sims Reeves, with Rudersdorff, Montem Smith, Formes and Weiss, establishing a connection with leading international singers which was to last throughout;[16] the orchestra was of 300 strings; nine each of flutes, oboes, clarinets and bassoons; twelve each of horns, mixed trumpets and cornets; nine trombones; three ophicleides; nine serpents and bass horns; three drums and six side drums – 'a force hitherto unprecedented'.[17] Just how unprecedented is made clear in a table of performance statistics published in the 1862 *Programme of Arrangements* which shows the remarkable growth in numbers which occurred with the inauguration of the Crystal Palace events.[18] The orchestra used in 1854 was already almost double that of the opening of Birmingham Town Hall in 1834 (100), a figure already well in excess of the established regional festivals; yet this figure was itself doubled by 1857, and the proportions were similar for the choir.

The works to be given, on 15, 17 and 19 July 1857, were *Messiah*, *Judas Maccabeus* and *Israel in Egypt*. The now customary royal patronage of Sydenham continued as the choral life began to develop, the Queen and Prince Albert attending on the second day, and creating another major public event as the royal progress moved through South London to the Palace; an infinitely vaster number of people waited between Dulwich and the Palace to glimpse their arrival than were present inside, a total recorded at 11,649; the return journey took until 6 p.m. Audience attendance on the first day was 11,129, and on the last, 18,000.

The event was extensively reported in the musical press, since the visual impact of the vast numbers filling the nave and galleries of the Palace and the terraces outside was overwhelming and quite unprecedented: as was the effect of the choruses,

as though the Palace itself were a great musical instrument ... The 'Halleluiah Chorus' could be distinctly heard nearly half a mile from Norwood, and its effect, as the sound floated on the wind, was impressive beyond description, and sounded as if a nation were at prayers ... The unison of the voices on the words 'For the Lord God omnipotent reigneth' brought out the full force and power of the orchestra – while the reposeful passage which immediately follows displayed to great advantage the precision of the performers.

On the second day, a spontaneous burst of applause for repetition of the 'Halleluiah' chorus which concludes *Judas Maccabeus*, was acknowledged by the Queen with a nod to Costa from the royal box, at the garden end of the transept, from whence it was observed during the performance that 'the Queen beat time with a fan, and Prince Albert with a roll of music'.[19] After the third oratorio, *Israel in Egypt*, the three-day festival ended with the National Anthem, Clara Novello repeating her by now legendary high note in the last cadence, to terminate 'a magnificent celebration, and a homage worthy of its illustrious subject'.[20]

But more important than the enthusiasm of the musical press was the attention of the national press, which immediately grasped the significance of the event. 'Such a mass of able and intelligent criticism has never before been elicited by any single musical cele- bration, not just in the United Kingdon, but the Continent and Colonies', reported *The Times*.[21] Musical performance in Britain had been put on a new footing, not only in the power of the effect of the music, but in the vastness and novelty of the location that made it possible, ensuring, moreover, a social mix – in performers and audience alike – that marked the dawn of a new era in British musical life: it also marked the establishment of *Messiah* as a national, rather than purely musical, symbol. It was to be predicted that such an event would prompt demand for another such meeting, even before the coming centenary of 1859. In July of the following year, 1858, with the choir increased in size to 2,500 (including 1,400 from the London contingent of the Handel Festival Choir and 200 from the Bradford Choral Society) and the orchestra now drawn from the Sacred Harmonic, the Royal Opera and the Guards bands, a programme of thirteen items drew on works by Mendelssohn, Rossini and Mozart, as well as Handel (*Acis and Galatea*) and Costa (the oratorio *Eli*) to an audience of 20,000.

ESTABLISHMENT AND EXPANSION: THE HANDEL
COMMEMORATION FESTIVAL OF 1859 AND THE FIRST
TRIENNIAL FESTIVAL OF 1862

Despite its vital historical significance for British music, little really critical response is to be had to the first Handel Festival. For most musicians accustomed to the familiar venues and contexts of musical life, it must have seemed more like a monster curiosity than a serious event and we have to wait for the Handel Commemoration Festival of 1859 itself to see the issues reflected upon. The *Programme of Arrangements* which appeared for this event makes it clear that the organizers considered the trial run to have vindicated the original conception: in matters of transport, the existing infrastructure had proved its capabilities with hitherto unimagined numbers; the accommodation, especially the central transept, had, despite problems, proved its size and potential; and, not least, the gamble of attracting to Sydenham 'duly qualified assistance, both from professors and from amateurs, which might be relied on for the Commemoration of 1859'[22] had paid off. The portents for rapid expansion of the event were favourable in the extreme. It was now time to undertake the improvements essential to the effective running of an even bigger festival. The Handel Orchestra created for 1857

was extended to such dimensions as experience had dictated to be best for the largest practicable choral festival. It was also enclosed at the side and back with screens of the most resonant material.[23]

In addition, a large oiled canvas awning was hung across the entire width of the performing area in the attempt to create the effect of a roof by the most direct means, and thus to help to contain and focus the sound. The orchestra was now 216 feet wide – twice the diameter of St Paul's Cathedral dome, and 100 feet deep, comprising over 10,000 square feet: and this area, of course, excluded several tiers of galleries, as the programme pointedly observed, and the sight of the enhanced orchestra captured the public imagination yet again, as the picture in the *Illustrated London News* makes clear. Work was complete by Good Friday 1859.[24]

Quite apart from its celebratory significance, the 1859 Festival can be regarded as the first true Handel Festival in that it established the pattern of events which was to last essentially throughout: three days in June, a Monday, Wednesday and Friday, known respectively as 'Messiah Day', 'Selection Day' and 'Israel Day', with a preliminary Saturday evening rehearsal, open to the public, thus providing four very substantial musical events, with chorus, soloists and organ. The purpose of the 'Selection Day' was to perform selections from other oratorios: the principal work in the selection was the *Dettingen Te Deum*, complete, which comprised Part 1: Part 2 included selections from *Judas Maccabeus*, *Belshazzar* and *Samson*.

The recruitment of singers followed the existing pattern, with a core from the Sacred Harmonic Society and picked London professionals and amateurs, and regional representation, now extended.[25] The size of the orchestra was now increased dramatically, with 2,765 voices constituted as follows: 725 sopranos, 719 altos (at least 418 of them male altos), 659 tenors and 662 basses. The orchestra was also bigger: 457 players, excluding the organ of 'vast power', as follows: ninety-two first, and ninety second violins; sixty violas, sixty cellos, sixty-one basses; ten each of oboes, flutes and bassoons; six trumpets, twelve horns, nine trombones, three ophicleides, two bombardons, eight serpents; three double drums, four kettle drums, one bass drum, six side drums. The soloists were as before, with the addition of Helen Sherrington and Giovanni Belletti. Their different qualities were a major feature of the performance: Clara Novello's classic simplicity and control in 'I know that my redeemer liveth', the agility of Rudersdorff's 'Rejoice greatly'; the special character of the alto Charlotte Dolby, for whom Mendelssohn had written the alto part in *Elijah*; a very different sound from the traditional male alto in England, which permitted Guadagni's version of 'But who may abide' to be performed;[26] the new young voice of Helen Sherrington. But the greatest star of all these early performances was Sims Reeves, especially in 'The enemy said' in *Israel in Egypt*, 'with a power of voice, truth of accent, and a well-sustained fluency of execution impossible to surpass'. To round off the days, Handel's *Royal Fireworks Music* and *Water Music* were played in the grounds.

To balance the performing forces, the seating accommodation for the audience had now been very greatly extended, including provision in the ends of the galleries.[27] The event instantly caught the popular imagination. The audience over the four successive days had increased dramatically: 81,319, which was 32,845 more than 1857 (made up of 19,680 for the public rehearsal, 17,109 on the Monday, 17,644 on the Wednesday and 26,826 on the Friday). The organizers now realized that they had something very special on their hands, recalling in a later programme (1862) that:

Apart from the superlative grandeur produced by hosts of players and singers, the charm of having one part after another taken up in different and distant portions of the immense Orchestra is a new feature of Festival music. Cathedral musicians know the advantages derived from the antiphonal character of anthems and services. But what in cathedral music could equal the sublime effect at the 1859 festival, in the chorus 'Lift up your heads, O ye Gates', with the enquiry *Who is this King of Glory?* responded to by 'The Lord strong and mighty', with trebles and altos in the centre of the Chorus answered by tenors and basses, so widely apart as to appear distinct choral forces was something without parallel in the history of music. It was the combination of numbers and distances made 'Israel in Egypt' so superlatively grand.[28]

In fact, *Israel in Egypt* was the real discovery of the Handel Festival, since it now found a place of equal prominence to *Messiah*, and was henceforth regarded as essential, in light of its large and appropriate choral writing.[29]

If the popular success of the first Handel Festivals was beyond doubt, it was inevitable that other reactions would be voiced in more specialist musical circles. Of central importance was naturally the question of acoustics and performance conditions, already domi-nant in the review of July. The major problem of the adaptation of accommodation had been overcome with characteristic industry by the authorities; but what were the effects of this entirely new kind of music-making on performance and reception? Opinions were not slow in formulating, not least in the columns of *The Musical World* which printed (though in order to challenge) a letter which is interesting in showing the reaction of the experienced chorister used to a different environment for his Handel:[30]

The Crystal Palace was not built for music, and no contrivance in the world will ever render it a place for music, for a reasonably-sized, or even a grand band and chorus would have been powerless, and only the mammoth noises of the orchestra could have had a chance. But as it was, except to a very small portion of the audience, the solos and duets were all but utterly lost, and half the grandeur of the great effects was wasted in empty air. We had a glorious sight ... but the real Handel effects ... there were none of these [as] I have experienced them in Exeter Hall, and ten times more in one of the old Cathedrals (Gloucester, or Hereford) ... or at the festivals.

The Musical Times went further in an article entitled 'The Power of Sound', which sought to reconcile the widely varying reactions to the effect through reference to the nature of the acoustics.[31]

Here we have 2,765 voices and 457 instruments, besides an organ of vast power, all performing together within a space comprising 77,760 square feet ... It was supposed by some that the noise produced by so great an orchestra would be perfectly deafening ... Nothing could be more falla-

cious than this notion ... the simple explanation is that the music produced
an entirely different effect according to the distance and position at which
it was heard. Those that were too near the orchestra necessarily heard only
a portion of the voices, and not all, consequently they heard but a portion
of the harmony instead of the united sounds that would have caused an
agreeable effect, and those parts which were heard were too loud to be
pleasant. [But for those] in the upper gallery at the furthest end, opposite
the performers ... this situation is removed beyond the fair extent of the
human voice ... [and] beyond those limits the sound does not arrive at the
ear at all. Surely no one would pretend that every singer in this great
chorus would be able to throw his or her voice to the opposite end of the
building – a distance of 360 yards; these voices, then, can never reach the
listener in the east gallery, and he is consequently listening not to 2,765
voices, but, in reality to a very reduced number of singers ... The consequence must necessarily be that the only proper portion of the building
for listening to the effect of the 2,765 voices must be within the limits of the
weakest voices.

And the problems were described as greater for the orchestra – 'that
some sounds travel quicker than others and therefore reach the ear
earlier than those sounds which ought to accompany them', though
in this case the writer prefers to ascribe these problems to performance: 'it is difficult to prove that such sounds have been emitted in
their proper places'. One observation was generally shared,
however: 'the well-defined period of time which elapses between the
beat of Mr Costa's *bâton* and the first note of each bar ...'
    The issues were to remain for discussion whenever the music of the
Crystal Palace was concerned. The problems were eventually to
prove indefensible in the face of new and more critical attitudes to
Handel performance towards the end of the century. But in 1859,
the effectiveness of one kind of music-making to the satisfaction of its
audience seemed proven beyond doubt, and there was nothing to
stop the steady development of festival choral music with extensive
solo participation based on a narrow repertory thoroughly known
by its performers and listeners in a unique acoustic and social
context. There was thus to be no rein upon the organizers of the next
such event, now determined to inaugurate a Triennial Handel
Festival, beginning in 1862. But in the prospectus that appeared
in the previous year this proven phenomenon was placed in a
broader symbolic public context still: that of another Great
Exhibition scheduled for the same period, 'a greater International
Exhibition of Art and Industry than the world has yet beheld',[32] an

event which caused the writers to reflect on the massive growth of
the Sacred Harmonic Society's activities since its precursor of
1851.[33] The previous Festivals are now seen as 'orchestral exhibitions', which this one must surpass, with the Society again providing the nucleus of picked amateur singers of the London district.

The motto . . . is . . . PROGRESS . . . At a time like the present this is
particularly necessary . . . English choral music should show what it is
capable of effecting . . . Handel too, in his Giant Majesty will then be displayed to the representatives of the assembled nations . . . There is a general
feeling that . . . it must be done by means of Handel's work, since his music
. . . rises in grandeur with every additional force . . . employed to develop
it.

Whilst formally acknowledging the dangers of 'exaggerated claims'
the Society expressed the belief that the festival of 1862 would be
'the most complete musical display ever witnessed . . . which could
be offered by no other country', in the realization of which the
Sacred Harmonic Society 'gladly enters the field'. Retrospective
comments in the later publicity show what an impact this moment
had: how the nation 'rose to it', and how Handel was seen to have an
extra musical significance, to be an embodiment of national
identity.

    In the attempt to master the acoustic, further modifications were
now made to the Handel Auditorium, to extend the benefits of the
1859 improvements. Recalling 1859, the Programme of Arrangements for 1862 observed.

there had first been a disinclination to roof it in with oiled canvas like the
ancient roman Coliseum and it was considered this would not be effective.
But when the orchestra was increased in size, clarity in the chorus was lost.
It was therefore determined to roof the entire orchestra and that the inter-
section of the grand transept and nave be solidly roofed as well.[34]

Thus the oiled awning of 1859 had yielded to a proper roof acting as
a sounding board and springing from the walls and back already
added then as solid and permanent. Performance was fixed for 23,
25, and 27 June, with the Saturday again a rehearsal day. The
numbers involved showed another increase: a total of 3,120 singers:
trebles and altos, 810 each, tenors and basses, 750 each. The band
now reached 505, thus making a grand total of 3,625 performers,
excepting the organ, which, counting the various officers, stewards
and librarians, made up the total 4,000.

The main talking point in connection with the performance was inevitably the effect of the completed Orchestra with its new sounding board. *The Musical Times* commented that

we need only repeat the universal opinion, that it is in every respect a magnificent success. The vocal parts are now defined as completely as if they were delivered at Exeter Hall; and the fugued passages and points are brought out with clearness and decision. Some of the choruses are no doubt heard with better effect than others; but the fogginess and uncertainty incident to the manifestations of the former festivals are wholly got rid of. The sound is wonderfully amplified, and there is an extraordinary richness in the tone, without any perceptible resonance. Whether from the alterations in the building or from the improved selection of the singers, the sound of the voices is considerably brightened ...

Occasional 'unsteadinesses' in the sopranos and ponderousness in the basses apart, 'it is really wonderful that so large a chorus should have been collected from all quarters, who could sing the music with so few mistakes'.[35]

Improvements in the auditorium continued until 1868, when *Illustrated London News* commented favourably on the acoustics:[36]

The finest solos and choruses were performed with a smoothness and effect which left the most fastidious listener nothing to desire ... the acoustical improvement of the Palace ... was solved to the satisfaction of the public ... the aspect of the great central transept, which had been enclosed on each side to form a vast concert hall, the glass arched roof being also screened by external coverings from the glare of the sun, was a novelty to the eye. The Royal boxes and adjoining raised seats were so placed as to not interfere with the general effect ... Since the objection to the Crystal Palace as a location for great musical performance, an objection hitherto deemed insurmountable ... has been so completely obviated, the Handel Festival has been placed on a permanent footing, and may be carried to a magnitude of which the world has not yet formed any idea.[37]

THE PRACTICALITIES OF A DEVELOPING FESTIVAL

If the musical characteristics naturally attract the greatest attention, the vast organization which made it all possible was just as important, and of more facets. That of choral and orchestral recruitment has already emerged, growing steadily from the extensive metropolitan and regional arrangements made for the opening ceremony. Records show the great expansion of the contributing cities and towns and the strict limitations on numbers. All the preparation

came together at the first rehearsal. At first, no publicity was
attached to this, not least because Costa treated it as a run-through:
performers were expected to know their parts before. Attention
naturally focused more on the soloists and their projection into the
great arena. But it soon became a crucial factor in the reminding of
the potential outside audience of the impending event, through the
speed of the press. Strict regulations were employed to control the
vast choral numbers, and failure to attend the full rehearsal by
leaving early, of transferring tickets once issued, from one chorister
to another, and by singing in any rival activity within two weeks of
the performance, were all the subject of printed and circulated
warnings by at least 1868.[38] Invitations to the orchestral players
were also accompanied by the fee of £3 by at least 1868. An
indication of how the orchestra appeared to the closer observer can
be gained from the description of a model displayed in the transept
during the Festival: though only nine feet wide by five feet deep, its
2,400 musical figures, each about two inches high, with music stands
and instruments, may well capture detail missing elsewhere, and
also confirms the important role of the Royal Opera in providing
players.[39]

Regarding the accommodation, it shows that of the 386 performers listed in the programme, the only ones provided with seats
are the cellists (the report suggesting that the remainder stood
throughout the three days' festival).

One or two violinists appear to be leaning negligently against the stand
behind, so one assumes that they found it a tiring job. The vocalists
were more fortunate, for they at any rate could sit on the steps ... The
double basses are in two rows round the back of the orchestra and also in
two groups in the aisles between the violins and violas. Each double bass
player has his attendant satellite in the form of a cello player seated
(apparently on a soap box) at his right hand side. Every fiddler stands with
his right leg slightly in advance of the left, in best grand opera style. Coats
of all cuts and hues [including coloured waistcoats], frock coats, cutaways
etc, grace their well-wasted manly figures.

Of the ten flutes and eight piccolos in the wind section

Four of them are sitting between the trumpets and the clarinets, while four
of the piccolos are wedged at the back between the horns and bassoons!
The rest of the wood and brass are dotted here and there in patches, a
fair number of them sitting entirely surrounded by string players. There
are three timpanists with seven drums between them and one eight foot

upright drum just below the organist's seat ... Standing in the gangway between the banks of vocalists and well to the back of the orchestra are six serpent players. A couple of bass horns are similarly placed, but nearer to the band ... [The serpents] are at least thirty feet from the orchestra proper and are separated from one another by solid masses of vocalists.[40]

Despite the efficiency of the accommodation arrangements, performance conditions could be problematic: the great building – essentially a winter garden – could become a hothouse in summer, and, at least initially, no protection was afforded, though it continued to remain a problem, as Hollins later recalled.[41] But a more pressing problem was that of transport, not least since the rehearsal took place in the morning. Most travelled by train. Providing that the trains were not disrupted, the arrangements went well: the Palace had been designed to receive and dispatch vast numbers, even before the addition of the High Level Station in 1864. A report of another event in 1859 shows how easily things could go: when 63,181 attended the Annual Meeting of the Foresters Club and Society on 23 August there was no great inconvenience and everything was conducted with surprising regularity. Fully two thirds went down by rail ... For some hours during the morning the passengers delivered exceeded 12,000 per hour, or 1,000 every five minutes'.[42] But delays on the railway caused problems, as at the commencement of the rehearsal in 1862, when trains failed to run for an hour from Victoria and likewise London Bridge. Anticipation of the great triennial event must always have been tinged with anxiety. None the less, the railway provision was such a major part of the whole undertaking that it was openly acknowledged in the Festival publicity in the Programme for the 1862 meeting.[43] Such were the numbers involved, that special arrangements on a nationwide basis were made, and financial incentives given. But as well as the rail facility, the authorities acknowledged the importance of the postal services and the telegraph, in reporting 'by the next morning the details of the rehearsal day nationally and on the continent'. It is claimed that this influenced the attendance: that a vaster number thus came than by forward planning.

The Festival was widely advertised from the first, through the normal channels of the national press, musical press and the Saturday programme;[44] advanced notice in the latter was from April for the June event and invited the purchase of advance tickets. By 1880 it was necessary to buy an advance ticket to get a reserved seat.[45]

The available seating must have gradually increased over the years to judge by the figures of attendance. For the 1859 festival, two areas of seating were advertised: the central numbered stalls in lettered blocks, and unlettered seats in side blocks. By 1880, these had been extended by at least the addition of gallery seats, so that four areas of seating were available, the corner gallery seats, having the better view, being priced with the two higher stalls seats; there were two grades of unnumbered seats; all areas were divided not into rows but into blocks. The cost of the seats in 1859 for each individual day, or two days of the three, was one guinea for the centre seats and half a guinea for the sides. The set of three days was reduced to two guineas and twenty-five shillings respectively. In 1859 there is no mention of a ticket requirement for rehearsal day. In 1880 the four price levels were, for single performances, £1.10s., £1.1s., 15s., 7s. 6d., reduced for the three days to 3 guineas, £2.12s.6d., 2 guineas and 15s. Separate prices existed for Rehearsal Day, though at only three levels: 15s., 10s. 6d., 7s. 6d. Considering the massive ticket sales, these prices indicate an affluent audience, as could be inferred from the social status of many choral societies.[45]

In addition to the cost of the ticket, the audience member had to buy a programme and obtain refreshments. The printed programme for the Festival performances soon settled into a regular pattern of information, as the new audience obviously became accustomed to the historical background to works at first hardly known.[47] The first Handel Festival had been the occasion for an explosion of information about the composers and their works. The programme carried an extensive commentary on the music by Macfarren, running as a half-page footnote under the texts of *Messiah* and *Israel in Egypt*. From 1859, these commentaries become more general – not a description of the music so much as a background to the work, its composition and the outline of the drama. And drama was obviously a major factor in the event, as reviews on the performances by the most favoured singers indicate. The vast number of attenders obtaining refreshments at the interval clearly gave the event a special excitement as a whole. The Great Exhibition of 1851 had inaugurated a new era of mass catering; the Handel Festivals now extended this business to hitherto unimagined size, numbers naturally multiplying with the commensurate increase in the attendance at subsequent Festivals. With the firm establishment of the event,

Punch took a special interest in such aspects, as in reporting the first interval in 1883, and in so doing capturing something of the festive atmosphere:

Between the parts there is a tremendous run on buns, ices, teas, coffees and sandwiches. Waiters do marvels in the way of carrying heavily-laden trays through obstructive crowds. They remember that 'Who breaks pays' – and I don't hear a smash anywhere. After a few refreshment bars' rest, the second part commences and we are 'all in to begin'.[48]

COSTA THE MUSICIAN

Neither the size of the auditorium nor the sheer numbers involved in performance could have made the Handel Festival a success by themselves: on the contrary, the success was that of the first and longest-serving conductor, Michael Costa. The response to the problems posed by the unique acoustic character of the Crystal Palace clearly suited Costa's commanding musical personality. But his ways were not to everyone's taste, even those with an obvious sympathy towards the large-scale performances at the Palace. None the less, George Grove, for one, was fair in recognizing the qualities of discipline which had made such a contribution to London orchestral life: 'he was a splendid drill sergeant; he brought the London orchestras to an order unknown before. He acted up to his lights; he was thoroughly efficient as far as he went and was eminently "safe".'[49] But this 'safety' went beyond musical matters and was achieved at a cost, financial and artistic. Grove thought his requirements unreasonable, commenting 'Surround yourself with the best possible agents, the best assistants that you can obtain, quite regardless of expense, and success is certain. In the zenith of his career, Sir Michael never moved without such men as Bowley, to prepare the whole scheme of the transaction for him, Sainton, Blagrove, Hill, Lucas, Howell, Pratten, Lazarus, the Harpers, Chipp and others of equal eminence at the principal desks, Peck and Henry Wright to distribute the parts. With the perfect organization and efficient execution of such lieutenants failure was impossible', though, as Grove adds, the method was 'horribly expensive and crippled the Sacred Harmonic'. But Costa was 'quite unable to train and develop second-rate materials – to educate an orchestra like Richter, Manns or Rosa'.[50] Indeed, many of his concerts were not even rehearsed by him but by his leader.

An intimate part of Costa's approach was a cavalier attitude to text. Grove was severe in his judgement: 'his interpolations were "shameful": his additions vulgar, unnecessary and brutal, and his ignorance astounding'.[51] Grove's remarks must be placed in the context of contemporary practice. The provision of additions to orchestral parts was commonplace, inspired, not least in the choral field, by Mozart's to *Messiah*: Costa was a notable practitioner – indeed, four months before his death, Novello had secured rights to publish all his orchestral arrangements, so there was clearly a market for them.[52] His additions to the orchestral parts of *Messiah* were based on the Mozart version.[53] The basic choral text used at the Festivals was that of the Novello vocal score, published in the year of the Palace's opening, 1854, for 4 shillings: five years later, the massive sales guaranteed by the Handel Festival would prompt a cheap octavo edition for use there, first at 1s. 4d., later at a shilling.[54] Though Costa's additions were in the orchestral parts, they must have affected the vocal performance through doubling, for it seems that some instruments (serpents and 'bass horns') were placed within the choir.[55] In like manner he added liberally to the orchestral requirement, inevitably so with such large numbers, apparently in continuation of his practice at the opening ceremony, when the choir of 1,500 was 'monstrously strengthened' by 200 brass instruments, as Chorley put it.[56] Most striking of his effects was the addition of bass drum and cymbal parts to the 'Halleluiah Chorus', as Wood later discovered.[57] This was clearly a major feature of the early performances, to judge by the illustration of the 1857 Festival which appeared in the *Illustrated London News* (27 June 1857).[58]

For all the criticism of Costa's Handel, he presided none the less over a crucial phase in the introduction to the public of lesser known pieces as well as the two major oratorios: for, if *Messiah* and *Israel in Egypt* had become fixed and immutable parts of the Festival by the 1860s, the Selection Day,[59] and to a lesser extent, the preliminary rehearsal, offered a range of items from the rest of the repertory which provided the major national focus for education in Handel's works, maintaining a continuity for the subsequent performance of these works as wholes in the twentieth century. The Selection Days of 1859–1874 saw a repertory becoming established, first with the most accessible and effective choruses and vocal items, grouped in such a way as to form coherent units in a programme of two parts lasting for about three hours, which also required appropriate opening and closing pieces and variety of content. By 1877 the repertory had become sufficiently established through repetition for the printed programme to identify which items were new and thus reflect the response to a changing demand; in earlier years, the purpose had simply been to give 'several pieces not so well known . . . with the intention of showing the universality of the composer's genius', but as time passed on, critics and audience had become more demanding.

Although the confidence of the advertising suggested that the Festival was established supreme for ever, with numbers steadily increasing through the 1870s, its days were obviously numbered in its existing form. It had to change to reflect changing attitudes towards performance based on growing musical knowledge. Yet the end of Costa's reign came surprisingly suddenly, the conductor succumbing to a paralytic stroke just before the 1880 Festival: and to the ongoing financial pressures created by him was added in 1880–1 the requirement on the Society to leave the Exeter Hall. The new location, St James's Hall, forced a reduction to only 300 performers. Though the Society drifted on with new arrangements for several years, its days of control at the Crystal Palace were over by 1880.[60]

A NEW BEGINNING: THE FESTIVAL UNDER MANNS

When Manns took over the Handel Festivals at very short notice in 1883, an entirely new spirit came to inform the music-making. Used to working with the Crystal Palace Orchestra on new musical scores, Manns's whole approach was more painstaking than that of his predecessor and he trained the choir with a thoroughness that enabled it to perform without orchestral stiffening. Moreover, he knew the building intimately, having attended every Festival since 1857. As he told an interviewer years later, he 'had fully studied the acoustical properties of the building and could have given Sir Michael many hints'.[61] Like Grove, Manns was aware of Costa's limitations: 'his parts were full of cues and it was more upon these than upon rehearsal that he relied for a successful performance'.[62] Manns always rehearsed the orchestral parts first, and only when satisfied that all was well would he rehearse with the choir. Although never seen as the equal of specialist conductors like Richter, Bülow, or Joseph Barnby (commonly regarded as the greatest of English choir trainers), he was certainly considered the

best all-rounder, and this was the quality most needed for the
direction of the Handel Festivals.

Though stalwarts of the old choir (from now to be invited to
participate by the Crystal Palace Company under Manns's overall
control) naturally greeted the change of leader with some reserve,
Manns established his authority at the first rehearsal at Exeter Hall,
not least by his humour in the Selection piece from *Acis and Galatea*,
practically demonstrating the pedestrian qualities of Polyphemus by
taking 'monstrous strides' across the platform and singing the notes
with polyphemic gusto.[63] His manner contrasted with that of Costa,
concluding the final choral rehearsal with the encouragement
'ladies and gentlemen, if you have as much confidence in me as I
have in you we shall have a great success'.[64] The results were a
justification for the efforts, for the Festival was deemed to have
maintained its former standards, no mean achievement in the circumstances. If Mann's beat had not quite the commanding sweep of
Costa's in the rehearsals, his pains guaranteed security in the performances: and in regard to some aspects of choral precision, the
standards were judged the best ever, not least by the players. The
press was enthusiastic as to the achievement of the 4,000 picked
performers and 441 instrumentalists. If slightly hurried in *Messiah*,
the orchestra and chorus were 'on the whole wonderfully steady in
Israel in Egypt, creating 'a great result' alike for executants and
audience, 'who sat all through the oratorio under the full impression
that the highest creative and executive art can make'.[65] And the
Selection music seems to have made the greatest impression of any
Handel Festival to that date. Like the standards, the receipts were
also the best on record, with an attendance of 22,388 for Messiah
Day (nearly a thousand more than in 1880), 22,290 for Selection
Day (205 less) and 23,000 for Israel Day (about the same).

With this success behind him, Manns continued to develop his
more rigorous approach to the great Festival, the next of which
occurred two years instead of three hence in order to coincide with
the bicentenary of Handel's birth in 1885. A major innovation was
Manns's insistence on the rehearsal of *Messiah*. Under Costa, the
work was always taken as read, with only one or two stoppages for
correction: but Manns insisted on rehearsal of detail comparable
with that accorded the other works. This was clearly necessary for,
as he told Walker, he had 'discovered a large number of discrep-
ancies in the orchestral parts which had been overlooked for

years'.[66] As was observed of later occasions, Manns arrested the march of his army when he pleased, and chose to do so very often, teaching alike by example and precept what should be done, occasionally to the amusement of the public, always to the advantage of the music. Another feature was the use of regional rehearsals, the conductor travelling extensively to rehearse the provincial contingents. However, as he observed in an interview, he found recent improvements in standards so great that no criticism was needed, as in the cases of the Leeds and Bradford Societies in preparation for 1885.[67]

By the time Manns's directorship of the Festivals was well established in the middle and later '80s, they had been taking place for all of thirty years. It was inevitable that certain problems of longevity would have set in: chiefly that of old singers continuing to attend and of the problem of finding new works for Selection Day. As Manns proudly observed during the 1888 Festival, there were still many singers in the chorus who had sung in the 1857 and 1859 Festivals. None the less, he adopted a more rigorous approach to the maintenance of standards and had already engaged a thousand new voices for 1885 to replace older ones. If *Messiah* and *Israel in Egypt* posed no special problems for the conductor of the Festivals, the provision of pieces for Selection Day represented one of Manns's chief problems. By his period it was growing increasingly necessary to find unfamiliar items to satisfy the purpose of the Selection Day, which had become the one occasion in the Festival when the needs of the more discerning musician could be catered for.[68] The fact that Manns drew special praise for his choices in 1888, including choruses from *Belshazzar*, *Alexander Balus* and the Ninety-Fifth Psalm, complete, brings home the immense changes which have taken place in our familiarity with Handel's music, as with so much else performed at this time. One of the most striking discoveries was for the 1888 performance: that of the 'Gloria Patri'. The original had been destroyed by fire in 1860, but a copy made, and this was purchased by W. H. Cummings in 1878 to form part of his private collection, from which he permitted copies to be made for the festival.[69]

Manns conducted two more Festivals, 1897 and 1900, but by this time he was losing some of the youthful qualities he had kept for so long (he had celebrated his seventieth birthday in 1895). Indeed, he had been battling with rheumatism in both shoulders since the previous festival, explaining to his friend Joseph Bennett that a most

uncharacteristic example of a false choral entry (in the chorus 'And
with the blast of thy nostrils' from *Israel in Egypt*) was due to this.[70]
The last Festival was notable in changing the weekdays of the
Festival performances: from Monday, Wednesday and Friday, to
Tuesday, Thursday and Saturday, still with the preceding Saturday
evening for rehearsal. Another change was in the increase of women
performers in the orchestra. Costa would have no women, but in
Manns's later years there was a dramatic increase from eight in 1891
to sixty-eight in 1900; of this sixty-eight, fifty-one were violins, ten
violas, five cellos and two clarinets. In the choir, on the other hand,
the long cherished male alto tradition had dwindled from a force of
no less than 418 in 1859 to a mere 73 in 1900 and 23 in 1903.[71]
Manns was by no means the only veteran either. Charles Santley
had reached his twelfth and Edward Lloyd his tenth Festival by this
year. Although the public could not have anticipated that Manns
would no longer be conducting three years hence, the immense
warmth of his reception after this festival may have reflected the
sense that time was moving on. Although he immersed himself in the
preparatory work for the 1903 Festival, introducing considerable
changes in the preliminary organization of the singers, the effort
made it clear that he could not take full responsibility and he agreed
to involvement only if Frederick Cowen assumed the responsibilities
of the conductor's desk. He took his final rehearsal of the Handel
Festival Choir on 15 June 1903 at Exeter Hall at which the extent of
his popularity was clear. He had but one last conducting appearance to make. In continuance of his appearances with the Crystal
Palace Festival Choir, intermittently to perform Haydn's *Creation*
and the two Mendelssohn oratorios and other choral works, he
directed Mendelssohn's *Lobgesang* at the concert for the Jubilee
celebrations at the Palace on 11 June 1904.

Although this was a fitting moment to withdraw, acknowledging
his vast contribution to the fifty-year history of the Palace and
surrounded by affection and support of his singers and players for
the musical ideals he cherished, in truth, audiences had been
showing a steady decline since 1886. Bennett shows audience figures
from 1888 to 1897 as follows: 1888, 86,337; 1891, 80,796; 1894,
76,406; 1897, 67,376 (though the big drop in the latter was partly
the result of the rival activities of Queen Victoria's Diamond
Jubilee).[72] The reasons are those which can be observed in other
aspects of the quality music making of the Palace: the development

of new, more accessible venues in London, and the development of national standards comparable and even sometimes higher than those of the Palace – though, ironically, significantly inspired by its achievements.[73] And attitudes towards Handel were now changing. Although the Festival had always had its critics, broader popular enthusiasm was now on the wane. For the newer breed of critical writers on music and performance, it held no real importance. Maitland,[74] observing English music in the 1870s, thought that, despite the high ticket costs and the 'brilliance of the Sydenham audience, the Handel Festival seemed more a spectacle for the eye than a real musical treat for the ear', though certain things like 'they sank to the bottom like a stone in *Israel*' remained vividly as thrilling moments; and the acoustic still served to show the 'value of a method' for the singer, with such a distinguished performer as Georg Henschel suffering in comparison with the veteran Santley. Bernard Shaw gives the broadest view of how things were towards the end of the century, writing of the 1891 Festival:[75]

Fundamentally, my view of the Handel Festival is that of a convinced and ardent admirer of Handel. My favourite oratorio is the *Messiah*, with which I have spent many of the hours which others give to Shakespeare or Scott or Dickens. But for all this primary bias in favour of Handel, my business is still to be that of the critic, who, invited to pronounce an opinion on the merits of a performance by four thousand executants, must judge these abnormal conditions by their effect on the work as open-mindedly as if there were only four hundred, or forty, or four.

If in the 'Halleluia Chorus', Shaw found the right feeling, he insisted that

The Messiah is not all Halleluia. Compare such a moment … with the experience of listening to the fiercely tumultuous 'He trusted in God' with its alternations of sullen mockery with high-pitched derision and its savage shouts of 'Let him deliver him', jogging along at about half the proper speed, with an expression of the deepest respect and propriety, as if a large body of the leading citizens, headed by the mayor, were presenting a surpassingly dull address to somebody … To get rid completely of the insufferable lumbering which is the curse of English Handelian choral singing, a spirited reform in style is needed. For instance, Handel, in his vigorous moods, is fond of launching the whole mass of voices into florid passages of great brilliancy and impetuosity. In one of the most splendid choruses in The Messiah, 'For he shall purify the sons of Levi', the syllable 'fy' comes out in a single trait consisting of no less than thirty-two semi-quavers. That trait should be sung with one impulse from end to end without an instant's hesitation. How is it actually done in England? Just as if the thirty semiquavers were eight bars of crotchets taken *alla breve* in a not very lively tempo ... When I had been listening for some minutes of Wednesday evening to the festival choristers trudging with ludicrous gravity through what they called Tellit Outa Mongthe Hea-ea Then, I could not help wishing that Santley ... had given them a taste of their own quality by delivering those chains of triplets on the words 'rage' and 'counsel' [in 'Why do the nations'] as quavers in 12/8 time in the tempo of the pastoral symphony.

Shaw was much less critical of *Israel in Egypt*, which he found closer to Manns's inclinations, and much more lively and articulated, reserving his chief criticisms for those choir trainers who inadequately prepared their singers, since little could effectively be done on Rehearsal Day with so many participants.

THE HANDEL FESTIVAL IN THE TWENTIETH CENTURY
COWEN AND WOOD

As a major musical institution with very strong participant support, the Handel Festival retained its vitality well into the twentieth century, with triennial meetings until 1912 (the 1914–18 World War interrupting the sequence), and from 1920 to 1926, making a total of seven. Frederick Cowen directed six and Henry Wood the final festival, though even after this there there were occasional large scale performances. Although Manns had greatly improved standards, the whole undertaking was prone to shortcomings which were largely unavoidable. The internal evidence for the slackness noted by Shaw comes from Henry Wood, who (as it emerges from his reminiscences published forty years later) was approached in 1899 by the aging Manns to largely take over the 1900 Festival by conducting *Messiah* and *Israel in Egypt* in his stead. From his own previous attendances at the Festivals, Wood did not like 'the way in which the accompaniments were scored – no middle harmony, no balance between chorus and orchestra – all top and bottom and no middle'.[76] And Walker recalls a choral participant's experience of 'an alarming number of wrong notes in her neighbourhood', adding for himself, 'I knew one of the violinists who was a very bad player, but in such an army his scratching passed unnoticed. The whole thing was a hotbed of pretence.'[77]

Like Manns, Cowen was a noted orchestral as well as choral

conductor, who kept strictly to the text and avoided interpolations and changes. He was highly efficient, as he showed over a considerable period as conductor of the Philharmonic. His achievement in carrying off the performance at short notice was acknowledged and some improvements also noted in the enunciation of words. 'But' (in emulation of Shaw) the critic of *The Musical Times* stressed

there is still a great deal of leeway to make up in this respect. Final and other consonants did not receive their proper value – e.g. 'le*d*', 'oppress'*t*', 'tribes'. A tendency to run one word into another manifested itself, sometimes with curious results. And then the important matter of feeling – entering fully into the dramatic significance of the words. To give two instances, one longed for '*He* spake the word' and 'Thy right hand, O Lord, hath *dashed* in pieces the enemy', such a rendering, for example, as one might hear with thrilling effect in the West Riding of Yorkshire.

Indeed, this critic went out of his way to stress the importance of the provincial contingent, listing them and stressing their superiority over the London choir. Out of 3,300 singers, 576 were from the provinces, as follows: Birmingham and Bradford, 90; Bristol 50; Leeds, 70; Sheffield, 220; Other Places, 56. Of sections, the altos were felt to be weakened by the handful of 'bearded altos' as Mendelssohn had once called them (only 23), but the sopranos were chief in the firing line

at least as far as the London contingent is concerned. The chronic faults of the old go as you please style were unfortunately in evidence in spite of the leavening of the great Metropolitan mass by the Provincial singers – but what are they among so many?[78]

In 1906 another sign of the need for reform appeared when *Judas Maccabeus* was given on Day 3, *Israel in Egypt* given in part within the Selection Day programme (most of its choruses within Part 1). The Handel–Mendelssohn Festival of 1909 required a more complete change, again with the choruses of *Israel in Egypt* playing a central part on Day 3. In this year, the combining of the two great names of the Palace's choral tradition finally took place through the celebration of Mendelssohn's centenary. The choir consisted of upwards of 3,000 voices, London and the suburbs contributing 2,700, with the remainder from the chief provincial centres: Sheffield, Leeds, Bradford, Bristol and, for the first time, South Wales. The orchestra now numbered around 500, of whom about 270 were experienced amateur performers; but the London Symphony Orchestra led by

W. H. Reed were specially engaged to accompany the solos 'and leaven, so to speak, the instrumental force'. The doyen of the soloists was Santley, who had first appeared in 1865. The pattern was as follows: Grand Rehearsal, Saturday 19 June; *Elijah*, Tuesday, 22 June; Selection (Handel) and *Hymn of Praise* (Mendelssohn), Thursday 24 June; *Messiah*, Saturday 26 June. This time, praise for Cowen's preparation was unstinting and *The Musical Times* commented boldly that

with a long experience of Handel festivals, we have no hesitation in saying that no finer choral singing has ever been heard at the Crystal Palace, that choral technique has very greatly improved during recent years with the result that, we venture to say, no other country could produce a choir so intelligent, so artistically vocal and so efficient.[79]

Whatever future such singing might have had was soon to be dashed by the First World War. By the time it had come and gone, the Handel Festival found itself in a strange position, if fulfilling an unanticipated role. As *The Musical Times* observed of the 1923 Festival,

there are those who scoff at the Handel Festival. Vain highbrows! The Festival is an overgrown giant. Nonetheless, it has something to be said for it ... To begin with, the Triennial Handel Festival is the only place you can nowadays hear Handel. Handel is under a cloud, and the sun shines on him but once in three years, for the stray wintry gleams of a Messiah performance hardly count, *The Messiah* being performed as *The Messiah*, and as a part of the British themselves, rather than as Handel. Now at the Festival this year could be heard not only *The Messiah*, but considerable chunks of *Israel*, *Jephtha*, *Samson*, *Acis* and *Galatea*, and *Alexander's Feast* as well as smaller selections from *Atalanta*, *Rodelinda*, *Joshua*, *Judas Maccabeus*, *Saul*, *Semele* and the *Dettingen Te Deum*, with the *Water Music* (in Hamilton Harty's arrangement for modern orchestra) thrown in.[80]

The enthusiastic critic did not pick up the irony that it was precisely the deficiencies of such giant performances (however relatively well done) which had lost the audience for Handel's choral works in the twentieth century, as another devotee of 'modernized Handel', Thomas Beecham, observed, quite independently.[81] And to a large extent, Handel's place had been taken by Bach, whose music had never allowed inflated performance and which, in any case, had no such traditional associations, even for the few Victorians who knew it. The traditions developing apace from the pioneering work of Otto Goldschmidt and the Bach Choir were of a far more 'serious' nature than those which had fostered Handel in England.[82] Still, the Festivals continued, with Henry Wood now succeeding Cowen in 1926. He had new ideas of performance, including a radically innovative Selection Day taken from the operas. Standards remained high, though the old problems remained to be solved, and the participation of the LSO to provide a nucleus had now become regular, no mean sign of the continuing importance of the Festival. For all its shortcomings and the attendant problem of finance, the critic of *The Musical Times* predicted no reason for the Festival not to continue, taking it very much for granted (as, in 1923, its critic had commented 'nobody needs a report on the Handel Festival'). No advance warning was published of the non-appearance of the 1929 Festival: in place of the customary *Musical Times* comment, there merely appeared a report on the exhibition of the 1859 Festival, with a description of the model of the Handel Orchestra and performers. Doubtless some practical factor inhibited the organization, and, once discontinued, the sequence would never resume.[83]

In retrospect the Festivals can be seen as lasting virtually the entire history of the Palace, longer than any other regular activity: in a mere ten years the building would be no more. The musical achievements cannot be gainsaid. The Handel Festival had seen Handel established in England in a new and modern social context. The sheer numbers involved had in turn created a climate in which a publisher could produce cheap editions of the music, thus enabling more and more people to get to know it. If it is impossible to know how influential in the long term were these monster performances as such, the spin-off effect was incalculable in its influence on a new world of mass dissemination.

CHAPTER 4

Other large-scale choral performances

If the passing question of a critic of the 1862 Handel Festival whether 'only Handel's music should be performed'[1] – was a rare one at the time, it could as well have been applied to the rest of Handel's music: for the Festival was not concerned with Handel the composer, as much as with Handel the composer of *Messiah* and *Israel in Egypt*: other music of his received only the very partial treatment of Selection Day, in which the choice of choral items was determined by effectiveness within a structured programme. The selection principle was to dominate all the large-scale choral activities at the Palace. Few other works in the regular choral repertory were appropriate as a whole for Crystal Palace festival-scale treatment. One such was Mendelssohn's *Elijah*, and its composer was the only other figure to receive comparable adulation. This is first manifest in the 1860 Mendelssohn Festival on 4 May 1860. The celebration was for the unveiling of a statue of Mendelssohn, in bronze, subscribed for by the friends of the composer. It had first been intended to position this in central London, first choice being The Mall; but the permission was refused and the Crystal Palace became an appropriate home, where it was erected on one of the terraces. At the end of the performance there was 'a simultaneous movement towards the statue' and the fountains gave forth for the first time of the season;[2] the unveiling was accompanied by a performance of the Overture to and Wedding March from *A Midsummer Night's Dream* played by the Band of the Coldstream Guards, and the evening concluded with a torchlight 'exhibition',[3] the whole event capturing national press attention.

For all the enthusiasm, performance of *Elijah* simply intensified the problems which already attended the more complex passages in the Handel works. With about 3,000 choral and orchestral performers on this occasion, the dangers in the more animated passages loomed even larger, critical response reflecting the limitations of popular taste in observing that 'the music of *Elijah* is of a more complicated and florid character than any which has hitherto been attempted by the colossal orchestra, and though the grander parts of the chorus were brought out with the most telling effect, there was a cloudiness and apparent unsteadiness in the most delicate passages'.[4] Only vocal soloists capable of projecting the full length of the auditorium were deemed successful by the critic and it is natural that a core of soloists should tend to dominate all performances. The audience numbered 17,192.

An early Saturday in May further establishes itself as a focal moment for large-scale choral performance outside the triennial Handel event with another Mendelssohn performance, of *Athalie*, given on 1 May 1863. This further served to show the value of the location. The band and chorus numbered 2,500 under Costa, with Parepa, Martin and Sainton Dolby as soloists. Critical reaction was consistent with the 1860 meeting, here regarding the audibility of the reciter of the illustrative verse, though 'the choruses went steadily and were well in tune. In the march, played by the band, splendid effect was produced by the organ at the close'.[5] This musical success probably influenced the decision to perform *Elijah* in 1869, though it was now generally agreed that the work was not appropriate to performance on a grand scale. But twenty years later, in June 1889, with Manns now establishing new standards with the Handel Festival, it was a different matter, the quality of performance suggesting that the fault was with the executants, not with the music'.[6] Manns's 900 performers now moved with 'marchlike accuracy and the volume of tone and unfailing precision in the "Baal Choruses", "Thanks be to God" etc. was not more remarkable than the beauty of the phrasing and delicate gradation in "He watching over Israel", "He that shall endure" and "After the fire there came a still small voice" ... Mendelssohn's music has never before been heard to such advantage'. The soloists too were effective, with Albani's penetrating tone exciting comment and Patey and Lloyd repeating their familiar success in the alto and tenor parts. And, at 24,133, this was the largest audience so far on record.

Encouraged by this success, the 21 June of the following year saw a similar performance of *St Paul* which proved that, allowing for the precedence of broad choral effect over projection of solo voices, 'there is now no reason why any work should be kept out of the Central Transept. All are possible with such perfectly-trained executants ... and so resourceful a Conductor'.[7] In due course, the 1909 Triennial Festival, bringing Handel and Mendelssohn together in (coincidental) celebration of Mendelssohn's centenary, would confirm the point, with a choir of upwards of 3,000 voices.

The only other choral work to receive any such regular performance over the years was Haydn's *Creation*. This was first given in 1860 to honour the retirement of Clara Novello. In being reviewed in terms of her performance, it gives a clear image of the issues for solo performers, and the attractions for the listening participants and audience.

the Directors having assigned to the members of the press as usual the upper gallery in the far-off distance, we were enabled to give our undivided attention to Madame Clara Novello, who, if the truth be told, was the only singer whose voice could be heard to advantage in that position. In the upper gallery choruses sound as if veiled, and the solo singers as if they were singing in the gardens [instead of] building. Madame Novello's voice is the only one which can be said to reach the further end of the building in all its purity of tone, undiminished by the vast area through which it has to travel. The softest accents are heard with distinctiveness and her voice alone stands out as the prominent and only voice of the oratorio.[8]

The next great choral performance was that to acknowledge the death of Rossini. On 1 May 1869, vast forces comprising the choir of the Sacred Harmonic Society, the London contingent of the Handel Festival Choir and 'numerous other amateurs and professionals of the first rank ... carefully selected, with the Crystal Palace orchestra, performed a concert of varied items, with the *Stabat Mater* as the focus.[9] It was to be conducted by Costa, who was a friend of the composer and whose March from *Naaman* was one of the other items (with three Rossini overtures, the Prayer from *Moses,* and the 'Blessing of the Banners' from *The Siege of Corinth*), but was in the event directed by Manns. Only one English composer could ever have competed with Rossini, to say nothing of Handel and Mendelssohn, in providing music for such events during this period: Arthur Sullivan. His fame by 1872 and special association with the Palace led to his being invited to write a large-scale setting of the *Te Deum* to celebrate the recovery of the Prince of Wales from illness in 1872. It was scored for soloists, chorus, orchestra and military band in the last movement, and was given on 1 May 1872. Sullivan was to retain his pre-eminence in being seen as giving expression to the voice of England at the Palace throughout his life, and on 24 June 1893, a performance of his Leeds-premiered oratorio *The Golden Legend* was the occasion for the employment of similar forces, with 3,500 performers. Of other native works of this kind, a notable performance was of G. A. Macfarren's setting of the *Te Deum* for the opening ceremony of the International Exhibition at the Palace in 1884.[10]

In all these large-scale choral performances till 1880, participants in the Sacred Harmonic Society played a central role. Only one other choir was destined to rival it in length of association with the Palace in later years; characteristically, it was another organization of dissenting tradition which favoured the Palace as a natural locale: the Nonconformist Choir Union. This existed with the purpose of 'the development and improvement of the music of our services, the mutual co-operation of our choirs, the holding of festival services on a large scale and annual choral festivals'.[11] It was an important initiative in the music of the free churches, which otherwise possessed no natural cohesive force in national organization. For them, the Crystal Palace was again an ideal venue for the numbers involved. The festival on 1 June 1889 boasted 3,000 singers mustered from over fourteen listed towns and cities from Manchester to Margate in a programme of fifteen oratorio items and church anthems, with the National Anthem as the climax. By the meeting of 1907–8 the name had been changed to the Free Church Choir Union. The programme of that year followed similar lines, though revealing more imagination, partly as a consequence of the inclusion of a competitive element: the winning choir of a previous competition singing a part song. Selections from a band (together with a distribution of choral prizes) also added contrast in an eleven-item programme of hymns, anthems, part-songs and vocal and organ solos. The repertory ranged from anthems by unknown names (presumably associated with one of the represented denominations) to part-songs by modern composers, Edward German and Frederick Cowen, choruses by Handel and, finally, Verdi: the soldiers' chorus, 'Hark the Loud Clarion'.

In the 1930s a new phase began in the life of the Union with the retirement of the long-serving conductor Frank Idle and organist Arthur Meale at the beginning of the decade. Eric Thiman was appointed organist in 1930 and Ernest Read conductor in the following year.[12] Instrumental music was now to play a bigger part, with regular solos from Thiman as well as the participation of an orchestra. The existing high choral standards were maintained and improved, with a marked rapport between choir and conductor, and the organization extended to encourage choirs from the provinces with special travelling arrangements, and invitations in the press to London choirmasters to involve their choirs, prompting comment that the Union was becoming 'a kind of all-England Choral Society'.[13] Throughout the rest of its life at the Palace the Festival programmes showed a broadening of repertory towards the mainstream of English church music old and new, as well as the staple Mendelssohn and Handel items. If the first year under the new conductor was more memorable for its instrumental than for its choral items (the orchestra played *The Mastersingers* overture and Boellmann's *Fantasie Dialogue* with Thiman as soloist), the 1932 advertised twelve-item programme included seven English works, four by modern composers (Bairstow, Geoffrey Shaw, Elgar, Charles Wood) and one sixteenth-century item, 'O Lord the maker of all things', though the review shows Thiman including his own 'Elegiac Melody' for strings and organ:[14] the orchestra also contributed the Overture to *Egmont* and March from *Tannhäuser*, and the Handel item, 'Let the bright Seraphim', was sung by all the sopranos of the choir. Though standards were thought to have declined a little by 1936, the event maintained its vitality; in 1934, the Festival Choir drew on 100 church choirs and in the following year, 1935, the event took up the complete Saturday, solo singing and choral competitions and a Junior Choir Concert during the day preceding the Grand Festival Concert at 6.30 in the evening. The Festival moved to the Alexandra Palace in 1937.

The greatest challenge in the days at the Crystal Palace was the provision of adequate audiences, and members were encouraged to form the nucleus from their own circle by the sale of visitors' tickets by choir members. By the 1930s *The Musical Times* played an important part in notifying of the event in advance. Singers were now required to attend at least nine rehearsals in order to participate. Preparation was aided by the advance publication of a programme book published by Novello containing the music as well as notes on its preparation and performance by Ernest Read, which it was stated as 'the duty of everyone taking part to read, mark and inwardly digest'. Many of the items were in standard Novello editions, bound together with uniform editions of the remaining items. The choice of Novello rather than Curwen as publisher reflects a difference of tradition and musical literacy: the Free Church Choir Union was at the more sophisticated end of the market than the institutions associated with Curwen's popular educational publications, increasingly so with the twentieth century, and by the 1930s *sol fa* transcriptions were no longer included with the published music.

If the choral tradition at the Palace had no special connection with the established Church in England, its facilities remained attractive to many organizations, and in 1933 and 1936 it played host to festivals of a very different kind from those previously described. The School of English Church Music had been founded by Dr Sydney H. Nicholson in 1929 at Chislehurst, Kent, with the aim of training choirmasters and improving the range and quality of church music.[15] After festivals at the Royal Albert Hall and elsewhere, the 1933 festival took place at the Palace on 21 July, the Archbishop of Canterbury dedicating a festival which involved 4,000 singers, some from cathedrals outside the United Kingdom (Singapore and Capetown).

The choirs assembled at ... 2 o'clock in the afternoon, and all the music was thoroughly rehearsed, beginning with the processions. At the service in the evening, the organization of this difficult part of the scheme was singularly complete. Two processions approached the central transept from opposite ends of the Palace, singing hymns in alternate verses, at first without accompaniment. They were faultlessly in tune and time, each led by a conductor with a long wand; when they had joined forces in the centre, a third procession of choirs, including the clergy and the archbishop, approached from the opposite end of the transept. To the musician it was interesting to note the steady increase of volume of tone as the choirs assembled.[16]

There followed an introduction on the work of the Society by the Dean of Windsor and a message from the King and Queen. The service was Evensong, with special psalms, and the other anthems were chosen to provide 'variety of style and date'; the excellent preparation gave smooth performances under Nicholson, unaffected by the great distances involved – clearly a reflection of the cathedral experience of the choirs. The organist was Dr Ernest Bullock of Westminster Abbey.

PART 3

August Manns and the Saturday concerts,
1855–1900

CHAPTER 5

The concerts, orchestra and conductor

ORIGINS, GROWTH AND DECLINE

It is a measure of the importance of choral music in Victorian England that, even at the height of his fame, Manns was best known to the public at large as the conductor of the Handel Festivals.[1] Yet, for all its public prestige, the Handel Festival was a limited vehicle for the expansion of the repertory. But in the field of orchestral music the situation was totally different. In frequency, standards of performance and range of repertory, especially of new music, the orchestral concerts of the Crystal Palace offered the major impetus to the development of British musical life. Only in Manchester, with the work of another German expatriate, Charles Hallé, was any comparable orchestral endeavour to be found, though far fewer performances were given. The Crystal Palace became a place of musical pilgrimage as well as conferring on its locality even more fashionable status, not least for musicians.[2]

In his later years, Manns commented that 'no special room for music or provision for full orchestra had entered into the ideas of the designers of the Palace'.[3] At first a brass band was thought quite sufficient to serve the various regular needs of the vast building and its grounds:[4] everything from outdoor performance of rousing marches to indoor pomp and ceremony for visiting dignitaries. Moreover, the original Palace band was far from impressive in standards, as is vividly recalled by the critic of *The Times*, J. W. Davison, who watched musical events at the Palace with a close and sympathetic eye.[5] He recounts that the new brass band (conducted by one Herr Schallehn, a German ex-military bandmaster) was performing programmes made up of marches, overtures, pot-pourris and polkas. But when, in the autumn of 1854, it played at a military fete at the Crystal Palace, it compared very unfavourably with the

English regimental bands playing on the same occasion, as well as with the French Guides, who were visiting London. Its problem lay with 'wearisome monotony' of its wholly brass composition, as well as its style, which was 'pompous, vulgar and exaggerated, and above all, – wholly guiltless of any approach to a piano'.[6]

At least one participant agreed, and his role was soon to be crucial: August Manns. Manns had been appointed sub-conductor in the previous May, and had played in the opening ceremony (as also for the opening of the Great Exhibition in Hyde Park itself). But his connection with the Palace band and its conductor at this stage was to be short-lived. For Manns soon found himself in dispute with Schallehn and duly dismissed by him in October 1854.[7] In fact, as later emerged, Schallehn's appointment was merely part of the casualness with which musical matters were handled in the early months.[8] Manns's strength of character was certainly to serve him well as he now responded to the Palace authorities in pressing his claim for reinstatement – and doubtless the glimpse of far greater musical opportunities in prospect too. He wrote a long and per- suasive letter appealing to Englishmen for the justice 'which I am denied by a countryman of my own'.[9]

But in the short term at least, no official response was forth- coming. Manns duly left, first to teach and perform outside London, and subsequently, in the spring of 1855, to travel to Amsterdam.[10] But the whole matter had obviously been an embarrassment to the authorities. In addition to Davison, Manns had the crucial backing of Grove, who 'kept him warm with the Directors during the Amsterdam period, and for many years afterwards'.[11] Grove sub- sequently offered him the post, writing

As you know the Palace very well, you should be considering what number the band must consist of . . . The number of our band is at present 58, but we should be very glad if possible to reduce it to 36 . . . If you should engage any of your present musicians you must consider that after 7 *in summer and 5 in winter their time is their own for other engagements* and this should be taken into account in fixing their pay. You must remember that as conductor of the band you will be bound to do all you can to make the music *economical* as well as *efficient*.[12]

Grove was impressed by the works that Manns had performed (the overture Op. 124 by Beethoven, Weber's Clarinet Concerto, Berlioz's *Invitation à la Valse* Mozart's finale to Gluck's *Iphigenie*), of which only the Beethoven had been heard in London in his recollection: 'I like them very much, and would give a great deal to have such music done in the Crystal Palace'.[13]

Davison spoke truer than he knew. For Manns conducted his first concert only a week after his arrival: and only the second part of his performance was given to the wind band. The first half was given by a string orchestra, made up from the double-handed players of the wind band and about half a dozen extra strings from London. Even Grove had not counted on strings and apparently thought them inappropriate for the Palace: only the results of the first year's concerts converted him.[14]

Concert patterns and locations through the first decade

Manns's sustained efforts were gradually attracting attention. For Saxe Wyndham the concerts had become 'an institution' by January 1859,[15] a view certainly to be inferred from the regular acknowledgement of the press and the initial completion of the Concert Room. In the four years since their inception, patterns had become established which would last another forty years till changing circumstances began to threaten the very foundations of the Palace's pre-eminence. But it was only after about ten years that they really began to receive their due, with the critic of *The Times* commenting at the end of the 1866–7 season that it had become the most brilliant ever known at the Palace – 'a succession of orchestral performances without parallel in this country and unsurpassed in any other. Never in England . . . have the symphonies of Beethoven been performed as under Herr Manns at the Crystal Palace'.[16] From this point too, the Crystal Palace advertisements begin to trumpet the reputation of 'the world-renowned orchestra'. Already the programme for the 1864–5 season had quoted from *The Times* on its front cover that 'a more agreeable means of passing Winter afternoons can hardly be imagined than is now provided every Saturday at the Crystal Palace'.

This reputation was intimately tied up with the establishment of the Concert Room. The first year had been full of problems of location as Manns later recalled. 'As far as accommodation was concerned the Court of Musical Instruments, since known as the Bohemian Glass Court, was the nearest approach to such a room that the building contained.'[17] Like all the courts it was of adequate size and it was the natural choice because of its musical associations.

It was situated on the east, garden, side of the nave near the south end. Manns explains that this room soon proved too small and that the concerts then moved to the north transept, near the fountains, during December 1855: and afterwards in 'a kind of lecture room formed in extempore fashion outside the Queen's apartments to the north end of the Palace'.[18] This was the part of the Palace destroyed by fire in December 1866 and never rebuilt. 'Here the Mozart celebration was given on 26 January 1856 and here the concerts continued to be given for some months.'[19] Wyndham indicates that they then moved 'to an enclosure upon the garden side of the centre transept'.[20] Since the Palace was designed for the free exploration of its patrons, the problem posed by the proper location for serious listening was crucial to Manns's ambitions. Disturbance was obviously a major problem. In the early printed programmes, the conductor appealed to his listeners: 'Visitors are earnestly requested not to leave their seats during the performance of the pieces.' He even encouraged his audience by pointing out how the location could best be reached from the gallery.

For the second season, beginning on 15 November 1856, the 'New Music Room', as it came to be called, became available, constructed in the same location as the enclosure already in use (see Plate 12). It provided a much larger area than the Court of Musical Instruments (situated in the same, south east, part of the building), though it was at first clearly only a provisional, partly enclosed structure. It was not till three years later, in 1859, that it was (still temporarily) completed. Work had to continue thereafter because of the persistent disturbances. It only needed two concerts of the 1862–3 season for the concert programme to note complaints about 'interruption to the concerts by visitors walking in the galleries during the music (which) is so great that it is found necessary to close the staircase and galleries absolutely after the commencement of the programmes. The entrances to the floor of the Concert Room and the entrance to the reserved seats will be kept open throughout.' The problem was not easily solved, for later programmes show that the disturbance has caused 'such strong remonstrances, both from the audience and from the eminent solo artists that the door will re-open at 5 p.m. or at the conclusion of the Symphony', indicating that by now the doors had been closed for part of the concert. Clara Schumann was one of those affected, noting to Grove that orchestra and conductor had let her forget 'quite all the trouble and noise of the visitors

DINNER TO THE 69TH REGIMENT, IN THE CRYSTAL PALACE.—(SEE NEXT PAGE)

12 The Concert Room in 1857, in use for a regimental dinner with musical entertainment. The stage was subsequently remodelled to accommodate over 300 performers.

walking outside the room' after her first performance at the Crystal Palace in 1863.[21] A note in the programme for 7 October 1865 states that 'by next Saturday, the Concert Room will be entirely enclosed, additional space being added thereto on the south side'.[22] Thus the process of the adaptation of concert facilities reflected that of the choral transformations of the great Handel Auditorium itself – directly across the nave. By 1868 the Directors could further state in their programme that 'the enlargement of the concert hall, which now includes an area twice the size of Exeter Hall and the erection of the new organ, together with the remodelling and extension of the orchestra, have enabled the conductor to produce, in all classes of music, works which were formerly beyond the powers of the Crystal Palace orchestra'.

But an element of adaptability obviously remained. Hollins recalls that during his first Handel Festival in 1880, 'the entire wooden wall of the Concert Room near the Centre Transept was taken down and a low barrier erected and the Concert Room was used as a Restaurant'.[23] He also remarks that one could always hear the great organ through the wooden walls. A description of the Room was provided with the 1911 Auction Catalogue of the Palace.[24] It had a gallery (a structural consequence of the existing design of the building, though access from the rest of the east side was removed), and thirteen entrances and exits. The stage was a sixteen-tiered orchestra for some 300 performers, with green and retiring rooms, and the main body of the room and galleries had accommodation for up to 2,000 spectators, though the evidence is that it held many more in Manns's earlier years.[25] The completion of the room was symbolized by the addition of its own organ, installed in 1867. By 1885, the building was provided with electric lighting.[26] Yet for all the 'countless first performances of standard works' heard there, it remained, for Walker at least, 'that ugly room', and hardly any illustrations of it survive, unlike those of the great transept outside its doors.[27]

The regular pattern of orchestral music-making soon established itself, with the daily concerts (advertised as. 'daily music') at 12.30 p.m. and 2.30 p.m., though the latter also took place at 4 p.m. The Saturday concerts began in the early years at 2 p.m., 2.15 or 2.30, but later at 3 p.m. or 3.15 on special occasions. The time of conclusion, flexible in the earlier years, became fixed in the 1860s, when the introduction of the 'fashionable promenade' to the accom-

paniment of the organ till 6 p.m. became a feature, after which the
Palace generally closed. As well as giving advance notice of the
Saturday concerts, the more substantial items to be given daily were
generally noted in the programme for the previous Saturday. Friday
became the day for the most extended weekly programme. Walker
recalls that

Symphonies and concertos were, as a rule, left to the afternoon concerts:
but at 12.30 in the morning, a handful of listeners, I never saw more ...
came in for an out-of-the-way overture by Berlioz or a Liszt symphonic
poem – or a brand new piece by, say, Ethel Smyth not to mention the
classics or Viennese waltzes or specimens of Spohr, Raff or Rubinstein ...
And such had been the routine ever since 1855.[28]

Despite the limitations, the establishment of a classical repertory
remained Manns's central goal. He remarks that

with this, so to say 'improvised' orchestra, the first attempt at the symphony was made at the sixth concert, on Saturday 1 December 1855, when
the two middle movements of Beethoven's 7th Symphony were performed
in the North Transept.[29] This attempt seems to have been successful, for
Beethoven's Nos. 2, 4, 8 and Mendelssohn's Scotch (the entire works) are to
be found in the programmes of the next four Saturdays and Schubert's 9
and Schumann's 4 had received their Crystal Palace christening before the
end of the first season had been reached in April 1856.[30]

These were likely very obscure for most of his audience and presaged
the bold approach to repertory that would distinguish the Saturday
concerts.

For years the experience of the Saturday concerts at the Crystal
Palace was to dominate the lives of musicians eager to know the new
repertory better. But, for all its pre-eminence in the 1860s and 70s,
the days of the Crystal Palace concerts were inevitably numbered.
Its very achievements had sown the seeds of its demise. Innovative
orchestral concerts had also begun to emerge in the life of the
metropolis. First the Richter concerts from 1879, setting new standards and bringing a more direct contact with the greatest modern
European traditions, and likewise Henschel's London Symphony
Concerts and finally, the Queen's Hall concerts under Henry Wood,
the first great native orchestral conductor, which began in 1895,
really sounded the final knell for Manns, because, unlike the other
concerts, they took place on Saturday afternoons. The journey to
Sydenham was no longer a musical imperative, even for the most
dedicated musician; and likewise the general public found other

attractions which marginalized the Palace in its provision and location. By the turn of the century, the metropolis could offer many new specialist facilities catering for activities, educational, recreational and domestic, with new exhibitions, forms of leisure, department stores and restaurants, reflective of a growing consumer culture based on the rapid expansion of the population, the growth of national wealth, and burgeoning technological innovation and transport links; the capital was changing and opening up suburbia and the countryside beyond. Above all, Saturday was the focal day of activity and so another part of the potential audience for the Saturday Concerts was significantly reduced. In addition, Manns had trained no successor, which naturally eased the decision regarding continuity. The daily orchestra was disbanded in April 1900. Manns's Saturday concerts could not continue in this way without this nucleus, and the final Saturday concert under his direction took place on 19 May 1900 at 3.30.

ORCHESTRA, CHOIR AND CONDUCTOR

The permanence of the Crystal Palace orchestra was the key to the achievements of the Saturday concerts. Although Manns had to start from scratch, with no existing structure (as had the concerts of the Philharmonic Society in London, or the Hallé Concerts in Manchester – with which Manns's work most often finds itself compared),[31] he had the unique advantage of daily contact with his players through the daily orchestral performances. This nucleus, which required relatively little augmentation for the Saturday concerts, enabled him to establish quickly a real sense of a functioning orchestra: nowhere else in Britain did a comparable situation exist.[32]

The constitution of the original resident (brass) band must have been changed at some time during the first year that the Palace was open, 1854–5, for Manns speaks only of a wind band for his first concert on 20 October of the following year, 1855, the opening of his first, and the Palace's second season. This concert marked the transition towards a symphony orchestra, for, as earlier noted, he states that it employed two bands: the wind band, which played the second half in the Centre Transept, and a string band, made up of the double-handed players of the wind band, which played the first half in the Court of Musical Instruments; this string band was augmented by four players.[33] This arrangement lasted until the end of November.[34] From 1 December 1855 a mixed orchestra played both halves of the concert in one of the various locations already described, permission having been given by the Directors for full orchestra.[35] The orchestral listing that appeared towards the end of the next season, 1856–7, shows an orchestra of forty-five players comprising twenty-four strings, eight wind (two each of flutes, oboes, clarinets and bassoons), twelve brass (cornet, four horns, two trumpets, four trombones, bombardon and kettle drum.[36] Assuming Grove's requirement of Manns to reduce the band from fifty-eight to thirty-six players had been fulfilled,[37] this leaves an augmentation by seven strings for the first Saturday orchestra.

By 1866, the strings of this orchestra had been augmented to thirty violins, ten violas and sixteen cellos and basses, to make a total complement of seventy-six players:[38] this significant expansion co-incides with the greater projection of the orchestra through the advertising in the programme and the press, as in the recognition of the critics. The augmentation of the orchestra had for some years taken place for special performances, when the complement was compared with that of the orchestra of the Leipzig Gewandhaus or that of the Philharmonic Society: for an early performance of the *Eroica* Symphony – clearly a special event – the programme indi-cates the band augmented to 'full Philharmonic size', though this must have been an approximate claim.[39] By the time the consti-tution and personnel of the orchestra is again, and now regularly, published in the Saturday programmes from 1885–6, the orchestra is of eighty-five players, fourteen each of first and second violins, ten violas, nine cellos, nine basses, two flutes, piccolo, two oboes, cor anglais, two bassoons, double bassoon, four horns, two cornets, three trombones, tuba, two harps, timpani and percussion.[40] By the last season, 1899–1900, the second violins had been reduced to twelve, but the wind extended, clearly to cope with the new repertory, to three flutes, three clarinets and clarinet in D, three bassoons. By this time a much larger proportion of the orchestra must have been comprised of Saturday players, since the daily orchestra had been reduced in numbers.

If early membership of the Crystal Palace Orchestra hardly offered a player a musical, to say nothing of social, status compar-able to that of membership of the Philharmonic orchestra,[41] it did offer permanent employment as an orchestral musician without the customary need to travel around. The lack of information on the early personnel makes it difficult to establish the level of stability in the orchestral personnel for the first thirty years. But the evidence of a partial reconstruction of membership of the orchestra in the 1867–8 season suggests that it remained relatively stable.[42] Of the seventeen names listed, six were present in the 1857 listing: assuming a measure of proportionality, this would give upwards of twenty players from the daily orchestra of thirty-eight. But the relevance of long-serving members to the stability of the orchestra diminishes somewhat with the great increase of Saturday numbers when the orchestra grows to full size in 1866, because it comprised so many additional London players who only appeared on Saturday. It is clear that the London orchestras shared personnel to a considerable extent. Even in the terms of Manns's appointment in 1855, Grove seems to have assumed that players would take extra work, in stressing that they should be free after 5 p.m. in the winter and 7 p.m. in the summer:[43] players could easily have worked in the London theatre orchestras in the evening, since London was only thirty minutes distant by fast train. The attraction of the professional status of playing with the Philharmonic Society must also have been a draw, though only three of Manns's players could be proposed as Philharmonic players in the first decade.[44] But with the augmentation of the Saturday orchestra in 1866 the problems naturally proliferated: in 1876 Manns experienced a major clash of personnel when the Philharmonic decided to rehearse on Saturday morning, the only rehearsal time of his full band; the clash was now of eighteen players. Certainly, by this time the deputy system was in full force and Manns seems to have been happy with it provided that it did not compromise his Saturday rehearsal and therefore performance; on this he was adamant.[45]

The Crystal Palace choir never attracted the same attention as the Saturday orchestra. Although it appears to have been adequate to the run of works it had to perform – many of them new works – the impression emerging from reviews is that it was never outstanding, and obviously vulnerable in demanding works: commendation is particularly guarded in the reviews of the last decade. An effective choir was an essential part of Manns's ambitions for the concert repertory of the Palace. Its first important performance was on 11 November 1865, when Beethoven's Choral *Fantasia* attracted special attention with Arabella Goddard as pianist, though the first two performances of the Ninth Symphony had taken place earlier in the year. Prior to this, choral works with orchestra under Manns (as opposed to the visiting choirs in the early Saturday programmes) had been given with outside forces, chiefly based on the 'Choir of the Royal Italian Opera' with other selected members of choirs, of which the performance of Lobgesang in 1860 was apparently the earliest. At full strength the choir was of 300 voices, the maximum with which the stage could cope after its final extension in 1868; when choir numbers were at their greatest, as in the most extreme case of the British premiere of the Berlioz *Te Deum*, requiring three choirs of 100 voices each plus a vast children's choir (which was obviously compromised), the stage was inadequate, and the performance suffered badly as a result. Numbers clearly affected Manns's performance standard throughout, his ambitions constantly outstripping his means: adverse reviews of early performances often attribute their inadequacy to his small resources, as when he performed Spohr's symphony 'The Power of Sound' on 18 April 1857.

Manns's achievements were the result of very sound musicianship, wide experience (he played several instruments) and total commitment to a vision of the musical possibilities at the Palace. He was never adjudged a conductor on a level with Richter or Bülow, the greatest pioneer virtuoso conductors in Europe. His background was of the military band and he was always portrayed with a military bearing, the *Spy* cartoon matching Walker's description of a 'gallant, picturesque figure with his symmetrical mane of snow white hair and his velvet coat'. As Walker further observed, 'his training had been that of the military band; he very nearly won his freedom, but not, I think, completely so; he was a disciplinarian first and foremost'.[46] Stanford seemed rather to identify Manns's limitations by inference, in emphasizing the special qualities of Bülow and Richter as masters of the orchestra – their marvellous memories for the score, and the fact that both would stop conducting and control their orchestras simply with a look.[47] One never reads such things of Manns. It was not so much the mystery of his orchestral control that impressed, as the precision and energy of the result. One reads repeatedly of the fire of Manns's performances. Rhythmic energy was his greatest resource, and he was at his best in music displaying this quality, the music he did most to promote. 'Specially favourite works, like Schubert's C major or Schumann's D minor symphonies, he could make positively blaze (except on full-dress occasions he

13 August Manns as seen by 'Spy' in *Vanity Fair* in 1894.

always, in his excitement, sang the four sforzando minims towards
the end of Schubert's finale).'[48] But he was not equally strong in all
music. Walker further notes that 'in the later Wagner and so, on he
was not happy, his conceptions lacked colour and undulation. Often
one felt that things might not disadvantageously have been subtler.
One noticed the difference when hearing Richter handle a band . . .
to a considerable extent, comprised of the same men.'[49] But for
Stanford, Richter had his weaknesses as well: 'With ... Schubert
and more especially Schumann [Richter] was comparatively a
failure ... The best conductor of them was Manns. Though by
nature more of a bandmaster than an orchestral virtuoso, Manns
had genuine sympathy with the romantic element.'[50] Indeed, seen
more broadly, Manns's temperament was far from solid and pre-
dictable. He would never have achieved his results had he been
merely an energetic disciplinarian.

The fire which so impressed his audiences was but part of a highly
strung personality. As Bennett observed, 'It was impossible to watch
Manns in the act of conducting without becoming aware that he was
supersensitive, and, in popular language, a bundle of nerves.'[51] And
this also applied to his own esteem of his achievements, more so as
the years threatened to dim the importance of his work. Thus he
writes to Bennett in 1893:

the musical critics seem to have been under the impression that the above
named Symphonic Poem [Smetana's *Vltava*] has never been heard in
England before last Monday, when it was included in the programme of
the Richter concert. Kindly examine the two programmes of our Crystal
Palace Saturday concerts of 1881 and 1882 and you will see that I
introduced *Vltava* and *Vigsebrad* as long as twelve years ago. I was much
discouraged by the musical criticism which followed my efforts (and my
musical self) to bring these works of, at that time, a perfectly unknown
Bohemian composer before the Crystal Palace audience, and I must adhere
that I did not fare much better in Glasgow where, in 1882, I gave *Die
Moldau (Vltava)*.[52]

In addition to its regular contact, the foundation of the success of
Manns's orchestra lay in his capacity to train it. This was particularly noted of the wind section. As Stanford put it,

Manns trained a number of players in his smaller band (that is, the daily
orchestra) which was independent of the old guard of the opera houses, and
they became the ancestors of our finest modern instrumentalists. Some of
the older generation were as good as could be found ... But Manns had his

younger men to boast of: Crozier the oboist, Clinton the clarinettist, and greatest of all, even to the founding of a school, W. B. Wotton the bassoonist.[53]

Shaw even held the tone of this section superior to that of the wind section of the Bayreuth orchestra.[54] Walter Bache, Liszt's greatest British champion, describes Manns's results with strings in Liszt's *Mazeppa*: 'Manns (formerly a fiddler himself) worked with the violin players ... fingering and editing all difficult passages: strings quite sufficient for the brass. Manns enthusiastic: a really magnificent performance.'[55] Though, according to Shaw,[56] Manns's strings seem to have been less consistent in performance standard, Hallé's strings on occasion superior, and Richter's mastery of the brass section unique,[57] the all-round standard of the orchestra gave it a major position in British musical life, quite apart from the unique range of repertory it performed.

The sheer energy and commitment of Manns was however only the minimum necessary to cope with his position. For, compared with Richter and Bülow, the range of his musical responsibilities as musical director of the music of the Crystal Palace was extraordinarily wide. While, once he had overcome the initial resistance to new music, he had the advantage of freedom from committees in planning the programmes, he paid a price in the responsibility he held for the vast range of Palace activities. He found himself perforce filling the musical gaps in the early years, and was always ready to use his skills to smooth the corners in making effective programmes. This did not stop with musical performance. He sometimes paid the expenses of additional rehearsals for works he wished to perform, or for the copying of parts.[58] He was the point of focus for all musical activity, and he emerges in every conceivable context in which the band found itself in attendance, from the fashionable Opera Concerts in the nave to the accompanying of the high-wire artist Blondin in the same location, to the Christmas pantomime, burlesques or theatrical performances with music in the Theatre. Just how much he was rewarded for all these extra activities is not recorded. His salary on appointment in 1854 was £30 per month (£360 per annum).[59] From 1 January 1864, he received what appears to have been his first rise to £500 per annum,[60] an indication of the permanency he now had, though the profits of his Benefit Concert had to be returned to the management. In May 1869 he received 'half of the profit derived from the benefit concert on the 24 April' – £115 –

though Grove's letter makes it clear that this is in acknowledgement of Manns's efforts for the conducting of the rehearsals for the Rossini Festival and the work attached to it. This was a major festival, seemingly the biggest so far at the Palace. In 1858 he conducted the intermediate days of the Handel Festival in selections from Handel's Italian operas and secular works. In April 1871 he had a rise from £500 to £600.[61]

By the end of his career, Manns had become widely acknowledged for his contributions to British music through his work at the Palace, and not least for his support for British composers. His achievements at the Palace were recognized in his last years with an Oxford Doctorate in 1903 (the report in the *Oxford Magazine* stressing his interest in the music of his adopted country) and, later in the year, a knighthood for his services to British music.[62]

CHAPTER 6

Programmes, performers, repertory, programme notes

PROGRAMMES

Building a programme structure

Manns faced two problems in building his repertory at the Palace. He had, on the one hand, to attract the kind of audience that would initially have looked down on the Crystal Palace as a place for serious music; and, on the other, to attract from the general audience of the Palace those listeners seeking more adventurous musical fare than was at first customary there.[1] The Directors would have been quick to recognize any failure to create an audience for the additional investment they had placed in the band. The taste of the time was more for a vocal miscellany than for orchestral music. To some extent a popular character never fully disappeared from the concert programme. Though its character changed – lieder gradually displaced ballads – a couple of songs still tend to be included, even if the programme features a concert scena and aria rather than instrumental pieces (the concerto soloist always played a separate instrumental group).[2] Only after the Manns period do the programmes change to fewer items, in line with the newer concert programmes in London, notably those of the Richter concerts.

The disposition of an ideal programme was hardly Manns's problem when he started. He was held by more immediate constraints, his very first programme determined largely by the instruments available. The second half of the first programme was devoted entirely to the kind of music associated with the wind band, which still constituted the official musical provision of the Palace: two popular overtures and three dance items, one by Manns himself. Only the mixed orchestral items of the first half show the possibilities for growth, the two overtures framing three solo items, of which only one, the Beethoven Romance, points towards the symphonic concert repertory.[3] The programme read as follows:

PART THE FIRST

(String Band in the Music Court)

1 Festival Overture   Leutner
2 Fantasia Brilliant on airs from Der Freischütz   Moeser
   Violin, Mr Manns
3 Solo for Pianoforte 'The Chimes of England'   Holmes
   Pianoforte, Mr Darlington
4 Romance for Violin, Op. 50 in F Violin, Mr   Beethoven
   Manns
5 Overture 'Oberon'   Weber

PART THE SECOND

(Wind Band in the Centre Transept)

1 Overture 'Ruy Blas'   Mendelssohn
2 Waltz 'Des Wanderers Lebewohl'   Strauss
3 Charivari   Zulehner
4 Marian Redowa   Manns
5 Overture 'Le Roi d'Yvetot'   Adam

The Mendelssohn, Weber and Beethoven items constituted a framework on which to build a programme structure; the other items belonged more to the popular audience which would be served in other ways at the Palace. With the establishment of his full, if small, orchestra by 1 December 1855, the programming possibilities opened up immediately. They are first apparent in the presence of grouped individual movements of symphonies: on this very day Manns gave the Allegretto and Presto from Beethoven's Seventh Symphony. The concert of 5 February offered movements one, two and four of the *Italian* Symphony as the sixth item of an eight-item programme framed with overtures – Beethoven's Overture in C and Rossini's *William Tell*. By 1 March the symphony comes complete as the final, seventh, item, the programme beginning with Costa's March from *Eli*. Concertos posing comparable musical demands were slower to appear; the Mendelssohn piano concertos, which were so frequent in the early years, were relatively straightforward to accompany, and appear complete from the first year. It was rather Mozart who appeared piecemeal, as in the first performance of part of the D minor Piano Concerto.

But the major factor influencing developing concert patterns was the presence of a choir, which offered the easiest way to achieve contrast and variety. Several choirs appeared in the first five years, contributing a selection of shorter items: they included the Glee and Choral Union at the beginning of 1856, Henry Leslie's Choir, and in 1860 the Cologne Gesangverein. And larger choral activity soon developed: by 1859 an entire programme is given over to extended works, as, on 26 March 1859, with a concert performance of *Fidelio*, and the music to Mendelssohn's *Antigone* on 19 April 1859. The establishment of a more consistent pattern, with the focus of a symphony as concluding item and an overture at the beginning, appears from the middle 1860s. Over the years the popular favourites tended to create regular patterns: for example, Beethoven's Fifth Symphony was invariably the final item of a seven- or eight-item programme which would begin with an overture and include a concerto or equivalent, and another substantial orchestral item.

The novelty item, special concert and series

It is ironical that the little-known works which Manns was first encouraged to avoid should so soon have become the mark of his concerts: for once the patterns had become established in the middle 1860s, the audience increasingly looked for the 'novelty', and the critics assessed the offerings for the coming season in the Prospectus: Manns was beginning to mould the taste of his audience, offering new works, alternative versions of known works, and programmes devoted to the full range of a single composer's works. If specialist concerts were not unknown in Manns's time, the range of the orchestral fare offered at the Palace, reflective of its educational ethos, eclipsed that of any other British concert-giving organization, with a unique record of new works by foreign composers given British first performances, and of new works by British composers likewise. And if the emphasis on novelties – such, for example, as the original version of Mendelssohn's *Hebrides* Overture, the alternative slow movement for Mozart's *Paris* Symphony or the alternative

CRYSTAL PALACE.

SEASON 1895–6.

PROGRAMME OF
THE TENTH
SATURDAY CONCERT,
DECEMBER 14th, 1895.

BEETHOVEN PROGRAMME
In Commemoration of the 125th Anniversary of BEETHOVEN'S *Birth.*

---

1. OVERTURE, "PROMETHEUS."

2. SLOW MOVEMENT FROM THE FIRST SYMPHONY.

3. CONCERTO FOR PIANOFORTE No. 5, IN E FLAT.
   Pianoforte—MONS. SILOTI.
   (Pianoforte by BLÜTHNER & CO.)

4. GRAND SCENA, "AH! PERFIDO."
   FRÄULEIN FILLUNGER.

5. SYMPHONY, "EROICA."

6. SONGS—
   "MAILIED" (MAY SONG).
   "MIT EINEM GEMALTEN BAND" (WITH A FLOWERED RIBBON).
   FRÄULEIN FILLUNGER.

7. OVERTURE, "LEONORE, No. 3."

AUGUST MANNS, CONDUCTOR.

A

14 The programme of the Beethoven Anniversary Concert of 14 December 1895,
with the pianist Alexander Siloti and the soprano Maria Fillunger as soloists.

score of his G minor Symphony – began to wane in the 1880s, the Palace could now afford to celebrate its special achievement in bringing new music to popular attention.

The special celebratory concert represented the natural extension of the feature of the novelty item into a complete programme. It took many forms: of the acknowledgement of an anniversary, most likely a centenary; of memorial to a recently deceased composer, or of recognition of a living composer (in which case a visit in person was an ideal event); of an 'historical' concert aimed at identifying a little-known earlier composer, or showing a sequence of musical development, as in concerts of German or English music. 26 January 1856 provided an early opportunity for a centenary celebration, that of the birth of Mozart, and no clearer indication of the educational ethos of the Palace exists than the way in which it was grasped by Manns and Grove in the programme planning and provision of programme notes. The ten items performed show the extension of the previous pattern to offer the most ambitious concert programme of the early months: in addition to an overture, two operatic items and duet and songs, the instrumental items are a violin sonata and a piano sonata, one movement of a concerto and two of a symphony. By the time of the centenary of the birth of Beethoven in 1870, the celebration took the form of a series of concerts, including all the symphonies and concertos and selected overtures, spread over six weeks. The unique connection of the Palace with Schubert led to a series in 1881 which included all the works introduced over the previous years in individual movements or as a whole, the series including one premiere.

PERFORMERS

Early years and international reputation, 1855–75

The emergence of the Crystal Palace orchestra coincided with the flowering of the profession of international virtuoso. The Palace was uniquely placed to benefit, through the sheer number and regularity of its concerts. They soon became a fixture on the London musical scene and, by the time of their decline, Sullivan could comment that 'all the singers and players of the world are heard at one time or another at the C[rystal] P[alace]'.[4] Pupils followed teachers in successive generations, and the unfolding of the Palace concerts gives a clear picture of the individuals who stocked the new international world of concertizing. But the important names would not appear until the concerts were publicly recognized. The difficulties associated with the general image of the Palace at its beginnings were recalled later by Manns in connection with his invitation to the leading soprano Madame Emilia Rudersdorff to sing for a series of six concerts, which she refused on the grounds that 'to sing at the Crystal Palace would injure her reputation'.[5] The Palace had to be prepared to pay for the quality it needed, and, as in other activities, clearly did, to judge by the performers who began to appear. A fee of £15 seems to have been standard for the leading visiting virtuoso, at least on the evidence of Manns this was the fee given to the Czech violinist Jan Ondříček, Manns commenting that he was not well enough known for more, and citing the name of Vieuxtemps, who 'had never received more'.[6]

It took five years to start attracting international performers: only after a series of London based players had gradually established the place of the concerto or concert piece in the programmes, albeit in a limited range of repertory, did they begin to come. Manns began with his own skills and those of his band, or those of any other adequate performer he could find. His is the most frequent name met with in the first year, whether as soloist (in works by Vieuxtemps, Beethoven, Leonard, or himself), as obbligato player with singers, or in instrumental duo. Then come his section leaders: his leader (the first-listed 'solo' violin), Van Heddeghem, in a Paganini Concerto on 24 November 1855; his second-listed 'solo' violin, Gravenstein, in the second season, on 15 November 1856, with the first-listed 'solo' clarinet, Pape, in the same programme: and on 25 April 1857 the principal cello and flute, Daubert and Svendsen, both appear as soloists. There seems to have been no resident solo pianist at the start, though the young prodigy Oscar Beringer was appointed in 1857 and held the position for nine years thereafter, playing in midweek concerts and giving daily recitals. Manns looked both to young and to established London players: to 'Master' John Francis Barnett,[7] who played the first movement of the Mozart D minor Concerto in the Mozart Commemoration Concert of 26 January 1855, and to the distinguished violinist Henry Blagrove,[8] who played Spohr's *Scena Cantante* on 13 December 1856. On 5 December 1857, the leading piano pedagogue Ernst Pauer played Mozart's D minor Concerto complete.[9] The season 1858–9 saw appearances by W. H. Cusins (later conductor of the Philharmonic Society Concerts), Arabella Goddard (an outstanding pianist, the wife of Henry Davison), the leading French violinist Wilhelm Molique and the Hungarian violinist Eduard Reményi.

From the point of view of the audience, the more popular performer was likely to be the singer rather than the instrumentalist, and accessible vocal items remained a constant throughout the life of the concerts (as they also did at the Philharmonic). The singers first widely known at the Crystal Palace were those associated with the Royal Italian Opera at Covent Garden and the Handel Festivals. Madame Rudersdorff obviously overcame her scruples very quickly, because her name is one of the most prominent, first appearing as early as 15 November 1856, to sing a scene and aria from *Der Freischütz*. Other established names appearing in the following year included May Banks, Anna Bishop (the wife of Sir Henry Bishop), and Charles Braham, now at the end of his career. By 1859 the first important vocal ensemble appears for the concert performance of *Fidelio* on 26 March, with Rudersdorff, Weiss, Madame Weiss and Wilbye Cooper in the leading roles.

The early 1860s saw the first appearance of outstanding string players. The leader of the Royal Italian Opera, Prosper Sainton, appeared in 1861 in the first performance of the Mendelssohn Concerto at the concerts. Two other established London Germans, Ludwig Straus and Adolph Pollitzer, appeared in 1864, respectively in the Mendelssohn concerto and in Manns's own Violin Concerto in E. Straus's partner in Joachim's London quartet, the cellist Alfredo Piatti, first appeared in 1867 playing the Molique and Sullivan concertos. Carl Rose (later Rosa, the opera producer) had appeared as violinist with the Adagio from Spohr's Eleventh Concerto. But it was visiting continental players who caught most attention from 1861: in that year the senior Norwegian musician, Ole Bull, played the second Paganini violin concerto, and Henri Vieuxtemps, unrivalled in technical mastery at this time, played a concerto of his own, as well as giving the first Saturday performance of the Beethoven concerto. 1862 saw younger names. Most famous was Joseph Joachim in the Mendelssohn concerto, known in London since his Philharmonic debut as a teenager in 1844. 1866 was an especially significant year for violinists at the Palace. August Wilhelmji, aged twenty-one, made his English debut with concertos by Lipinski and Paganini, as did his exact contemporary Leopold

Auer in the Mendelssohn. The season 1866–7 also saw the first important visiting cellist, Friedrich Grützmacher, in his own concerto. The new decade saw in 1871 the first appearance of a now resident continental player who would make great contributions to the music of the Palace: the Bohemian violinist Wilma Norma Neruda, later Lady Hallé. But genuine native violinists were few: to the name of Blagrove is added that of Thomas Weist Hill in his own concerto, and the more famous Henry Holmes in the Mendelssohn, both in 1867. Another important name in London music, making his debut in 1875 in the Macfarren Concerto (from MS) was that of John Carrodus, who, with Straus, had played in Joachim's London quartet.

Leading continental pianists were much slower to come. Manns had likewise a background of resident Germans to call on by the 1860s. In 1864 Fritz Hartvigson, a pupil of Bülow, played the Liszt–Schubert *Fantasia*, and Otto Beringer made his debut in a Saturday concert in 1867. Perhaps the most renowned German resident pianist, Karl Hallé (now Charles Hallé), appeared in 1869 in the Mendelssohn *Rondo Brilliant*, though he had performed earlier, with Stephen Heller, in the Mozart two-piano concerto in 1864. Of the three outstanding young players beginning their careers in England, two were of German origin. Edward Dannreuther was born in Germany though educated in the USA before going to Leipzig in 1859; Agnes Zimmermann, a longer resident, was educated at the Royal Academy of Music. Only Franklin Taylor was strictly a native player, though, unlike Arabella Goddard, he had a Leipzig training. Dannreuther and Zimmermann both made their professional concert debuts at the Palace, Dannreuther in Chopin's F minor Concerto, given for the first time complete in England, on 11 April 1863, and Zimmermann on 5 December 1863, in two movements of the Beethoven E♭ Concerto. Taylor played the Hiller Concerto in F♯ minor concerto on 18 February 1865. All played frequently at the Palace through the 1860s to 1880s, Dannreuther making a speciality of the demanding new virtuoso works, giving the British premieres of the Grieg and Tchaikovsky concertos.

The new era of continental pianists begins about five years after that of the violinists. Clara Schumann appeared in Mendelssohn's G minor Concerto, later in Chopin and Beethoven, before playing the Schumann Concerto on 8 February, 1868, her sister, Marie Wieck, having already given its first Saturday performance at the

Palace on 5 March 1864. Clara's much younger compatriot Marie Krebs made her Saturday debut in 1865 in Carl Krebs's fantasia *Lucretia*, long before her first appearance at the Philharmonic. Another early visiting performer of the Schumann was Emma Brandes, 13 April 1872. Of the male players, the senior figure was Karl Reinecke, who played his own Concerto in 1869. The second important year for visiting pianists was 1873, with the London visit of Hans von Bülow, who played the E♭ Concertos of Beethoven and Liszt in November and December respectively, having earlier played at St James's Hall to great acclaim. A significant moment for the development of the organ repertory was the installation of the organ in the Concert Room. The first concert performers were the resident Palace organist James Coward and John Stainer, organist to the University of Oxford, whose first notable contribution was the J. S. Bach 'pedal fugue' in G minor in 1868, though his contributions also included the performance of new British works for organ, giving the Gadsby Organ Concerto in F on 21 January 1874. With the appearance of large-scale choral works from the same time, the role of the concertizing vocal soloist increases significantly, with groups of leading names appearing more often: prominent names in the later 1860s are Julia Elton, Euphrosyne Parepa, Edith Wynne, Edward Lloyd.

The high period and a younger generation, 1875–1900

Numerous as concerto performances had become, and rapidly as the repertory was expanding, the concerts had been dependent upon the contribution of relatively few players, with some stalwart figures becoming firm favourites, not least the English players. But from the mid 1870s, a steady increase in the number of new visiting players occurs, with more of them appearing at the Palace before the Philharmonic, or making their British debut there. Pianists now become much more prominent. Of special interest are leading composer–performers, exciting names old and new, bringing their works with them, whose visits were specially important in the Crystal Palace calendar; also apparent are increasing numbers of other instrumentalists.

Of the pianist–composers, the Crystal Palace had hosted two established figures and one very new figure by the later 1870s. The major figure was Anton Rubinstein, not merely one of the great pianists, but also a significant composer in his time: he came in 1877 for a concert in which he conducted his *Ocean Symphony* and played his second piano concerto. A much younger figure was Ignaz Brüll, a pupil of Epstein and Dessoff in Vienna, and an intimate of the Brahms circle, who introduced his own piano concerto to Britain in 1879. The dominance of German contacts finds an exception in the case of the French composer Camille Saint-Saëns, who came in 1878, playing his Second Piano Concerto, and returning several times more in his own works. Britain too had its outstanding young players, none more so than the Glasgow-born composer–performer Eugen d'Albert, who played his own piano concerto in 1882. But not all composers played their own music first. Giovanni Sgambati, whose music was often played at the Crystal Palace, appeared first in the Beethoven E♭ Concerto in 1882; likewise Ludwig Scharwenka gave this work in 1879, also appearing in the Weber *Konzertstück* in this year. Of the violinist–composers to visit to Palace, the outstanding names were Henri Wieniawski and Pablo de Sarasate. Wieniawski was aged forty-one in 1876 and played the Beethoven Concerto; Sarasate, aged thirty-three in 1877, the Bruch G minor Concerto: though Sarasate had made his London debut in 1874 at St James's Hall and later played at the Philharmonic in 1877, he was long since known at the Palace, having, like Marie Krebs, appeared as a youngster in the Italian Opera Concerts.

In the pianistic tradition, the two extremes were represented by the names of Liszt and Clara Schumann, with Bülow as an independent figure – a Liszt pupil devoted to Beethoven and Brahms. The traditions were equally reflected by the outstanding men and women players. From the middle 1870s, three women command attention: in 1875 Anna Mehlig, a pupil of Lebert and Liszt in the Beethoven E♭ Concerto; in 1878, Schumann's pupil Nathalie Janotha in Beethoven's G major Concerto; in 1881, Sophie Menter, a pupil of Bülow, who married the cellist David Popper and gained great popularity in London, with the Liszt A major Concerto. Karl Barth, an intimate of the Brahms circle, initiated the appearance of a sequence of Bülow pupils when he gave the Brahms Second Piano Concerto in 1880; Walter Bache, another Bülow pupil, appeared in Chopin's F minor Concerto in the following year. Other important names were Louis Brassin, Franz Rummell, Clothilde Kleeburg. Two very distinguished pupils of Leschetizky were Annette Essipoff (whom he married), who first appeared in the Mendelssohn

G minor Concerto in 1875, and Vladimir de Pachmann, who first appeared in the Beethoven G major Concerto in 1883.

No one player dominates the pianistic tradition as much as does Joachim the violinists. Outstanding pupils of his from Berlin begin to appear in the 1880s. Hugo Hermann introduced the Goetz Concerto in 1880, Tivadar Nachez played the Mendelssohn Concerto in 1881, and Richard Gompertz premiered the Mackenzie Concerto in 1886. However, Joachim's unwillingness to play the outstanding modern concerto after the Bruch and Brahms, that of Dvořák, presumably accounts for the visit in 1886 of Jan Ondříček, the Czech violinist who had made the work his own. Other virtuoso string players remain rare, though a clear continuity is apparent. Piatti's pupil Robert Hausmann appeared in 1877 in two movements of Molique's Cello Concerto, which he repeated complete in 1883, and, in April 1880, in the Schumann A minor Concerto, previously played only by Piatti, in its first modern performance in England. English players too reflect the influence of Clara Schumann and Joachim from the end of the 1880s, notably through the former's outstanding pupils Leonard Borwick and Fanny Davies. Davies, who made her first English appearance at the Palace in 17 October 1885 in Beethoven's G major Concerto, became the outstanding stalwart native British player of the later years. Borwick, seven years younger, made his first appearance at the Palace in 1891 with the Brahms First Piano Concerto.

Perhaps the most striking development on the performing stage in the period is the emergence of a wider repertory of vocal music. The later 1870s saw important works new to the Palace by Brahms, Liszt and Wagner: and one notes the interchangeability of German and English singers in their performance. The tenor Edward Lloyd, who had made his debut at the Palace in the Handel Festival to great acclaim, sang *Rinaldo* in the first English performance in 1876; the *Alto Rhapsody* is given first by Louise Redeker in 1878, rather than by Amalie Joachim, its first performer, who rather sang her husband Joseph's scena *Marfa*. The first vocal Wagner is Isolde's 'Liebestod' by Maria Fillunger, which she sang in 1877, and again later. Throughout the 1880s the increasing Wagner performances gave new opportunities for singers. They received a great stimulus through the first English appearance at the Crystal Palace of the great German baritone Franz Betz, who had created the roles of Sachs, Wotan, the Dutchman and Telramund; he sang the recitative and aria 'Der Abendstern' as well as items from Spohr's *Jessonda*, and songs by Schumann and Schubert. Most prominent of Wagner singers is Lloyd, singing Walter's 'Preislied' from *Die Meistersinger* four times, as well as the Quintet: he also sang the Prayer from *Rienzi*. Barton McGuckin appeared in Lohengrin's 'Farewell', and Watkin Mills in the final scene of *Parsifal*; Anna Williams followed Fillunger in *Tristan*. Of the Germans, notable was Georg Henschel in Pogner's address from *Die Meistersinger*.

In 1896, Sarasate, by this time the leading violinist of his generation, gave the first of the twenty-five concerts of his United Kingdom tour at the Crystal Palace. Just what status the Palace now possessed is clear from the number of great players of the early twentieth century who, on the threshold of their careers, filled the programmes. By now a high percentage of foreign players made their London debut at the Palace or included it in their first season. More were now pupils of figures previously associated with it, not least the English pupils of Bülow, Schumann and Liszt.

Composer–performers continued to be prominent: Cecile Chaminade played her *Concertstuck* for piano and orchestra in 1896 and Erno Dohnányi included his Scherzo in C♯ minor in his programme in 1899. But when Ferruccio Busoni came in 1899, it was as a pianist not in his own music, but in that of Liszt. Liszt pupils made a feature of his concertos: Bernhard Stavenhagen in 1893, Moritz Rosenthal in 1898, Arthur Friedheim in 1900 – though some played other works, as when Alexander Siloti played solo works by his fellow countryman Antony Arensky in 1893. By comparison the German pupils of Clara Schumann are less prominent: only the Viennese Ilona Eibenschütz was truly a visitor when she played the Brull Concerto for the second time in 1897; Mathilde Verne was a resident when she played the Saint-Saëns Second Concerto in 1900.

It is rather the increasing presence of pupils of Anton Rubinstein and the Vienna based Theodor Leschetizky which attracts attention. Outstanding were Anton Rubinstein's pupils Emil Sauer in Beethoven during the 1894–5 season, Vassily Sappelnikoff in the Chopin E minor Concerto in 1896, and Josef Silvinski the Tchaikovsky Concerto in 1893. His Polish pupil Ignaz Paderewski played the Chopin E minor Concerto in 1897 and, also in 1897, Ossip Gabrilowitz the Liszt E♭ Concerto. Mark Hambourg played the Rubinstein D minor Concerto in 1896 and Agathe Grondahl the Grieg Concerto in 1890. Of outstanding names of other traditions, the most notable was certainly the Venezuelan born Teresa Carreño; she first appeared at the Palace in 1895 in Weber's Polonaise Brilliant. Of French players, Roger Miklos apppeared in 1892 in the Beethoven C minor Concerto.

Of the violinists, the outstanding player was Eugène Ysäye, who played the Mendelssohn Concerto in 1891. Of Joachim's leading pupils, Gabriele Wietrowetz made her English debut at the Crystal Palace, and Willy Hess in the Mendelssohn in 1888; Hugo Hermann gave the Brahms Concerto in 1890. Wieniawski's pupil Serge Rivarde played the Lalo *Symphonie Espagnole* for the first time in England in 1895. Cellists assume a much stronger profile by this time, particularly Julius Klengel, who came in 1890 with a Fitzenhagen *Perpetuo Mobile*, David Popper with the Haydn Concerto in 1894 and the French cellist Jean Renard with his own Concertino in 1899.

As he encouraged English composers, Manns also encouraged young English players: an outstanding pupil of Clara Schumann and of Fanny Davies, Adelina de Lara, appeared in Rubinstein's D minor Concerto in 1891 and often thereafter. Of others, Kendall Taylor's RCM pupil Ethel Sharpe played the d'Albert Concerto in 1895, and two other RCM pupils appeared: Dora Bright made her public debut with her own piano concerto in 1891, while Marmaduke Barton gave the third Crystal Palace performance of the Brahms second concerto. The Bülow tradition is felt most strongly through the Scottish pianist Frederick Lamond. He played at the Palace Saint-Saëns Second Piano Concerto in 1890, appearing at the Philharmonic on 14 May 1891 in the Brahms Second Concerto. Evidence of the cultivation of a native school of players is especially clear with violinists, with the Palace as a nursery for aspiring talent. Virtually all Joachim's English pupils played the Max Bruch Concerto in G minor, though none of these names became established.

Vocal participation increased markedly in the last decade. Wagnerian performances continued to increase in regularity, with the same singers who had established them in the previous decade as well as new native names: for example, Andrew Black in Wotan's 'Abschied', and Henry Plunkett-Greene in Sachs's Monologue, parts previously sung by Henschel. But more opportunities existed with new music, whether of the present day or earlier music finding modern performance; and these works might be sung by either native or German singers, the latter invariably having close English

connections. MacCunn's cantata *The Cameronian's Dream* featured
Henschel, and his dramatic cantata *Queen Hynde of Caeldon* featured
Fillunger, with Black, Emily Squire and Henry Piercey. Eugen
Oudin returned to the Palace in 1892 near the end of his life in 'The
Templar's Soliloquy' from Sullivan's *Ivanhoe*. But some works were
only sung by British singers: Lloyd and Black in Goring-Thomas's
The Swan and the Skylark, Black in the Sword Song from Elgar's
Caractacus, Ben Davies in Cowen's *The Dream of Endymion*. And
singers become involved in the increasing presence of music from
before the regular concert period: Henschel in Schütz's 'Lamentatio
Davids' and Maria Brema (the English singer Minny Fehrmann) in
Purcell's 'Mad Bess'. As well as some established names – Raglioli,
Albani – there are, in minor roles or short pieces, an increasing
number of English ones: notably Clara Butt, Clara Samuell (winner
of the Parepa-Rosa scholarship at the RAM), the baritone Kenner-
ley Rumford (husband of Clara Butt) and the tenor Gregory Hast.

REPERTORY

A basic repertory

Manns's ironic reference to 'the sanctified Haydn, Mozart, Beethoven and Mendelssohn'[10] identifies the prejudice against any other
symphonic composers which he had to face in building towards his
goal of a modern orchestral repertory for the Palace. The works of
these composers were not at this time equally known, however.
Central were the symphonies and concertos of Beethoven, given
very regularly in the first five years, as thereafter, though the Ninth
was first performed at the Palace only in 1865. In contrast, the
symphonies of Mozart and Haydn were represented by few works.
Of the works which then, as later, constituted the core of Mozart's
symphonic repertory, only the G minor Symphony (No. 40) was
regularly given, twice in 1856 and thrice in 1857, the E♭ (No. 39)
and the 'Jupiter' (No. 41) having, by comparison, only two performances and one respectively in the first five years; otherwise only the
'Linz' and 'Prague' symphonies were given (once each) in the first
five years, and this pattern continues later. Haydn performances
were even less regular: though there had been three performances of
the Symphony in G 'Letter V' by 1860 and two of the 'London'
Symphony in B♭ (No. 9), only two other symphonies appear in

the first five years and, with few exceptions, the performances thereafter are of different single symphonies – as representing the genre – rather than of a canonical group of works.[11] Mozart piano concertos were also only marginally known; even the D minor Concerto comes only once (complete) by 1860, though regularly thereafter and more so than any other concerto. A violin concerto was a real rarity throughout, as was the *Sinfonia Concertante*, given only once in Manns's period. The only Haydn concertos (those for cello) come in the 1890s.[12] The most striking feature is the popularity of the much more recent composer Mendelssohn. The *Italian* and *Scottish* symphonies were repeatedly given, whole or in part, and achieve figures comparable with those of the most popular Beethoven symphonies, Nos. 4, 6, 7 and 8. But the first symphony was much less performed, and striking is the absence of any early performance of the *Reformation* Symphony, which was not given till 1867, though then it received both its English premiere, and only second world performance; *Lobgesang* appeared in 1861.

The operatic and concert overture constitutes the one genre in which the concert repertory was considerably enhanced by works by other composers. Of German works, Weber's operatic overtures dominate; of Italian operatic works, those of Rossini are omnipresent. But there were many other composers as well: the French operatic school from Cherubini and Meyerbeer, through Auber, Halevy and Flotow, as well as the emerging Russian school with Glinka. Of special interest is Manns's devotion to the technically challenging overtures of Berlioz, which he gave with great frequency. But by its nature, this repertory was not as stable as others, and patterns later change; only the German repertory remains consistent throughout. Manns's way forward in broadening the repertory lay in substituting for these familiar works comparable unfamiliar works, and in extending the proportion of the concert programme given to them. This he first began to do through his favourite modern German composers, Schubert and Schumann.

A new repertory

Schubert; Schumann and his contemporaries[13]

The Crystal Palace was to become nationally and even internationally pre-eminent in the dissemination of the orchestral music of Schubert and Schumann. But this was at first regarded by Grove as inappropriate to the Palace and he discouraged Manns's early enthusiasm for performing Schubert's Great C major Symphony.[14] Apart from its two early performances (the effective British premiere on 5 April 1856 and on 11 July 1857), Manns duly refrained from further peformance for a decade. Grove's reference to the performance on 21 April 1866 as 'the first great performance at Sydenham' reflects the limitations of Manns's early performing forces and facilities,[15] for, as he remarked of an intervening performance given in the daily music, 'the location was then so unfavourable and the band so small that it is not wonderful that it should have achieved no success and awakened no enthusiasm'.[16] Manns also gave the B minor Symphony (No. 8) its British premiere on 6 April 1867, soon after publication. Both works were to be performed annually from this time almost without exception, more frequently performed and more closely associated with the Palace than with any other institution.

By this time Grove's enthusiasm had grown apace and was soon to achieve a Schubert association with the Palace which became part of its tradition as well as a remarkable chapter in the history of English music. Having recently read of the extensive unpublished MSS symphonies and other works of Schubert,[17] Grove entered into correspondence with the Viennese publisher Spina and arranged to visit Vienna to seek the scores. Not only did he find what he particularly sought – the complete Rosamunde music (the overture having already been performed and having enchanted him), but all the unpublished symphonies; what is more, he was given the permission to copy and perform them, and prohibited from allowing copies to be taken from the Palace copies or performances given from there, without express permission.[18] Thus the Palace found itself in the position of having performance rights not only in England, but in Europe as well. Over the following years, all the symphonies were given, either as single movements or complete, sometimes repeated, virtually all for the first time in England, culminating in the complete cycle given in spring 1881. Three of those were world premieres, since they had never been given in Vienna complete: No. 1 in D, 5 February 1881; No. 2 in B♭, 20 October 1877; No. 3 in D, 19 February 1881. The complete *Rosamunde* music was also a world premiere, that of 'The Song of Miriam' on November 14 1868, a British premiere.

For the real enthusiasts the year 1867–8 was the Schubert season.

As Bennett put it 'work after work unheard of in this country was produced at the Palace with loving care and received with fervent admiration. We were fortunate in those days, for it seemed to us that the shining glasshouse at Sydenham had become the temple of a new and gracious gospel . . . How the audience of connoisseurs gloated on this precious new music!'[19] Grove was also to achieve a form of premiere with the first ever performance of a realized score of the Symphony No. 7 in E major, left in sketch form by the composer, which he owned, having obtained it through the Mendelssohn family:[20] though he offered it first to Sullivan, the work was done by John Francis Barnett, whose connections with the Palace were likewise intimate. Barnett's completion was given at the Palace on 5 May 1883, when the autograph was also displayed in the Centre Transept. Orchestration rendered two other works available for inclusion in the programmes: the Octet was given with full strings in 1874, and the F minor *Fantasia* for piano duo for full orchestra in 1894.

Resistance to the Schumann symphonies was similar to that experienced by the Schubert Ninth. The first real acknowledgement comes only in November 1878, when we read of a 'magnificent performance of Schumann's great Symphony in C [on 12 October]. The work itself is now, thanks chiefly to the Crystal Palace concerts, too well known to need criticism.'[21] From now on the praise for Schumann came easily. Against this background, Manns's determination seems the more striking. Despite Grove's advice, he had given his first Schumann symphony, No. 4 in D minor, on 16 February 1856, and thereafter five times till 1865. The 'Spring' Symphony was given on 10 March 1860, and again on the 24th, thereafter three times till 1864. Predictably, the longer symphonies had to wait: No. 2 till 1865, No. 3 till 1866, and neither quite matches the frequency of performance of the others overall. The overtures, including the *Overture, Scherzo and Finale*, were also given more frequently than at other venues, as was the extremely popular Piano Concerto. Other concerto works were much less common, though single performances were given of the Cello Concerto and *Fantasie* for violin and orchestra, the latter with Joachim, the former effectively the first modern British performance, by Hausmann. Schumann's choral music was rarely done, no more than at the Philharmonic. *Paradise and the Peri* appeared in 1867, then 1873; the *Manfred* music in 1874, though this was the first English performance of the music other than the overture.

There remained other composers of Schumann's generation with whom Manns's contacts were direct. Ferdinand Hiller conducted his own symphony 'Es muss doch Fruhling werden' on 26 March 1870, and it was again given on 18 March 1871. Quite soon after he gave other symphonic works, *Symphonisches Fantasie* in February 1872, and *Dramatisches Fantasie* in 1873 and again in 1875, both in MS. Hiller had already been known by shorter pieces, including overtures from 1857. His Piano Concerto in F♯ minor received three performanes, in 1865, 1876 and 1879, and his choral work *Loreley* was given in 1866. But the symphonist who received the greatest Crystal Palace exposure was Joachim Raff, one of the most prolific of modern symphonists. The Crystal Palace not only gave performances, but quite a proportion of first performances, of his works. Manns performed nine of the symphonies from 1874 onwards, though only one received more than one performance (*Leonore*), seven times till 1898. Karl Reinecke was well represented from the middle 1860s, especially in his incidental music, with items from *King Manfred* and solo works with orchestra, though only the Piano Concerto in F♯ minor was played as many as three times, once by the composer himself.

Brahms, Dvořák and Smetana

Important as respect for the established figures was to Manns, the ultimate sign of the vitality of the concerts was a personal appearance by a major figure of the younger generation. Pre-eminent here (apart from the great composer–performers, who probably commanded greater interest for the average concert-goer) were Brahms and Dvořák. The Crystal Palace made Brahms's name in England. When Manns gave movements from the recently published Serenade in D for the first time in 1863 he was effectively unknown in England, and his first English performance of the D minor Concerto on 9 March 1872 significantly pre-dated that at the Philharmonic on 23 June 1873. The following year saw the *St Antoni Variations* for the first time in England on 7 March, and the second Serenade on 10 April 1875. Around this time Manns had invited Brahms to come to conduct. Brahms declined, but indicated how much he knew of Manns's work on his behalf. By now the rumours of a Brahms symphony had long been circulating and Manns and Grove were well placed to hear the latest through their close contacts with Joachim and Clara Schumann. But clearly their enthusiasm exceeded their judgement and materially influenced Brahms's decision not to come and receive a doctorate at Cambridge with Joachim, who was to conduct the symphony for the first time in England: 'the Crystal Palace authorities publicly announced that they hoped for a special concert of his works conducted by himself ... As soon as he saw what the Crystal Palace meant to do, he retired into his shell, and the opportunity was lost for good.'[22]

But Manns obtained the second performance of the work on 31 March 1877 and the first performance in England of the Second Symphony on 5 October 1878, drawing the comment that 'the rendering of the exceptionally difficult music was one of those, we might almost say, miracles of performance, which, in this country at least are to be heard only at the Crystal Palace'.[23] The work was repeated by popular request on 22 March 1879. The contact with Joachim next yielded the British premiere of the Violin Concerto on 22 February 1879, repeated at the Philharmonic Society on 6 March, though not as well received as the symphony. British premieres now followed of the two overtures opp. 80 and 81 and the Second Piano Concerto, given by Beringer, and soon by Brahms's friend Karl Barth. Thereafter Palace premieres were less frequent: Manns first gave the Third Symphony (after Richter) on 18 October 1884 and was even more slow with the Fourth, which the Saturday audience heard for the first time only on 9 March 1889. Of choral works, Manns secured the British premiere of *Rinaldo*, with Lloyd. But the greatest of the Brahms choral works, the Requiem, first given privately in London in 1872 and at the Philharmonic in 1873 and often thereafter, was never given at the Saturday Concerts, a sure reflection of the limitations of the choir, given Manns's love of Brahms.

If unsuccessful in enticing Brahms to England, Manns did succeed in attracting his prominent contemporary Max Bruch, whose G minor Concerto was given repeatedly. For his visit, Bruch conducted his cantata *Fritjhof*, as well as the prelude to *Loreley*, on 8 June 1878. Earlier in 1878 the Palace had hosted another young composer, the pianist Ignaz Brüll, who played his own concerto on 23 February.

News of Dvořák's music came much more quickly than that of Brahms. When Manns gave the English premiere of the first set of 'Slavonic Dances' (Nos. 1, 2 and 3 of the original version for piano duet) on 15 February 1879, the programme remarked that 'it has been found impossible to obtain any information as to his position or antecedents, or the nature of his works'. But that situation did not last for long. On 22 April 1882 Manns gave what was apparently the first performance of the Symphony in D (No. 6), 'No. 1' in the programme,[24] pre-dating both Richter's performance at St James's Hall on 15 May and the Vienna first performance in February 1883. 12 May 1883 saw the first British performance of the symphonic poem *My Home*. Unlike Brahms, Dvořák was keen to make contacts and to travel. The next Crystal Palace connection came through Beringer,who wrote to Dvořák to commission a piano concerto about a month before the Philharmonic Society issued their invitation to him to visit London. Since such a work already existed, Beringer took the opportunity of giving the first British performance at the Palace.[25] Around the time of his meeting with Beringer, Dvořák offered to Manns performances of three new compositions, the Violin Concerto, Nocturne for Strings and *Scherzo Capriccioso*, of which the latter two were given first British performances.[26]

Rivalry with the Philharmonic was to continue. Manns obtained what appears to have been the second English performance, on 31 October 1885, of the D minor Symphony, the work 'written expressly for the Philharmonic Society', and secured a triumph with his performance. With the revised version of the F major symphony (No. 5) he obtained the first performance on 7 April 1888. Manns did not obtain the first performances of the G major or 'New World' Symphonies, but he was successful with his performance of *In Nature's Realm*, which he gave on 28 April 1894; and he was preceded by only days in performances of *Otello* and *Carnaval*. He secured the first performance with the original soloist, Leopold Stern, of the Cello Concerto on 12 December 1896, the work having been first given by the Philharmonic. Though the Palace could not claim priority in performing choral works, which were commissioned by the provincial festival organizations, Manns gained an early performance of *St Ludmilla* on 11 March 11 1893 and the first English performance of the Mass in D, admittedly not as difficult a work as the Requiem, first given at Birmingham in 1891. Manns was equally interested to follow up the new works of Dvořák's compatriot Smetana as they became known. He secured the British premieres of the symphonic poems *Vltava* and *Vysherad* on 5 March 1881 and 11 November 1882 respectively, repeating the former in 1898; he also secured an early performance of the 'Lustspiel' Overture (*The Bartered Bride*) on 18 October 1884, repeating it twice in the next four years, performances significantly ahead of those at the Philharmonic.

Wagner, Liszt and Richard Strauss
Although the critics favoured Manns less in the works of the New German School than in the symphonic repertory, his record here is impressive and he gave a wide variety of works by Wagner and pioneering performances of Liszt and Richard Strauss. The early resistance of Grove to new repertory was certainly stronger against Wagner than against Schubert or Schumann. Though Manns presented Wagner in his very first season, with a *Tannhäuser* selection, on 26 April 1856, giving the overture in May of 1857, Wagner was not to be played again in the Saturday concerts until 1866, when the overture was repeated; the only other work in this decade is the 'March' from *Die Meistersinger*, which received its first performance in 1868. From the 1870s appears a steady sequence of overtures, and a great variety of separate items and selections from the music dramas, and one notes the quick response to works that were then new to England: for example, 'Siegfried's Death' in 1876, 'The Ride of the Valkyries' in 1878. However, the first concert to feature more than an isolated item or selection was the Memorial Concert devoted entirely to Wagner's works on 3 March 1883, which included the 'Good Friday Music' from *Parsifal*, only recently premiered and published, receiving its British premiere.[27] But orchestral Wagner was clearly more acceptable than vocal Wagner to the Crystal Palace audience. Only one item appears in the 1870s: Isolde's 'Liebestod' in 1878, repeated in 1883. The first real year of vocal Wagner performance at the Palace is 1885, with items or selections from *Tannhäuser, Tristan, Die Meistersinger* and *Parsifal*, but performance is not at all regular until the 1890s, when an item is given in every year, whether set piece or selection.

Manns's contribution to Liszt performance is more striking, with a significant number of orchestral works in early and first performances. The earliest Liszt at the Palace was naturally dominated by virtuoso piano works, the ideal vehicle for the emerging virtuoso player. Apart from solo works, it was not until 27 January 1872, that Dannreuther gave the E♭ Concerto; he also gave the A major concerto on 21 November 1874. From the middle 1870s all the Liszt piano works with orchestra become common, featuring some of the greatest pianists of the day. The orchestral works, apart from the various Rhapsodies in the Hungarian manner, were less common. After *Mazeppa*, which came on 9 December 1876 (and was repeated in 1886), the next symphonic poem was *Hunnengeschlacht*, performed on 17 May 1879, symphonic poems then coming at roughly five-year intervals: *Les Preludes* was the most repeated, appearing five times between 1884 and 1894. The Liszt connection was destined to find more tangible expression, however, albeit at the end of Liszt's long life. He visited London for performances of his music at a Saturday concert on 10 April 1886 and also for a performance of *St Elizabeth* at St James's Hall several days later, staying (like Dvořák) at the house of Littleton of Novellos, close to the Palace. Manns had arranged an all-Liszt programme for his concert, and his orchestra 'surpassed iself ... the players were determined to let the Abbé know what an English orchestra could do, and the result was a magnificent performance'.[28] As well as those of Manns, Liszt also attended the rehearsals for *St Elizabeth*, but, in Mackenzie's memory as conductor, there were still bad faults to correct after the performance. He recalls that 'rapidly-made arrangements for a repetition at the Crystal Palace gave opportunity for a more perfect rendering of the work before an immense crowd of listeners on April 17. On the platform, when responding to the last of many ovations and shaking my hand, the courtly old man whispered to me 'Nun am Ende haben Sie dass besser gemacht' ['Well perhaps after all you would have written it better yourself']. It was a historic moment for the Palace and musical London: within months Liszt had died.[29]

The strength of Manns's commitment to the new in music is revealed most clearly in his willingness at a late age to take on some of the most challenging of new works: two symphonic poems of Richard Strauss, only published shortly before. He gave *Till Eulenspiegel* on 21 March 1896 and *Also sprach Zarathustra* on March 6 1897, both for the first time in England. The critics did not disguise the limitations of the performance. Indeed, Manns had commented to his audience to the effect that this was the most difficult piece he had ever had to perform. Doubtless he was much closer in spirit to Strauss's F minor symphony, his performance of which was also a striking initiative in 1896.

French, Italian, Scandinavian and Russian composers
Despite Manns's commitment to German music, he also showed interest in other emerging repertories, most notably the French: French composers were conspicuous as visitors to the Palace

(Meyerbeer came as early as 1859). The overtures of Berlioz were especially prominent in the early programmes. If the *Marche Hongroise* on 22 March 1856 was not specially demanding, the appearance on 10 January 1857, in only Manns's second season, of the overture *Le Carnaval Romain*, followed by that to *Benvenuto Cellini* on 9 May and *Les franc juges* on 6 June, was very unusual; and they were repeated as regularly as any German works in the following two years, with a steady addition thereafter including *Waverley*, *Le Corsair*, *Beatrice and Benedict*, *Rob Roy* and other smaller pieces from *Faust* and *The Trojans*. Larger works were obvious candidates for Manns's graduated performance-preparation, the three symphonies appearing piecemeal in individual or paired movements before the complete work was ventured on later. But most remarkable of all was Manns's interest in the choral works, reflective of his commitment to this field, not only in the large festivals, but in the Saturday concerts as well. He gave the first English performances of the Requiem Mass in 1883 and the *Te Deum* in 1885, as well as, also for the first time, two of the three choruses from *Tristan* in 1889 (No. 3) and 1891 (No. 2). The performances were not faultless, and the requirement in the Mass of 'an orchestra of 140 four small brass bands, eight pairs of kettle drums, with ten drummers, two double drums, four tamtams, ten pairs of cymbals' with a six-part choir of 210 voices proved too much for the Concert Room platform, 'though the reduction . . . was only slight'.[30] But the work was soon repeated on 1 December through the great interest it aroused. *The Childhood of Christ* was given in 1886, *Faust* in 1888, *The Death of Ophelia* in 1881, *Lélio* in October 1881 and repeated, a record without equal in British music in the nineteenth century.

Of the younger generation, Gounod had much stronger English connections, not least through his religious choral works, which became as popular as those of Mendelssohn for a long period. He was performed at the Palace from early years, his first symphony appearing in 1857, the second in 1864. In later years numerous instrumental items from the choral works were performed, including, in 1882, a specially composed royal wedding march. Gounod obviously realized that he could rely on Manns for performances and wrote to request them.[31] Of the complete choral works, Manns gave the Te Deum in 1872, and the oratorio *The Redemption*, which received the most performances, four times from 1882 to 1897. *Mors e Vita* came in 1886. Of the newest French composers, Manns gave two selections from Bizet's *Carmen* in 1882 and 1891, the 'Egyptian Dance' from *Djamileh* in 1893, and the *Suite Roma* in 1880; Chabrier's rhapsody *Espagna* was given in 1888. The Palace had a special connection with Massenet and Saint-Saëns. Incidental music to Massenet's operas appeared frequently from 1877, though without repetition. Massenet visited in 1878 and conducted selections from *Le Roi de Lahore* and *Les Erynnes*, apparently for the first time in England, selections from *Le Roi de Lahore* (Overture, Divertissement, Cortege). Saint-Saëns's first London performances were at the Crystal Palace, where he conducted selections from opera and ballet in 1877. But his concertos were his most popular works, especially No. 2, which he introduced to England in 1879, No. 3 likewise on 6 December 1879, coupled with its predecessor.

Though Italian music was more closely associated with the opera house, Manns explored this repertory fully, giving ten opera overtures by Cherubini, the most frequent of them (*Les Deux Jour-nees, Anacreon, Faniska*) regularly through the decades from 1856 into the 1890s. Verdi appears from 1878, with the ballet music from *Don Carlo*, Mascagni with the Intermezzo from *Cavalliera Rusticana* in 1892. Of vocal works by these composers, Verdi's Requiem was the earliest and greatest, appearing in 1878; but only the ballet *The Four Seasons* is of note thereafter, appearing in 1896, two years before Manns gave the Prologue from *Pagliacci*. But these names are all eclipsed by that of Rossini; even allowing for his belonging to an earlier generation, performances of his most popular orchestral overtures match those of the German repertory: *William Tell* was given four times in the 1850s, and in total thirty-two times by the end of the Saturday concerts; *The Siege of Corinth, Semiramide* and *La Gazza Ladra* also achieved frequent performances. Of choral works, the *Messe solennelle* was given in 1869 in the memorial concert.

Just as the music of Dvořák had introduced a new regional voice in the 1870s, so, to a lesser extent, the music of Grieg and Svendsen made a special impression in the 1880s. In this case, Grieg's precursor Gade (b.1817) was already well established in England, and especially known at the Palace, his Symphony No. 4 in B♭ having been given its British premiere on 14 March 1863, his Violin concerto would be likewise introduced in 1886. But this music was eclipsed by the appearance of Grieg, whose youthful Piano Concerto swept all before it. It received its English premiere by Dannreuther at the Palace in 1874, coming five times again thereafter, with the

Allegro separately on one occasion. Other Grieg included the overture *In Autumn* in 1888, the Norwegian Dances and selections from the *Peer Gynt* suites in the late 1880s and early 1890s. If the Grieg Concerto was prominent, the omission of the Violin Concerto by Sinding is notable, since it was significantly more often played in Germany than other new concertos given at the Palace. But Sinding's Symphony in D minor had its English premiere on 18 April 1896.

The full effect of the emerging Russian orchestral repertory was to be the discovery of the early twentieth century in London, through Henry Wood and Nikisch. But the Palace had its part in the reception of Tchaikovsky, the central figure in the new orchestral repertory of Manns's time, a repertory previously only known through a few overtures, such as Glinka's *A Life for the Tsar* given at the Palace from 1860. Manns gave the Fantasy Overture *Romeo and Juliet* its British premiere in 1876, and this year also saw the British premiere of the First Piano Concerto with Dannreuther, subsequently given three times, once by Lamond in 1892. Other works were the *Capriccio Italien*, and *Serenade Melancolique* for violin and orchestra in 1879 with Sarasate. The symphonies were more of a technical challenge, and Manns was never fully successful with them, though No. 6 is particularly prominent, first given in 1894, then five times till 1900; his performance of the Third Symphony in D also attracts attention.

Towards a native school[32]

First steps and establishment, 1855–1880

The Saturday concerts provided an immediate stimulus to the growth of English music, to composers as well as performers, in the period later described as the English Musical Renaissance. As Maitland put it 'as far as its source can be ascribed to any one spot, that honour must be ascribed to the Crystal Palace at Sydenham'.[33] As time passed, the riches of European music became increasingly familiar to the younger British generation, and a performance of a new work under Manns became a goal of a young composer. The development can be seen in three phases: first the early years, when Manns perforce leant on established names in the attempt to give the Crystal Palace concerts credence with the musical public, though also taking opportunities to invest in the young; from the later 1860s a second and larger generation comes forward with a much greater interest in symphonies and concertos, reflective of the increasing importance of European works; finally, from the middle 1880s, a rich crop of names working in all the major forms, especially the more extended ones, reflects the full impact of continental influence at that time, and the role of the Palace concerts as a focus for music in England. But this final stage took years to achieve: it was different when Manns started.

In Manns's early years, the dominant concert genre was the operatic or oratorio overture. Manns gave such works by the leading composers from early years, including those of William Sterndale Bennett (whose overtures were by far the most frequently performed), George Macfarren and lesser names like Harold Thomas, Henry Hugo Pierson and Charles Horsley. Larger-scale works appeared later, Bennett's Piano Concertos appearing in the 1870s, Macfarren's Violin Concerto in 1877 and Symphony in E minor in 1883 (both in MS). There was no special distinction for Manns and the Palace in performing works that had been given previously elsewhere. He needed new British works and the interest of young British composers to give the new venue a distinctive character. He did not have to wait long, for he soon established a close working relationship with Arthur Sullivan, who rapidly established himself as the great hope of British music and was the first native composer closely associated with the Palace. Grove and Manns decided to put on the complete incidental music to *The Tempest*, first performed only in part at Leipzig in 1862. The performance was an outstanding success for Sullivan, and a signal moment in the emergence of British music at the Palace. Sullivan's symphony was first given under Manns on 10 March 1866, then subsequently at St James's Hall under Mellon. The Cello Concerto was given its premiere on 24 November 1866 with Piatti, for whom it was written, and was soon repeated in Edinburgh.[34] The overture to the opera *The Sapphire Necklace* was given on 13 April 1867, and on 7 December the revised version of the overture *Marmion* played. Over the years these and numerous other works would be performed by Manns. In contrast, none of the major works of Sullivan's fellow Leipzig-trained contemporary John Francis Barnett, who also had close connections with the Palace, seem to have been given first performances, chiefly because they were written for choral festivals, where they were first performed. But his works figure strongly in the programmes, including many overtures and cantatas, such as *The Ancient Mariner*, *The Raising of Lazarus*, and *Paradise and the Peri*, and a piano concerto (played by his wife, Emma Barnett).

From the later 1860s, the number of young composers regularly represented in the programmes increases steadily; though concert overtures and suites of incidental music remain the most common types, there now appears an increasing body of symphonies, of which a number aspire towards the programmatic, bearing titles, though there are as yet no titled symphonic poems. Concertos are also more frequently found. Many of the names are known today only through their church compositions, or as academics and administrators, but this generation begins to look to the Palace for a first, or first London performance of a work premiered elsewhere. Of the older generation who come to prominence in the 1870s, Ebenezer Prout (b.1835) had four symphonies performed between 1874 and 1887 – the last a premiere, W. H. Cusins (b.1833) a scherzo and two overtures between 1863 and 1875, Alfred Holmes three overtures between 1874 and 1877, Henry Gadsby (b.1842) two symphonies in 1871 and 1888 and five overtures in 1869–87 (two for the first time), Swinnerton Heap an overture in 1879, and William Shakespeare a piano concerto in the same year. The most highly regarded orchestral composer of this generation was Thomas Wingham (b.1846), who had two symphonies and five overtures performed between 1872 and 1883, as well as an elegy for his teacher Sterndale Bennett. Important younger figures were Frederick Corder and Frederick Cowen. Corder was represented by overtures and smaller orchestral pieces, Cowen, later a leading conductor, by four symphonies between 1870 and 1884, overtures and smaller orchestral pieces, as well as many choral works in later years.

These composers were eclipsed by three figures destined to dominate British musical life into the twentieth century: Stanford, Parry and MacKenzie. The Crystal Palace was important to each, though in different ways. Stanford came to the Palace with the brightest image of the three, already established as a brilliant Cambridge organist, and active as an influence on new music.[35] It was in glowing terms that Grove introduced his audience to the composer in the programme note of the concert of 17 November 1877, when Stanford's *Festal Overture* was given. The work had been written for the Gloucester Festival, and only one of Stanford's major works given at the Palace was in a first performance, the Symphony in F, on 23 February 1889; other works included the Symphony in B♭ (MS), Symphony in D, 1895, Serenade in G, 1883, and the Overture and a Selection from *The Veiled Prophet* in 1882.[36] Stanford retained a close interest in the Palace and greatly admired Manns's achievements. In contrast, the achievements of Alexander Campbell MacKenzie were less known at first. Mackenzie's first performed work was the Scherzo for orchestra, written for the concerts of Edinburgh University. His Scottish Rhapsody No. 2 was given on 26 March 1881, and its companion, No. 1 on 21 April 1883. Mackenzie was quickly to become very well known at the Palace and had many more works performed there than his peers from 1879 numerous overtures and three works for violin and orchestra, including a concerto on 13 March 1886. He was commissioned by the Palace to write an ode for Queen Victoria's Jubilee in 1885 and had close contacts with the orchestral concerts. Of the three, it was Parry who owed most to the Palace for early performances, since his first work performed there, the overture *Guillaume de Castebanh, Troubadour*, was a first performance. But it was another first performance, of his substantial Piano Concerto in F♯ major by Dannreuther in 1880, which really made his name, and other works soon followed, including a selection from incidental music to Aristophanes' *The Birds* in 1883, the Symphony in G major (written for the Birmingham Fesival) in 1883 and three oratorios in 1888.

The younger generation, 1880–1900
By the middle of the 1880s a great momentum of British composers coming forward with major works had developed, and Manns was inundated with new works for consideration, few of which ever got as far as a Saturday concert, though more were given in the daily music. Two features dominate the repertory: the vast increase in dramatic cantatas and oratorios, which almost treble proportionally, and the appearance of the first British symphonic poems, with the work normally regarded as representing the first British example, Wallace's *The Passing of Beatrice*, in 1892. Concerto compositions remain about the same, but there are slightly more overtures and significantly more symphonies and texted works, though few of the names mean much today. Of concert overture composers, only one name stands out, that of Hamish MacCunn, whose *The Land of the Mountain and the Flood* is the only one to have held a place in the repertory, though that strongly; it had its British

CRYSTAL PALACE.

SEASON, 1895–6.

PROGRAMME OF
GRAND CONCERT

(THE SECOND OF THE FORTIETH ANNUAL SERIES OF SATURDAY CONCERTS)

OCTOBER 19th, 1895,

IN CELEBRATION OF THE FORTIETH ANNIVERSARY

OF THE

INSTITUTION OF THE CRYSTAL PALACE SATURDAY CONCERTS,

The First of which took place on the 20th October, 1855.

---

1. CONCERT-OVERTURE, "THE LAND
   OF THE MOUNTAIN AND THE FLOOD" *Hamish MacCunn.*

2. CONCERTO FOR PIANOFORTE AND
   ORCHESTRA . . . . . *C. Hubert H. Parry.*
         Pianist—MR. FREDERICK DAWSON.
         (Pianoforte by ERARD.)

3. SELECTION FROM THE INCIDENTAL
   MUSIC TO "THE TEMPEST" . . *Arthur Sullivan.*
         Introduction.
         Banquet Dance.
         Song. "Where the bee sucks."
         MRS. HELEN TRUST.
         (Her first appearance at these Concerts.)
         Dance of Nymphs and Reapers.

4. SYMPHONY NO. 1, IN D, MS. . . *H. Walford Davies.*
         (First time of performance.)

5. ROMANCE, "THERE'S A BOWER OF
   ROSES" (*The Veiled Prophet*) . . *C. Villiers Stanford.*
         MRS. HELEN TRUST.

6. SELECTION FROM SUITE FOR
   STRINGS, "IN THE OLDEN TIME,"
   NO. 2, "THE LUTE" . . . . *F. H. Cowen.*
         (Composed for these Concerts.)

7. SCOTCH RHAPSODY NO. 1, IN G . *A. C. Mackenzie.*

AUGUST MANNS, CONDUCTOR.

A

---

15 The programme of the concert for the fortieth anniversary of the Saturday Concerts, held on 19 October 1895, and devoted entirely to British works first performed at the Palace.

premiere at the Palace on 5 November 1887. Of symphonic composers, Frederick Cliffe created a strong impression with his first
Symphony when it was premiered on 20 April 1889 at the Palace, a
second appearing in 1892. It seems to have created more interest
than the symphonies of Edward German and Walford Davies, given
British premieres at the Palace on 13 December 1890 and 19
October 1895 respectively. By the time the Palace organized a
concert consisting entirely of British music, featuring the composers
with a special connection (Stanford, Parry, MacKenzie, Sullivan,
Davies, Cowen, MacCunn) hardly any composer of significance had
failed to have some place in a Saturday concert.

But one who had was destined to be the most important of all:
Edward Elgar, whose early provincial life had given him far fewer
opportunities than many other figures. He constantly sought unsuc-
cessfully to have small pieces performed, despite the support of his
violin teacher Pollitzer, who was a member of the orchestra. The
role of the Palace was more one of education than of sponsorship for
Elgar and therefore more crucially important to his development.
As his friend and colleague, the violinist W. H. Reed, recalled, 'I
think it was the attendance at those concerts ... that fired his
ambition and turned the scales on the side of serious composition.'[37]
Elgar himself recalled the practicalities later in life, in 1927.

I lived 120 miles from London. I rose at six, walked a mile to the railway
station, the train left at seven; arrived at Paddington about eleven, underground to Victoria, on to the Palace arriving in time for the last three
quarters of an hour of the rehearsal; if fortune smiled this piece of rehearsal
included a work desired to be heard, but fortune rarely smiled and more
often than not the principal item was over. Lunch, concert at three. At five
a rush to Victoria, then to Paddington, on to Worcester, arriving at 10.30.
A strenuous day indeed; but the new work had been heard and another
treasure added to a life's experience.[38]

Nothing was more important to Elgar than to study the powers of
the modern orchestra. October 1881 saw Berlioz performances at
the Palace, including the first British performance of *Lélio*. The
programme note emphasized the orchestration, referring to Berlioz's
treatise: Elgar duly purchased it.[39] The death of Wagner in 1883
was the occasion of a Wagner Memorial Concert on 3 March;
against the words of the 'Liebestod' in his programme he wrote 'This
is the finest thing of W's that I have heard up to the present. I shall
never forget this.'[40] May and August saw two more Berlioz events:

the English premiere of the *Requiem* and three movements from the
Fantastic Symphony. Soon he too was engaged on a giant orchestral
work. His orchestral interests were further stimulated by the performance for the Liszt visit in 1886: on 10 April, Manns's orchestra
surpassed itself in *Mazeppa, Les Preludes* and other works. But his
interest was not only in big orchestras: 1883 also saw the first English
performance of Brahms's Third Symphony, though not in a first
British performance, and he was deeply affected by it.[41]

But performance of Elgar's own music at the Palace proved more
elusive. Though, through Pollitzer, he obtained a performance of his
Sevillana in a daily concert on 12 May 1884, his ambitions for
Saturday performance were constantly frustrated. In 1893 he left
the score of *The Black Knight* with Manns,[42] and in 1896, went
through the score of *King Olaf* with him.[43] Only in 1897 were the
latter and Three Dances 'From the Bavarian Highlands' given.[44]
But it was now too late for Manns to play a part, though an item
from *Gerontius* was given before the end of Manns's last season.

A feature of the programmes of the last decade is the support that
Manns gave to women composers. One of the most prominent of
them, Ethel Smyth, had her first public performance anywhere at
the Palace when Manns gave her Serenade in April of 1890,[45] and in
the following October he included her overture *Anthony and Cleopatra*
in the Saturday programme, repeated in Manns's Benefit Concert
on 26 April. He also produced works by Maud Matras, Alice M.
Chamberlayne, Alice Smith and Rosalind Ellicott.

Manns's desire to encourage young composers continued una-
bated to his old age. One of the most promising was W. H. Bell,
whose titled symphony 'Walt Whitman' was given its first performance, as were his symphonic poems *The Pardoner's Tale* and *The
Canterbury Tales*. Other premieres were of Herbert Bedford's symphonic poem *Kit Marlowe*, overtures by Charles Vincent and
Herbert Bunning, and Reginald Steggall's Suite in E. Of names to
become prominent in the twentieth century, that of Samuel Coleridge Taylor complements that of Arthur Sullivan in his having
special connections with the locality (he grew up in Croydon) and
teaching in the School; but only one of his works was given by
Manns (though many after his time), the Ballade in A minor for
orchestra on 5 November 5 1898. Joseph Holbrooke (b.1878) did
achieve a premiere by Manns, of his symphonic poem *The Raven* on
3 March 1900,[46] in Manns's last season: doubtless many others were
still in line.

THE MUSICAL PROGRAMME NOTE

No greater contrast could be imagined than that between the range of the popular events advertised in the Saturday programmes and the specialist information on the orchestral music provided through the programme note and the additional material on the day's music. For the Saturday audience was offered a unique range of information about the works performed. There is no clearer confirmation of the essentially educational spirit of the musical enterprise at the Crystal Palace than the character and scope of these musical notes. They began in connection with the centenary of Mozart's birth in 1856; prior to that, only texts of the vocal works had been provided. Grove recalls that Manns asked him 'to write a few words about Mozart himself and about the works to be performed. I tried it and that gave me the initiation: after that, as the Saturday concerts progressed, I went on week by week'.[47] In fact, relatively few works received notes before the mid 1860s, and many of these are by Manns, always prompted by a concert with a special feature, as several times in 1859: on 9 March the performance of the *Eroica* Symphony, with expanded forces, drew comment on the music; on 2 April, Mozart's Symphony in D prompted an article of two sides on 'Instrumental Music'; the Spohr Memorial Concert on 5 November recalled Spohr's life and work. The initial emphasis on biography was gradually broadened to include discussion of the music itself. As Grove pointed out in 1880 'I wrote about the symphonies because I wished to make them clear to myself, and to discover the secret of the things that charmed me so and then from that sprang the wish to make other amateurs see it in the same way'.[48]

Though Grove's printed notes were not the first such writings – nor claimed as such by him – he put the genre on a new plane. Amateur of music that he was, George Grove was a scholar and brought a high degree of accuracy of reference and precision of expression to his work, allied to extensive and carefully produced music examples. His method was narrative with examples and relied on assumptions of formal norms, to which he constantly referred, thus presupposing a fair degree of musical literacy on the part of his readers. Clearly his own theoretical background was very basic, with little chordal analysis, though he does draw attention to recurring themes and the re-use of material, hinting at deeper organic factors, though informally. His most extensive notes were on Beethoven, which gradually developed in length over the years, new background material being regularly incorporated. Notes on the longer works, such as the *Eroica* or Ninth Symphonies, expanded to upwards of twenty pages, with several examples per page.[49] Manns's notes are much shorter, rarely exceeding two sides. They tend to focus on notable characteristics of the piece in its effect, rather than offering a detailed successive account. Manns is particularly sensitive to orchestration and to the background and inspiration of works, giving a clear sense of the kinds of issues which attracted him in his response to music, and thus in searching out new music for the programmes.

The expansion of the repertory required new writers with specialist knowledge and several important musicians of the period began to contribute after a decade or so. The sheer practicalities of keeping abreast of new musical developments clearly tested the ingenuity of the writers. The achieving of a first performance of a new or unknown work was a high priority, and always stated in the programme: this could lead to difficulties in the provision of information. The resort to the previous notes of other concert-giving bodies was sometimes unavoidable, whether from the Philharmonic for new European works or from regional sources for British works. But it was against the ethos of the Palace, which would go to great lengths to make the authenticity of the notes match that of the performance, as when Manns wrote to Liszt in May 1879 to find out more about *Hunnengeschlacht*, to be played on 17 May 1879 as 'The Battle of the Huns', receiving something of an authoritative statement on the work in turn:

Kaulbach's world-famed picture represents two battles – one of earth, the other in the air (or sky), according to the legend that the warriors continue to fight after their death, as spirits. In the centre of the picture the Cross is seen with its mysterious illumination, and upon this my Symphonic Poem is based. The chorale 'Crux fideles', with its gradual development, expresses the idea of the final victory of Christianity in love to God and Man. Thanking you for your kindly interest, I remain, Yours very sincerely, F.Liszt'.[50]

Additional material

From about the middle 1860s to the 1880s, the notes on the works themselves are regularly complemented by various kinds of additional material, providing a variety of background information, either closely related to the composer and the circumstances of the works performed, or more broadly educational in tone. This co-incides with the establishment of the concerts as a national force in music and subsides when much of the material has been drawn into the programme notes themselves, their much more expanded format and more scholarly character offering the clearest sign of the new stage in the education of an audience. From the middle 1860s hardly a week went by without some fascinating insight into the world from which the music came, so the audiences were informed as to the contours of musical tradition and circumstances of first perform-ance, as well as contemporary trends in the provision of musical information, to an extent which was unique in Britain at the time. Two types of information dominated: on the one hand, the kind of material extracted from books, often recently printed, such as regu-larly appeared in the music journals; on the other, material that was unique to the Crystal Palace through its leading figures and their many contacts.

Information on the lives of composers, lists of works of a featured composer, and extracts from biographies, letters and reminiscences were already familiar from musical journals such as *The Musical Times*, but the Palace targeted its material more closely, matching its frequent acknowledgement of anniversaries and special dates with relevant notes. Where the Crystal Palace really came into its own was in the provision of material to which only it had access through its leading figures, or which was given to it as a consequence of its status: to Grove pre-eminently, but not only so. Thus one can read a recollection of the first night of *Der Freischütz* by Karl Reinecke, or Mendelssohn to the Handel Society of London, provided by Mac-farren. And Grove and Manns through their contacts with Joachim and Clara Schumann were likely to hear of anything relevant to a new work. The programmes soon became the repository of unique educational information and were regarded as collectors' items. And in time the programmes came to document the history of the Palace performances themselves, reminding the reader of when a work was last given, especially if it had been relatively little performed. The final programme of the year listed works performed and the prin-cipal soloists. But the significance of the programme did not end on the collector's shelf. The notes of Grove and his contributors were directly influential in the creation of the *Dictionary of Music and Musicians*. The particular strength of the entries on Schubert, Schumann and Mendelssohn, and the wide coverage on performers, reflects the detailed grasp he had gained through researching the concert notes since the middle 1850s. Just as Grove's Beethoven notes had resulted in a book on the symphonies which became a standard work of reference, so his devotion to the Crystal Palace programmes had stimulated his scholarly and bibliographic nature to a comprehensive coverage of the subject. And thus was created another vital link between the music of the Palace and British musical education through the agency of Grove.

CHAPTER 7

The Crystal Palace and its audience

THE MUSICAL CONTEXT

Looking back at his early years, Manns commented that 'I found neither orchestra, library, concert room or musical audience in 1855; and ... had to battle with strongly-rooted prejudices against the so-called classical instrumental music ...'[1] Present-day reaction to Manns's statement is likely to be very different from that which he would have assumed in making it. A modern response would tend to stress rather the social context than the achievements of the individual: Manns's audience must have existed, if only potentially, and he was merely the agent of forces of musical change. While there is obviously truth in this view – the initiation of a vastly broader audience for a culture previously the preserve of an educated class was everywhere apparent – his remark still retains some force: he went beyond what could have been expected at the Palace, and in his more extreme acts of musical exploration could never guarantee his audience. Manns could still have fulfilled a significant musical role in a much less demanding way, closer to the lines first envisaged by Grove. Moreover, one could well imagine the Palace as a musical showcase for high quality performers and composers whose music more directly reflected bourgeois entertainment culture in the way analogous to that to be found in other comparable locations, whether in German spa towns like Baden Baden (where Johann Strauss regularly played and was part of the highest musical circles) or in English metropolitan leisure settings, as at the Vauxhall Gardens (with which the Palace occasionally compared itself) or the Surrey Gardens, where Jullien regularly played promenade concerts in the years before the Palace's opening.[2] Indeed, as Davison relates, this is exactly what was suggested in the Palace's first year, when its musical direction was not as yet fully clear, the *Daily News* proposing in January 1855 that Jullien be engaged for a few months to make music inside while the Palace brass band played outside in the grounds.[3]

That comparison of Manns's achievements is made rather with the concerts of the Philharmonic Society, the Hallé Orchestra, and later the Richter concerts sets him apart. All these organizations had their musical and social contexts: when Manns began, the Crystal Palace had no such musical context. 'It was really a matter of patience, prudence, perseverance, and pluck on my part by which prejudice could be conquered and the road for high class music could be opened.'[4] But proud as Manns was of his achievement, it must be kept in perspective. He was not alone in his vision of a new national focus for orchestral music and a new audience at the Palace. The names of Davison and Grove have already emerged in this regard, not least that of Davison, who clearly saw the national implications of a new concert venue with a resident orchestra: 'Herr Manns is too intelligent a musician not to appreciate the nature of his resources and the requirements of his public.'[5] It was in the latter area that Manns stands out. And even though the practical support of Grove was vital in advancing the music, as was the scholarly prestige provided by his programme notes, it was in challenging 'the requirements' of his public that Manns gave the Palace its place in musical history.

Bennett's recollection of the significance of the Palace to music enthusiasts in the late 1860s gives a clue to the needs and the type of Manns's intended audience: 'We hankered after better things than could be found in town.'[6] Bennett and his fellows were essentially in pursuit of new orchestral music as well as high-quality performances of the repertory to be heard at the Philharmonic Society, firmly the province of a cultured class, who were in an economic position to travel to find it. The state of orchestral music in London 'sufficiently accounted for the Saturday rushes to Sydenham, not only of cultivated amateurs but of professionals also.' As for the critics, of which Bennett was one,

the whole army, nay, we were not an army then, the whole band moved upon the southern height as regularly as some of them frequented the Albion Tavern or the Edinburgh Castle ... All that was great and good in the London musical world might be seen at Victoria Station on the Winter Saturdays, as the special trains were backing to the departure platforms.[7]

The programmes clearly expressed Manns's high aims: 'a careful selection of orchestral and choral compositions ... the most remarkable novelties; an orchestra of Beethoven's day ... [which he] considered most efficient for refined performance of his orchestral compositions.'[8] The orchestral programmes of the Palace were never 'popular' in the sense that the Palace itself was popular: it is misleading to interpret them purely as the musical expression of the new popular educational spirit: opportunities for experience of music of all kinds were to be available to different audiences at the Palace, as the totality of the musical life shows. For example, Nettel's view that Manns's programmes were based on 'a careful study of the public and the use of every means to make good music attractive to them' is only partly true. He was clearly ahead of public taste.[9] Rather it was that he knew what was good and would find a response with a certain audience, which he then wished to expand. And his judgements were sound with regard to the European repertory, anticipating later concert fare with great accuracy. The supportive response of his audience by the middle 1860s is clear from the evidence of an advertisement that appears in *The Musical World* for Saturday, 10 March 1866, in respect of that day's concert. It informs its readers that 'the last four of these increasingly popular reunions have been attended by nearly 2,800 persons. The demand for reserved seats being much larger than can possibly be met, to prevent disappointment they should be booked for early.'[10] This figure indicates that somewhere in the region of 700 people attended each concert, a considerable number, though how much it filled the room it is impossible to say without more knowledge of the facilities at this period.

But if things were going well for the newly fashionable concerts in the 1860s, provision of music for the programmes was never a one-way or guaranteed process. Neither Manns nor the Directors could take an audience for granted and rely on a relatively small core of informed critics and musicians in building an audience and keeping it, in order, in turn, to sustain the quality of performers needed. They had to know what the audience thought. As the Palace attracted musical attention from the middle 1860s there seem to have been few problems in pleasing or attracting an audience. And as Manns pressed on with some much more demanding new music in the 1870s, it is obvious that his audience would have varied in its capacity to respond. Vivid evidence of how things must have stood emerges from the plebiscite which was taken at the end of the season 1879–80, the results appearing in the list of works performed during the entire year which was published, as usual, in the final programme in April. The list is divided into four classes: symphonies, overtures, miscellaneous works, concertos. Of the twenty-two symphonies listed, two works dominated: Beethoven's *Pastoral* Symphony, with 247 votes, and Mendelssohn's *Italian* Symphony, with 227. Of the only other works in three figures, Schubert's Ninth narrowly beats Beethoven's Fifth, with the *Eroica* achieving just 101; Beethoven's Second Symphony came second to last with twelve votes. Of the overtures, Manns's early championing of that to Wagner's *Tannhäuser* is vindicated as it sweeps the board with 247 given for seventeen works; *William Tell* received 155 votes, Leonora No. 1, 160, *A Midsummer Night's Dream*, 157. In the following year Manns used the plebiscite to gauge reaction to his recent performances of Berlioz, as well as their programming, with a view to their repetition. In the programme of 8 November 1881, he records 'votes for the repetition of both the Sinfonie Fantastique and Lelio, 951; votes for the repetition of one only, or of portions of the works, 151; votes for repetition of one only or a portion only of works: 25. The two works will therefore be repeated on an early Saturday.'

TRANSPORT, ACCOMMODATION, ADVERTISING AND COST

The provision of adequate rail connections was the key to the success of the Saturday concerts as to that of the whole Crystal Palace endeavour. The concerts could never have attracted a London audience without them, and only a London audience would have been able to generate the wider interest necessary to sustain the programmes: a purely suburban audience is unthinkable for these concerts and would doubtless have led to a different policy towards the provision of orchestral music. The management remained sensitive to the transport needs of the concert-goers, obviously in direct conjunction with the railway companies. Thus as early as January 1857 the concert programme informs its reader that 'special trains extra to those on ordinary days will be run on Saturdays, both from and to town, as the traffic may require'. Thereafter the programme kept the patrons fully informed of new rail provision, the possibilities of which had been greatly increased by the opening of the high level railway line and station in 1865, thus bringing patrons on this line directly to the Palace, and to their seats literally in seconds. Travellers from Victoria, like Bennett and Elgar, thus had two lines to choose from. In 1867, the accessing of the East London Railway connecting Wapping to New Cross brought the Palace within 'easy accessibility of the East End and the Metropolis via the Brighton Company's line'. In the 1871–2 season the south west of London was also made available by the direct line from Kensington and Hampton Court. And towards the end of the century, as the need to stem the declining attractions of the Palace increased, advertising is even stronger: the programmes for 1895–6 list all the evening departures on both lines, including the special trains for Thursday and Saturday evenings, which served the newly emerging evening concerts. A programme for 1900 notes that on Saturday afternoons, 'a special fast train departs Victoria at 3.00 p.m. and arrives at the Palace at 3.23', presumably a facility which had long been available.

Even more important than the means of transport in attracting an audience was the means of communication: how to capture the attention of the audience and how to keep it. Both internal and external channels were available. The weekly printed concert programme provided notice of coming concert events and, in time, a prospectus anticipated the coming season. Externally, notices in the press broadcast this information more widely and the constant reviews in the musical press kept attention focussed on the concerts, as they did for all London's concerts. The musical press also gave a great deal of intelligence of musical happenings which further directed attention towards concert life. There is a perceptible pattern in the Saturday advertising over the years. With the confidence that attended the flowering of Manns's orchestra and its international recognition much more information is given of the daily music, listing the bulk of the programmes. From about 1880, advance notice is given of the two respective series, with works to be performed and artists. By the 1890s this advertising had become more intense, clearly aiming to commend the concerts more powerfully in an increasingly competitive situation. Though there are now fewer concerts to advertise – only six in each series towards 1900 – they receive much more attention: notable is the attention to unusual coming works, as when the English violinist John Dunn plays the Gade Violin Concerto, or the growing attraction of child prodigies, like 'Little Bruno Steidel' or 'the amazing Maud McCarthy'. A particular strength of Palace advertising was the flexibility of its press, which was able to publish programmes very late and therefore take in cancellations and changes. But one feature of the advanced publicity was that players would not commit themselves to precise works: thus the reference to, for example. 'the Beethoven or Mendelssohn Violin Concerto', or simply 'a well known concerto'.

By the later 1860s, the interest of the press in the Saturday concerts had become intense, such that when the prospectus for the 1868–9 season was issued at the beginning of the year, *The Sunday Times* for 27 September 1868 responded with generous quotation and comment. So striking a moment was this for the musical life of the Palace that the programme of the first Saturday concert duly reproduced it at length, noting with approval the continuation of Manns as conductor, the maintenance of the choir at a level of 300 voices and the prominence of new works, indeed, 'a pledge, as far as we know unexampled in musical history [that] each miscellaneous programme will contain one work new to the Crystal Palace audience the composition of a living writer, or of a departed master, which, from some cause or other, is not yet known to the public'.

Although the Crystal Palace was intended as a popular venue, it was never as fully so as other places of cultural recreation, not least as regards its music. At its opening in 1854, admission was 2s. 6d., only children under twelve being admitted at 1s.[11] Bank Holidays or other declared 'shilling days' were the only occasions on which the popular rate applied and only later did this rate become customary. The regular facilities available in the entrance cost included the performances of the band and also the daily music, which seems to have been variously performed in the concert room or the centre transept. But other performances normally incurred a charge. Here again, the Palace was not cheaper than other comparable venues for quality music: on the contrary. Admission to the concerts was initially 2s. 6d., which continued through the 1860s; by comparison, the concerts at St James's Hall cost 1s. from its opening in 1859. Only with the full completion of the Concert Room in 1868 does a two-tier pricing appear. The completed Concert Room offered seating in the main stalls (called The Area) and the side Galleries. The end gallery facing the stage was kept for critics, directors and their guests, though it became available for seating by the end of the century, indicative of the decline in critical interest. The price distinction was between front and back seats, numbered and unnumbered, rather than between Gallery and Area, which were priced the same. From the opening of the Concert Room the cost of a numbered single stalls or gallery seat was 2s. 6d. and an unnumbered seat 1s. By 1881, the top price is divided, at 2s. 6d. and 1s. 6d., with an unnumbered seat for 6d. By the last years there is a considerable increase, with a division of 4s., 2s. and 1s. – almost double in twenty years years – and these prices continued till the end. All these prices were additional to a 1s. admission charge to the Concert Room itself. The programme was an additional 6d. The prices were subject to modification for special occasions, either down for popular events or up for special ones. The Special Summer Concert in May 1881 offered seats at 2s. 6d. and 1s. In contrast, the visit of Rubinstein, the biggest musical event of the same summer, doubled the prices to 5s. and 2s. 6d.

The central way of attracting a regular audience was through the provision of season tickets. Monthly and annual season tickets were available to the Palace from the beginning and were widely advertised in the programmes. Season tickets to the concerts, available not only at the Palace but also in central London, at Exeter Hall, are advertised from the season 1867–8: subscription for the double series of fourteen concerts each, two guineas each stall (transferable). Purchasers of tickets on 30 September 1871, are informed of transferable reserved stalls for the series of twenty-six concerts at two guineas, and that 'purchasers of stalls for this day's concert will be allowed the half-crown paid if purchasing serial stalls on the afternoon after the concert'. During the 1870s the price range is between two and two and a half guineas in accordance with the higher individual seat prices. By 1897 the prices have accordingly risen considerably: one guinea for a series of eight. The provision of combined rail and concert tickets was another way of making concerts attractive, offering further reductions. But the railway system did not serve the interests of all would-be musical visitors, since third-class travel was never available to the season ticket holder.

A SOCIAL PERSPECTIVE ON THE CONCERTS

Just how far the readers of *The Sunday Times* would have been interested in the musical aspirations of the broader mass of the populace is open to question. Bennett and his fellow music enthusiasts, amateur and professional, constituted a socially privileged class: there must have been other reactions by those who would have wished to attend, but were unable to for financial reasons. A view to set beside that of Bennett was that of Bernard Shaw, who was uniquely placed to express it, both as a music critic (albeit of a younger generation) and as one with a concern for the need for new social structures, as a Fabian socialist. Already in June 1885 his view of the social aspect of Palace music is trenchant:

When Herr Richter disbanded his orchestra on Monday last, London was left to face three months without concerts of high class music. Only the well-to-do amateurs will be any the worse, for there is practically no regular provision made at any time throughout the year for the mass of people who like good orchestral music, but who cannot afford to spend more than a couple of shillings a week on gratifying their taste. Of weekly concerts of recognized excellence we have two sets: the Saturday afternoons at the Crystal Palace in the winter and early spring, and the Richter concerts from Spring to midsummer, with a few extra performances very late in the autumn or early winter. These concerts are not cheap enough for the people. A Crystal Palace Saturday Popular, taking place on a half-crown day, with an extra charge for admission to the concert room, a sixpenny programme, and a railway journey makes a larger hole in half a sovereign than many amateurs care to make in five shillings. The lowest charge for admission to a Richter concert is two-and-sixpence; and the analytic programme, though fattened up by six pages of advertisements, costs an additional shilling, for which it is perhaps the worst value in London. The consequent dependence of both series of concerts on the patronage of comparatively rich people is shown by the fact that they cease when the moneyed classes leave London, and recommence when they return.[12]

At the recommencement of the concerts for the 1892–3 series he was able to commend favourable new arrangements aimed at culti-vating a wider audience, the existing charges being

absolutely prohibitive for four out of five Londoners [so that] regular frequenters of the concerts are very rare outside the ranks of the season ticket holders resident in the neighbourhood of the Palace [and that] in general social value the free orchestral concerts given on the other after-noons, with the smaller band, are probably much more important than the Saturday ones. This season, however, the railway companies have consen-ted to issue twenty first-class return tickets from London to the Palace, available on concert Saturdays only, for a guinea for holders of the two guinea serial stall tickets. By this arrangement I shall save nineteen shillings if I go to all the concerts.[13]

PART 4

Other orchestral, vocal and instrumental concerts

CHAPTER 8

After Manns: the Crystal Palace amateur orchestra and choir

THE END OF THE SATURDAY CONCERTS

Although the Crystal Palace Orchestra had been disbanded at the end of the 1899–1900 season, after forty-four years, a professional Saturday orchestra continued with diminishing regularity until the first series of the 1902–3 season. There was clearly some resistance to the breaking of the Saturday tradition simply because the daily orchestra no longer performed.[1] Of the two sets of six concerts scheduled for the 1900–1 season, Manns conducted most, the fourth and fifth in the first series and all of the second, though his orchestra was not named nor listed. Hans Richter took the last of the first series on 17 November. The season began on 13 October with three concerts by Robert Newman's Queen's Hall Orchestra under Wood, a significant choice, since no orchestra had benefitted more from Manns's work, and Wood was the first native conductor of international standing.[2] Manns's spirit was undiminished, Wyndham noting that he conducted his first two concerts 'with all his old fire and *verve*'.[3] It is interesting to compare his programmes with those of his successors. His programme-patterns remained the same, including more first performances of European works, such as Becker's Cello Concerto on 9 March 1901. Of new British music, the outstanding example is Elgar: the Prelude to the first part of *Gerontius*, the work Manns had hesitated to give complete. Its composer is now given full recognition on 10 November 1900, as the programme for the previous week heralds a performance 'when the orchestra will be increased to 108 players'. Younger composers continued to be represented, with the first major performance of Joseph Holbrooke's symphonic poem *The Raven*, and the 'Love Song' from Coleridge Taylor's *Hiawatha*. In contrast to the Richter programme, Wood followed Manns in offering a variety of contrasted genres and

127

composers, though it tended to be slightly shorter with six or seven items, by reducing solos. Richter's single programme was purely orchestral, its six items being entirely from Wagner, except for Beethoven's Seventh Symphony as the final item. Wood also stressed Wagner, though Tchaikowsky figures strongly as well, with performances of the Fifth and Sixth symphonies within a month. And he brought the *Nutcracker* Suite and 1812 *Overture* to their first Crystal Palace performances, also giving the work which Manns had first introduced in England, the overture *Romeo and Juliet*, its second Palace performance.

But this was to be Manns's last season with a professional orchestra at the Palace. For the 1901–2 series, beginning on 12 October, the Queen's Hall orchestra under Wood is the only listed orchestra, now quoting a complement of 110 players – bigger than Manns's even when augmented. New works still have their place, with more Elgar (the *Enigma* Variations for the first time at the Palace) and the English premiere of a work by Pauline Viardot Garcia (*Scène d'Hermione*). But the days of the big orchestra were rapidly coming to an end there, though there had been no hint of it in the previous year when *The Musical Times* had greeted the 'new departure' under Wood as promising success through his 'magnificent interpretations' of Tchaikovsky's Sixth and Beethoven's Fifth symphonies.[4] But despite the prestigious soloists, the advertising is notable for drawing attention more to Newman's Queen's Hall performances than to those at the Palace, announcing Promenade concerts on every evening at 8 from 6 December to 1 February. Rather it is vocal and chamber music which catch the attention. Mark Hambourg appeared on 14 December with seven items shared between voice and piano with Blanche Marchesi. On 16 November 1901 no lesser names than Ysaÿe, Busoni and Becker appear in a programme comprising five items in which Schubert's Trio in B♭, op. 99 and Rubinstein's Trio in G frame instrumental solos, with Chopin's Op. 58 Sonata as centrepiece.

By the 1902–3 season, Newman and Wood had withdrawn, the advertised orchestra being that of London Philharmonic under Cowen. The first eight concerts of the forty-seventh series were advertised for 11, 18 and 25 October; 1 and 15 November; 1 and 13 December. But the priority of a Palace orchestral performance seems no longer to have been great; Cowen's advertised appearance on 11 October is not reported as having taken place. He first appears on 1 November with a Grand Orchestral Concert, followed by a second on 15 November. Standards continued to be high and new music was performed, reviews of the concerts recalling 'excellent readings of Tchaikovsky's *Romeo and Juliet* overture and Beethoven's 7th symphony'. And new music continued to be represented through Arthur Hervey's tone picture *On the March* and Cowen's own *Fantasy of Love and Life*. But it is solo names which now attract attention, groups of such players also continuing to form chamber ensembles: outstanding names of the autumn series of 1902 are Jan Kubelik, Wilhelm Backhaus, Leopold Godowski, Fritz Kreisler and Garcia on 8 November 1902. By 1903–4 there is no advertised orchestra at all; Saturday concerts are now given entirely to solo performers: as well as those already named, Pachmann, Busoni, Petri, Gerardy, Dohnányi, Arnold Foldesy, Raglioli, Wolfstahl and Tillerand, as well as younger English performers, notably the violinist Marie Hall.

THE CRYSTAL PALACE AMATEUR ORCHESTRAL AND CHORAL SOCIETY

Although professional orchestral music soon declined at the Palace, a new era had already begun to dawn in the year of Manns's retirement which would be equally representative of Crystal Palace music in its day. The first Saturday programme of the 1900–1 season features an advertisement for the foundation of an Amateur Orchestral Society with Manns as conductor. It stated that 'by permission of the Directors the rehearsals and concerts will take place at the Crystal Palace and the company's extensive musical library will become available for the Society'. Membership was to be by subscription of one guinea per annum for the orchestral members and two guineas per annum for honorary members, with entitlement to four tickets for each concert for the member and six for each honorary member. Initial enquiries were to be directed to Henry Gilman, Manager of the Palace, though the name of Saxe Wyndham soon appears as Honorary Secretary. Wyndham himself informs us that its establishment was 'chiefly through the initiative' of Gilman.[5] Applicants had to satisfy the conductor as to their competence prior to election. It must have been a shock to Manns to be now dealing with amateur applicants, and he was obviously concerned to maintain standards as best he could in the new setting.

Wyndham recalls 'the kindly but vigorous way in which [Manns] heard and disposed of the trembling amateurs who aspired to join the Society'.[6] Just how vigorous he still was is clear from the programme of the first concert of the Society, given on Tuesday, 30 April 1900 at 8 p.m. Two halves of seven and six items respectively with choir and orchestra: in the first the orchestra gave Schubert's Overture and Second Entr'acte to *Rosamunde* and Sullivan's incidental music to *Merchant of Venice*, and the choir Mendelssohn's eight-part motet *Judge me, O God*, with instrumental and vocal solos; Beethoven's First Symphony opened the second part, the orchestra also contributing Mackenzie's *Benedictus*. After part songs and solo songs, the concert ended with choir, orchestra and organ in the chorus 'Sink and Scatter' from Sullivan's *Shore and Sea*.

But such exertion soon proved too much for Manns's strength, and his friend, the Palace organist Walter Hedgcock, took up the baton, which, as Wyndham stressed in 1909 'he has since held with much distinction to himself and advantage to the ladies and gentlemen of the Society which he directs'.[7] From now we read of no concerts conducted by Manns. Wyndham's view of Hedgcock is confirmed in the concert reviews for the period which Wyndham covers,[8] 1900–1909. The first is of a concert in the Theatre on 23 April 1902 when, for *The Musical Times*, the conductor had his orchestra of seventy-two performers 'well in hand'.[9] The tradition of the performance of English music at the Palace was obviously set to develop under Hedgcock, and the programme (admittedly for St George's Day) included Sterndale Bennett's G minor Symphony, Cowens's *Four Old English Dances*, Sullivan's music for *The Merchant of Venice* and Elgar's *Imperial March*. On 6 December the programme comprised Bridge's Ballad *The Flag of England* for soprano solo, chorus and orchestra, Elgar's *Three Bavarian Dances* and Mendelssohn's Cantata *To the Sons of Art* for male chorus with brass.

The choral initiative was soon destined to have broader consequences: on 6 February 1904 the concert room was filled with 250 voices of the Crystal Palace Choir and 75 in the orchestra for the sixth Concert of the season. The programme included Sullivan's *Overture Di Ballo*, three movements from Sterndale Bennett's Symphony in G minor, Stanford's *Three Choral Songs*, a Wilbye madrigal *Sweet Honey-Sucking Bees*, and Manns's orchestration of Schubert's setting of the Twenty Third Psalm and ended with Thomas's 'rarely performed' ballet-pantomime suite *Les Noces d'Arlequinne*. By 1910 the Society had become the Crystal Palace Orchestral and Choral Society, performing about six times per season, dividing between choral and orchestral music. Sometimes concerts were titled, as on 27 November 1910, when a 'Bohemian Concert' was given. Other concerts featured the young composer who had just missed the Manns era, Samuel Coleridge Taylor, whose music was to be very frequently performed, *Hiawatha* being given in 1911. Nor did the tradition decline after the war. In 1921 there is still a great range of music on offer: Coleridge Taylor's *A Tale of Old Japan*, Verdi's Requiem, Bach's cantata *Sleepers Wake*, German's *Theme and Diversions*, Delibes's *Sylvia*, Elgar's *Dances from the Bavarian Highlands*. Of the performance of *A Tale of Old Japan* on 1 April 1921, *The Musical Times* informs its readers that it was 'one of the best evenings of choral singing in the Society's excellent record. The tone was agreeable, and the expression notably elastic and responsive'.[10] And the Society maintained these standards with enthusiastically reviewed performances of Elgar's *King Olaf*, Dvořák's *The Spectre's Bride*, and, again, Coleridge Taylor's *Hiawatha*, as well as in many purely orchestral works.

As it neared its quarter century, the Society had established its own tradition such that *The Musical Times* could comment in its November issue of 1924:

Music at the Crystal Palace suggests to most people Handel Festivals, Brass Band Contests and similar large-scale doings. The Report and Prospectus of the Crystal Palace Choral and Orchestral Society reminds us of a more modest but a more sustained type of activity. The Society is one of the oldest in London and has to its credit a long list of excellent performances of first class works. Last season, for example, choir and orchestra combined in Grieg's Olaf Trygvasson, Hiawatha's Wedding Feast and Dvořák's The Spectre's Bride; the orchestra played about a dozen works by Tchaikovsky, Glinka, Schubert etc and the choir was heard in short unaccompanied pieces by Holst, Vaughan Williams and Grainger. Three concerts are promised for the coming season at which the chief items will be Blest Pair of Sirens, The Black Knight and From the Bavarian Highlands, A Tale of Old Japan, a liberal selection from Prince Igor, a concert version of Merrie England, the Pathetic symphony, Saint-Saens' Algerian Suite and short works by Delibes, Messager, Bizet and Tchaikovsky. There are vacancies for performing members. Rehearsals are held in the School of Art (South Wing, Crystal Palace) on Mondays (orchestral) and Wednesdays (choir) at 7.30 ... Mr Walter Hedgcock is, of course, the conductor. We are frequently asked for particulars of such societies. Here is one that should meet the needs of a large number of amateurs in the southern suburbs, and we hope they will make the most of the opportunity.[11]

Thus things had come full circle, back to music for a local suburban audience after the initiatives of the earlier generations had completely transformed the status of orchestral music in Britain; after 1928 the Society attracts no special press notice, rather a local orchestral society (which had long been noted in the musical press), the Dulwich Philharmonic Society, takes its place, along with the Sydenham Choral Society and the South West Choral Society.

CHAPTER 9

Popular concerts

THE OPERA CONCERTS AND BALLAD CONCERTS

If the regular Saturday concerts of Manns's era provided something
of a framework for the musical year, and the Handel Festivals for the
decade, they were but a part of a much fuller concert life at the
Crystal Palace. For the management lost no opportunity to arrange
extra concerts. Since concerts were so much easier to organize than
major choral events, a wide range of concert music soon came to
characterize the Crystal Palace year: both regular concerts in a
short season, and a special concert for a particular performer. The
attraction of 'the commonplace vocal miscellany' seems to have died
hard in the expectations of those Crystal Palace habitués who
formed most of the potential audience, and they were quickly
satisfied by a management sensitive to any new opening: the press
constantly acknowledges the 'great exertions' made to maintain
interest, especially during the summer months, when more visitors
could naturally be attracted. The first means was by increased use of
the Palace's own resources: organ recitals and band performances
intermittently from morning till evening, often complemented with
military bands from elsewhere. But outside performers soon played a
more prestigious part.

The most important concerts of the early years were those given
by the Royal Italian Opera Company from Covent Garden, beginning in May, 1856. Yet despite the strong links that already existed
between Covent Garden and the Palace as a result of the arrangements for the opening ceremony, the beginnings of what became
known as the Opera Concerts were fortuitous, occasioned by the
burning down of the Covent Garden Theatre in March 1856 and
the need for new accommodation.[1] The organization at the Palace
was extensive:

A large portion of the nave, north of the great central transept, was converted into a theatre, with stage, proscenium, orchestra etc. There were elevated seats behind the orchestra for the chorus – an admirable plan, by which the sound of the voices was projected into the area occupied by the audience without being disturbed ... That the sound might not be lost in reverberation – as inevitably it must have been – the whole stage and orchestra was covered overhead by a thick and impervious canvas awning, suspended by cords from the roof; and on either side, from end to end, huge canvas screens, painted blue, were placed so as to shut out the courts from the nave and prevent the sound from travelling beyond.[2]

The concerts drew a fashionable opera audience and totally out-shone the Saturday orchestral concerts in press attention. Reference to Manns's concerts in December 1856 in *The Musical World* amply supports his gloomy assessment of critical attitudes to the beginnings of the Saturday concerts: 'these weekly entertainments do not pretend to compete with the Grand Concerts of the season. They are put forth merely as collateral amusements for the visitors on the Saturday.'[3] Rather, for these Grand Operatic Concerts between three to four thousand subscribers were present, and these included nearly all the rank and fashion of London. Tickets were expensive relative to the cost of admission to the Palace and to other concerts. In May 1857 transferable tickets are 7s. 6d. (children under twelve 3s. 6d.), with a two-guinea season ticket for the season of twelve concerts. But also, further to popular request, reserved seats are now available for the series by additional subscription of a guinea or half a crown for a single concert. By 1868 a reserved numbered stall was 2s. 6d., with a subscription for the series of nine concerts at one guinea. Admission on the day was 5s., or 2s. 6d. in advance. The first seasons comprised six or seven concerts in May and June, beginning on Friday afternoons, but by 1864 ten concerts are advertised, beginning 14 May, at 3 p.m., doors opening at 1 p.m. The attractions remained the same for many years. A review of the 1864 season states 'the union of flowers and music in the highest perfection seems likely to render the lovely Palace at Sydenham a formidable rival to the London concert rooms during the height of the season'[4] while an 1868 programme confirms that this is by 'its delicious contrast with the heated atmosphere of London music rooms'.[5]

The whole point of the concerts was to hear the great stars of the Italian Opera in the attractive new location; the programmes were designed to balance musically, in two parts of seven or eight items (arias, duets, ensembles) with an orchestral overture at the beginning of each part and a finale at the end of the second. The eight soloists for the first concert included Mario, Grisi, Formes and Graziani. The programme of the first concert, on 16 May 1856, was as follows:

Part 1: Overture, *Oberon*, Weber; Air (with chorus) *Die Zauberflöte*, Mozart; Duet, *Don Pasquale*, Donizetti; Madrigal 'Down in a flowery Vale', Festa; Aria 'Della sua pace', Mozart; Scena, *Der Freischütz*, Weber; Solo (with chorus) 'Inflammatus', Rossini.

Part 2: Overture, *Masaniello*, Auber; Cavatina 'Ernani involami', Verdi; Duet 'Linda', Donizetti; Brindisi, *Lucretia Borgia*, Donizetti; Aria *Il Trovatore*, Verdi; Duet, *I Puritani*, Bellini; Finale, *Il Conte Ory*, Rossini.[6]

In the second concert, for which the audience doubled, a more extensive programme featured Mario and Grisi in the duet 'Tornami a dir' from *Don Pasquale*, and Mario in 'Il mio tesoro' from *Don Giovanni*, as well as Gardoni, Tagliafico and Formes in the Meyerbeer trio 'Pensa e Garda'; non-Italian items were 'In diesen heiligen Hallen' from *Die Zauberflöte* and the madrigal 'Now is the month of Maying' by Morley. For the second series in 1857, there were six female and ten male star singers, again including Grisi, Mario and Formes. The orchestral performance was always noted in the press and, as it grew in reputation, Manns often conducted his own orchestra in place of the Covent Garden orchestra under Costa or his assistant, Sainton.

The attractions of the Palace soon drew fresh performers. In July 1859, after the completion of the Covent Garden series, another series of Grand Opera concerts took place on Wednesdays, with all the leading singers of the Italian Opera under Arditti: that is, the Drury Lane Company. These began on 23 July with leading singers headed by Titiens and Piccolomini in what was reviewed as 'a pleasing selection of operatic music, suited to the tastes of all'.[7] A second concert on 30 July was received similarly. Of all the seasons of Italian opera music in concert, the most widely publicized took place in June 1868, when both companies appeared in what was by then the most highly publicized season: the Drury Lane Company included Titiens, Kellogg and Nilsson, with other singers including Lyall and Santley; two concerts with the Royal Italian Opera featured Patti, Lucca, Mario and Graziani. The advertising still sought a wide audience of former years:

The Directors are confident that these arrangements cannot fail to give the greatest satisfaction to the season ticket holders and to the other Patrons of the Crystal Palace ... These concerts will frequently be aided by the well-trained Crystal Palace choir, and the complete Chorus of Her Majesty's Opera, and by Eminent solo instrumentalists ... The Band of the Company will be considerably increased and the performances will be as before CONDUCTED BY MR MANNS.[8]

There had never been any attempt to build a dramatic programme, or to reflect new developments towards a more unified presentation of opera in a concert setting.[9] By the 1870s, the impact of Manns's orchestral planning had put the loose organization of the Opera Concerts under pressure, and attempts were made to give them more weight:

The Series of concerts which thus terminated was in some respects more attractive than its predecessor, the experiment having been made of giving classical operas as concert music, thus avoiding the usual *potpourri* of isolated tunes. The repertoire should be confined to those works in which dramatic interest is not paramount.[10]

For some time, however, the isolated items had included more than vocal and orchestral music. From 1861 we read of instrumental items by visiting virtuosi being included. Of special interest is the appearance of young aspiring virtuosi, given their chance of a first or early platform at a now prestigious location. Sarasate first appeared at the Palace in 1861 aged seventeen playing a piece by his teacher, Alard (*Fantasia sur les motives de Masniello*) as well as the violin part in Gounod's *Meditation*. The juvenile pianist Marie Krebs appeared:[11]

Childlike in appearance, but with the strength of a woman, she executed with marvellous effect some showy music of the day, and was received with acclamations by the audience. We trust that we may shortly have the opportunity of hearing her in compositions more calculated to test the higher capabilities of an artist

though this had not happened by the time she appeared later in the series:

Marie Krebs has advanced rapidly in public estimation as an intelligent and thoroughly well-trained *pianiste*. We shall be glad, however, to hear her in music of a higher character than she has yet attempted.[12]

For much the same reasons as the operatic potpourris, the popularity of the English ballad also came to be expressed through separate concerts. Ballad Concerts were more generally available because appealing to a broader audience and relating more closely to domestic music making. Unlike the Opera Concerts, they took place in the Concert Room of the Palace. Their popularity seems to have been established in the middle 1860s, a programme of 1868 referring to their success during the last two seasons. The great draw was again the most popular singers; thus of the performers in August 1869 we note Sims Reeves, contributing several of his 'best songs' in his 'best style'.[13] As with the Opera Concerts the programme did not consist exclusively of solos. Thus when in 1870 the concert followed Bruckner's organ recital at 4 p.m., it included solos and ensembles, such as the quartet 'Lo, the early beam of morning' by Balfe, as well as the ballad 'Our bugles sang truce' by Attwood, sung by Cummings. The two other participants were Patey and Edith Wynne.

Ballad concerts were easily adaptable to special days of celebration, such as St David's Day. Thus on 11 March 1878 is advertised a Welsh Ballad and Harp Concert. By the 1880s they were becoming more extensive, with a series of five advertised through May and June. These were priced at a subscription of 12s. 6d. for five concerts, or individual seats at 2s. 6d. and 3s. 6d., unnumbered at 6d. and 1s. Like the Opera Concerts, their elements were easily absorbed into larger concert contexts, and chief of these were the Summer concerts, when the facilities of the Palace were at their most attractive to the fashionable visitor.

THE SUMMER ORCHESTRAL CONCERTS

The transition of the Saturday Opera Concerts and Ballad Concerts into full-scale orchestral concerts is a sign of changing taste. Even if they remained more popular in content than the Saturday concerts, which were now featuring very adventurous programmes, they showed a preference for a wider range of music which would eventually minimize the distinction between the two types of concert. Manns's Saturday concerts officially lasted through two series the autumn and spring series, comprising about twenty-six concerts for most of the forty years. But from quite early on it is clear that additional concerts for the orchestra were arranged in the earlier summer months before the summer break, which seems to have covered the three months July to September. This was an inevitable consequence of the success of the Saturday concerts. Even in much later years, the return of the concerts in the autumn was eagerly awaited by their supporters, so the lack of an official summer series was a gap which was bound to be filled sooner or later. They were already under way in 1856. An advertisement announces a shilling day on Saturday 31 May 'in order to offer an opportunity of visiting the Crystal Palace Sydenham to the numerous Excursionists now in London as well as to Londoners having a holiday on that day'. The concert included seven popular operatic items for orchestra: two marches, an overture, a waltz, a quadrille, a solo and a finale. Later such concerts were extended into longer series, so that from 1869 a series of eight Grand Summer Concerts is advertised, inaugurated by the special Grand May Day opening Festival in honour of Rossini, conducted by Costa, with which it offered combined tickets. On 4 May 1871 the First Grand Summer Concert and Fashionable Promenade advertises eight vocal stars conducted by Manns, inaugurating seven other concerts. Serial stalls were 1 guinea each, individual stalls 2s. 6d. For 1 May 1880, the opening concert is described as a 'Grand Italian, Ballad and Military Concert', with five soloists, the Crystal Palace Orchestra and three bands, conducted by Manns. A special feature was the first display of the Great Fountains of the season; and at dusk a Grand Venetian Fete in the gardens.

In 1874 there is a clear attempt to impose a greater sense of unity with the introduction of thematic planning in a series of nine concerts from 2 May to 25 June. *The Musical Times* responded to the announcement on 1 June 1874 with some interest:

The idea of illustrating the music of England, Germany, France, Russia, Denmark, Norway and Sweden during this series of Summer concerts is an exceedingly happy one and certainly a welcome change from the Italian Opera Concerts which have so long come in with the warm weather at this establishment. Besides these, two Saturdays are to be included in the series ... the second to be devoted to the quaint and humorous in music.[14]

However, by August the critic was not quite as keen:

The illustrations of National Music ... have proved perhaps somewhat too exclusive to achieve unqualified success. This was more especially observable when the programme was limited to the works of Russian and Polish composers and also when the concert was strictly devoted to quaint and humorous works, most of the audience feeling, on the latter occasion, that a few bars of serious music would have been a positive relief. The experiment however has been an extremely interesting one; and although it may not be repeated praise must be given for the originality of the idea. The concerts have been invariably well attended.[15]

The humour was identified through literary rather than intrinsically musical means: as a 'Foreword', Mozart's *A Musical Joke*; The Clown's Music from Mendelssohn's *A Midsummer Night's Dream*; buffo songs; concert pieces from operas; old catches etc. But it was only in the following year, summer 1875, that the character came more closely to that of the official Saturday concerts, and this may be taken as the point at which another stage of the moulding of Crystal Palace taste in music had been achieved: the informal programme had yielded to something more demanding of its audience.

We have often wondered why the classical character of the Winter Concerts ... should be abandoned in the summer and music lovers be compelled to seek for good works at other places, or listen to operatic scraps in an atmosphere where they have been taught to expect only the highest specimens of the art. At last we are able to record that the seasons of the year are no longer to influence the nature of the music. The programme of the first Summer concert (on the 15th) could scarcely perhaps be distinguished from the one of the series just terminated; and when we say that the following Saturday is to include Beethoven's Choral Symphony, it may be concluded that these entertainments can be fairly accepted as models of those which are to follow.[16]

By 1881, the concerts appear completely in line with the official Saturday concerts, with star players, orchestral music and first performances of continental works in England. A series of four concerts on Saturdays from 7 May to 4 June includes the first English performances of three important works by European composers. Rubinstein's Russian Symphony, No. 5, Raff's Symphony No. 2 and Gounod's ballet airs from *La Tribut de Zamora*, as well as Cowen's orchestral suite *The Language of Flowers* for the first time at the Palace and Sullivan's *The Martyr of Antioch*, by request. The Gounod is paired with the Mendelssohn *Scottish* Symphony in the first concert and the Liszt Second Piano Concerto with Sophie Menter making her first Palace appearance 'with the full orchestra of the Winter Saturday Concerts'. Seats were 2s. 6d., 1s. 6d., 1s. A serial subscription was available, with the option to holders of season tickets for the series just ended to retain their seats on advanced application.

EVENING CONCERTS: SATURDAY, SUNDAY, WEEKDAY

The appearance of evening concerts, like that of evening opera, signals the appeal to a wider audience no longer able to attend during the day: for the concerts so far described were for the leisured classes. In advertising its Evening Local Popular Ballad and Instrumental Concert, the Palace made its aims clear: 'In order to meet the wishes of the many residents in the neighbourhood an Evening Concert has been arranged for the Opera Theatre on Monday Dec. 6 at 8.00 p.m.' It featured six soloists and the orchestra. Since the Palace was closed from 6.00 p.m., just three entrances were made available, the main entrance, and the high level and low level railway entrances. The doors of the Theatre opened at 7.30. Tickets were numbered at 2s. 6d., unnumbered at 1s. with admission to the Palace additional at 1s. as usual.

And as well as broadening the time of the event, the character of these evening concerts also changed somewhat. If the earlier years of the summer orchestral concerts represented something of a rapprochement between the traditional Saturday concerts and the traditional operatic concerts, an altogether more popular and public kind of concert appears in the later years. These evening concerts offer a link between the military and marching band tradition of the Palace, still represented in its wind band, and the popular repertory of vocal music. The Saturday and Grand Evening Promenades at 8.00 p.m. are advertised in 1895 for fourteen weeks from October to December. They usually featured a male and female singer or an opera company. The soloists were supported by the organ or an orchestra, the band playing separately. By the turn of the century Sunday evening concerts were regular, and took in the late afternoon as well. A visitor would have had three Sunday concerts available, at 4.00, 7.00 and 9.00 p.m.: at 4.00 two singers, piano and organ accompaniment, with the string band of the Royal Engineers; at 7.00 a vocal and instrumental concert, with two different singers and the same accompaniment; at 9.00, in the north nave, the Military Band of the Royal Engineers. These were all for no extra charge.

SPECIAL CONCERTS

The interest of the special concert at the Crystal Palace lies not so much in the fact of it – concerts additional to the regular patterns were frequent – so much as in the variety of its forms. Since the Palace was more a venue than an institution, no prescribed limits existed on what could be performed, and the performance contexts were wide: concert room, nave, transept, gardens, bandstands, permitting a complete range from solos to vast festivals. The visiting principle early applied to the programmes of the Saturday concerts. But any important group that would attract an audience was invited outside this context, especially vocal groups. For all their prestige, the Handel and other performances of the Sacred Harmonic Society did not represent the highest standards of vocal performance: they could hardly do so with such numbers. London boasted a number of smaller choirs directed by leaders of the choral movements, active in education or connected with other aspects of London's musical life. The great names of the mid-century were Henry Leslie, Julius Benedict, and, a little later, Joseph Barnby. The first native choir to attract great attention was Benedict's Vocal Association, which flourished between 1855 and 1865, and was modelled to some extent on the German Gesangverein, Benedict being a native of Germany. It had been founded in March 1855, having for its directors Benedict and Henry Smart and for its object 'the realization of the beautiful and extraordinary effects derivable from large bodies of voices under a state of discipline'.[17] Five concerts were given during the year 1856 at the Crystal Palace, and the size of the audience grew from 6,000 to three times that number. However *The Musical Times* was unimpressed with the results, suggesting that a German choir would have produced 'far more noise in the world'.[18] It did not last out ten years. But in 1859 it got a good review for a performance of 'great precision' in a programme which included Welsh harp music and piano solos by Arabella Goddard, with 1,000 singers to an audience of 15,000.[19]

The success of Henry Leslie's choir was altogether more impressive, because it was more elite. Leslie, a go-ahead choral conductor of a new breed, developed an ensemble of sixty members which soon established a quite new standard of choral execution, and, in turn, devotion to a new repertory: the English madrigal and part song. He visited the Palace with his choir on 9 July 1859, in a programme including part songs by Hatton, Thomas Morley, Arne, Smart, Pearsall, Weber. But apparently no choirs, native or visiting, could compete with the impression made by the French Orpheonistes in June 1860: they came from a more competitive tradition, closer to that of the British brass bands, and were thus appropriate to some aspects of the Palace ethos. They were far bigger than any choir heard in the Palace apart from the Handel Festival Choir, numbering 3,000 singers drawn from one hundred and seventy distinct choral societies all over France. They gave three programmes at the Palace and one at Exeter Hall. Their *pianissimo* singing seems to have aroused special admiration and the audience at the Palace expressed its enthusiasm 'with waving of hats and every demonstration of good feeling'.[20] But they were only part of a broader picture: musical entertainments for every audience came to the Palace, whether to hear the Distin Family performers in 1857, or the 'unrivalled choir of vocalists and instrumentalists' called the Christy Minstrels in 1871, and again in the following year.[21]

Concerts for special occasion or to honour special individuals pepper the life of the Crystal Palace, especially in the early years. The first decade witnesses several such occasions: the retirement of two great singers – Clara Novello and Giulia Grisi – and the celebrations in honour of the Italian patriot Garibaldi and the Tsar of Russia. Clara Novello's farewell performance of *The Creation* related to the choral world. Giulia Grisi was connected with the Palace through the Italian concerts and, retiring in 1861, gave a benefit concert at the Palace at 3.00 p.m. on 31 July during her final tour. The extensive programme was in two parts involving thirteen other singers of the Royal Italian Opera under Costa. The programme included arias, airs, duos and two Finales to the two parts from Rossini. A much less publicized retirement in the same period was that of the pianist Thalberg, interesting for throwing light on another aspect of performance at the Palace:

the concert [on 11 July, 1863] was given as M. Thalberg's 'Farewell Recital', the great performer having pledged himself never to play in London again. There was an unusually large attendance, but the difficulty of hearing the instrument in the large orchestra was felt by all who had omitted to pay for reserved seats. He played the fantasia on *Mose in Egitto*, 'A te o cara', 'The Last Rose of Summer', 'Home Sweet Home', and an arrangement of Russian airs, in all of which he was rapturously applauded.[22]

Events to recognize visiting dignitaries were on a much larger scale and show how the Palace had begun to assume a status as the venue best suited to project a sense of collective national feeling. It regularly received visiting royalty, and such visits were accompanied by lavish musical performance, as when the Tsar of Russia appeared in 1864. As *The Musical Times* wryly observed, 'Mdlle Titiens, Madame Parepa, Mr Lloyd, Mr Santley were merely there to receive him with musical honours. The orchestral force numbered about 500 performers, consisting of eleven military bands, besides that of the Crystal Palace, and the chorus was composed of the London contingent of the Handel Festival Choir.'[23] *The Musical Times* was more attracted by some other events in 1864, commenting that the Palace 'seems to be fast growing into one of the principal musical establishments in the country. During the past month it has been called upon to represent the feeling of England on two occasions: one in honour of the great hero Garibaldi and one in honour of the great poet Shakespeare.'[24] The Garibaldi concert, which took place after the Garibaldi reception on 16 April 1864, at which he was presented with a sword, was given by the principal artistes of the Italian opera under Luigi Arditi and included an anthem specially written by him. The Palace was full to overflowing. Arditi recalls

How picturesque he looked in the grey capote which he wore over a red shirt, a costume which had grown so familiar to us that it would have seemed strange to everybody had he appeared otherwise attired ... His manner was reserved, almost shy, when he came forward in his box ... to salute the house, a fresh burst of enthusiasm was the result, to which he bowed his head with a mute, yet eloquent mien, betokening his heartfelt appreciation of the honour that was being conferred on him by the British public.[25]

For the Shakespeare concert, a much less reported event, the status of Henry Leslie's choir re-emerges as it hymned the bard with suitable vocal music, including Leslie's own setting 'Soul of the Age, Shakspere [*sic*], rise'.[26]

CHAPTER 10

Solo instrumental music

THE FUNCTION OF INSTRUMENTAL PERFORMANCE

Instrumental music at the Crystal Palace was of two kinds, function related to location. That which took place in the concert room was related to the orchestral activity: that elsewhere was on a larger scale or of a more popular character. Solo instrumental music in the concert context had only a limited role at the Palace. Instrumental solos appeared as items to complement the main concerto or concert piece in the programme: this is where the many performances of solo pieces by Chopin and Liszt found a place, alongside the small vocal items which the soloist often accompanied. Only occasionally are larger works given, as when, in the early 1870s, Beethoven's thirty-two Variations in C minor appear to give evidence of a new impetus in the programming, though it was short-lived. For solo performance the devotee went elsewhere, chiefly to St James's Hall.[1] It was only in the post-Manns years that the Crystal Palace seems to have had a place for the solo or chamber player, either in the Saturday concerts in 1902–4, or in the concerts given in the School of Art. But the Palace did recognize a solo function outside the Saturday concerts in creating the post of 'solo pianist', which was held by the prodigy Oscar Beringer from 1857 for nine years.[2] His duties involved 'giving daily recitals and playing with the orchestra' (that is, the daily orchestra). But as the reception of the Thalberg farewell concert shows, the Centre Transept was entirely unsuitable for any but the most powerful musical effects. Here the presiding instrument was the great Handel Festival Organ. And with the completion of the Concert Room, a smaller organ would be built to enable organ participation in orchestral music, or in a solo role:[3] thus by the late 1860s the Palace had provision for both aspects of organ usage. But before turning to them, the continuing and revitalized role of the

Palace's initial musical representation – the 'Company's [military] Band' – must be recalled. After its transformation into an orchestral band by Manns in the autumn of the first season, 1855–6, the 'Crystal Palace Military Band' must have been to some extent reconstituted,[4] for advertisements for its performances appear by the late 1850s. It seems unlikely that the 'double-handed players' with which Manns created a symphony orchestra could long have coped with his expanding repertory, and his orchestral players were doubtless soon 'picked', to use Walker's term. Many must have returned to the wind band. Its regular daily role was to play wherever needed. Bandstands existed in the building and in the grounds for set performances. Any special occasion involved the band, often several times during the day, and it frequently appeared with other, visiting bands, of which those of the Grenadiers, Royal Engineers and the nearby Royal Artillery at Woolwich were most common.[5]

THE HANDEL FESTIVAL ORGAN

The unique physical character of the Centre Transept determined that any organ installed would have to be of vast power – a major instrument from a major builder in a period of rapidly developing organ technology: perforce a status instrument. The Directors commissioned a company with special interests in continental developments: Gray and Davison. The instrument of the Crystal Palace was one of three of their major concert organs of the immediate period, the others being at Glasgow and Birmingham. Perhaps more than with other instruments, considerations of function and context were especially pressing: the instrument was not installed with the building for a specific function, since no function originally existed in 1854. The instrument came from need, being specifically designed for the trial Handel Festival of 1857 and situated atop the choral auditorium: hence, the 'Handel Organ' on the 'Handel Orchestra'. The consequence is stressed in Macfarren's extensive description in the Festival programme of that year.

It was, of course, no part of the present design to produce a mere musical monster, capable of overwhelming the 200 voices and instruments with which it was associated; such a result, however practical, would have been as absurd as unnecessary. The aim of the builders has been to produce an instrument, the varied qualities of which should combine all desirable musical beauty with force and grandeur of tone sufficient to qualify it for the part it is specially designed to bear in this great commemoration; and should the result be pronounced successful, it is presumed that the very unusual difficulties of locality and employment to which the instrument is subjected will be felt to sufficiently enhance the credit due to its constructors.[6]

But, given the functional considerations, the instrument had to be very large, and the opportunity for symbolic status through rich provision of resources, with an eye on future recital use, could never have escaped consideration by those influential in its installation. Macfarren could certainly not resist pointing out its significance in size and modernity: 'occupying more ground than is allotted to most houses, 1200 feet of standing room ... it has four manuals, 64 registers ...' As a consequence of its exposed position it had no architectural casework. Though this was not uncharacteristic of Gray and Davison's other instruments of the time, it would have been difficult to design anything visually satisfactory, since the whole performing area was so exposed and in need of transformation, which gradually took place. It was left with its major pipes in towers, giving a stark impression.

Gray and Davison's design is seen by Thistlethwaite[7] as representing the apogee of French influence in their building. Such was the speed of events that its pre-eminence as to size was soon undermined by the instruments installed in the Royal Albert Hall, St George's Hall, Liverpool, and the Alexandra Palace, London. But its status remained enormous and it was to be widely used. Two features stand out in the design: the mechanical technology and the character of the stops.

Instead of the traditional composition pedals, the instrument employed combination pedals after the model of Cavaillé Coll. Macfarren claims that they were unique to England at the time.[8] These acted as ventils controlling the wind supply to the two or more soundboards appropriated to each department of the instrument; as Thistlethwaite points out,[9] 'the stops were grouped so that some kind of progression from *piano* to *forte* was possible, and the player set up his registration knowing which stops were winded through the agency of particular pedals; when a pedal was depressed, a pre-set register could thus be brought into play'. The increasing pressure system was adopted, and, in view of the vast power required to support the voices and instruments of the Handel Festival, wind was provided at a pressure considerably higher than that normally employed. The higher pressure gave the opportunity for the introduction of some modern French stops. 'As well as seven harmonic flutes throughout the organ, there was a Flute à Pavillon 8' on the Great and some of the trumpets were harmonic; the 32' was a free reed, the first made in England, an import from France: the trombas in Solo and Swell were horizontally disposed.' French infuence permeated the comprehensive provision, with many mixtures and many reeds. The specification is shown in Table 1.

That the instrument held its own in adding a distinctive resonance to the choral sound emerges from the descriptions of choral performance. Registration would have been influenced by the additions to the score introduced perforce by all conductors of the choral festivals, and its greatest value may have been in diapason tone to avoid clashing with the orchestral brass in giving support to such a large body of singers. Indeed, the only record of its ever being drowned out is by the full range of brass instruments in consort during brass band festivals.[10] But with the few exceptions that emerge, it hardly had a solo role. This came to it through the Saturday concerts. An audience for large recitals was traditionally associated with large municipal buildings and churches; the location of the Crystal Palace hardly fitted this essentially metropolitan role. The rapid development of the orchestral concerts came to create the context, and the recital on the great organ soon took its place in association with the Promenade which followed the concert, when the building was 'brilliantly illuminated': a recital sometimes took place before the concert as well. Thus the recital became a means of articulating the Saturday events: the instrument both welcomed and accompanied the visitors, and, as with a religious service, it could harmonize with the atmosphere – even help to create it through choice from the very wide repertory which was coming to characterize the use of the modern orchestral organ. In this sense it shared much in function with the Palace military band, and also some of its repertory through transcriptions: but it also had its own traditional repertory, distinctive to the instrument. Whenever there was a special occasion, the organ was likely to appear in this public and confirmatory role. Central to its success was the mastery of the acoustic: with the completion of the Concert Room and the Theatre on either side, the Centre Transept had itself become more like a vast concert hall, as noted by the critic of *The Musical World* in 1871.[11]

Table 1. *The Crystal Palace Handel Festival Organ.*
Gray and Davison, 1857

Great Organ (C to a³)

Double Open Diapason, metal	16
Double Dulciana	16
Flute à Pavillon	8
Viol de Gamba	8
Octave	4
Harmonic Flute	8
Clarabel Flute	8
Flute Octaviante	4
Super Octave	2
Flageolet Harmonic	2
Quint	5⅓
Twelfth	2⅔
Mixture	IV
Furniture	III
Cymbal	V
Bombarde	16
Posaune	8
Trumpet	8
Clarion	4
Octave Clarion	2

Choir Organ (C to a³)

Bourdon	16
Gamba	8
Salicional	8
Voix Celeste	8
Clarionet Flute	8
Gemshorn	4
Wald Flute	4
Spitz Flute	2
Piccolo	2
Mixture	II
Cor Anglais and bassoon	8
Trumpet (small scale)	8

Swell Organ (C to a³)

Bourdon	16
Open Diapason	8
Keraulophon	8
Concert Flute	8
Octave	4
Flute	4
Vox Humana	8

Table 1 *continued*

Twelfth	2⅔
Super Octave	2
Piccolo	2
Mixture	IV
Sharf	III
Contra Fagotto	16
Cornopean	8
Oboe	8
Clarion	4
Echo Tromba	8

Solo Organ (C-c⁴)

Harmonic Flute	8
Flute Octaviante	4
Mixture	II
Corno di Bassetto	8
Grand Tromba	8

Pedal Organ (C to f¹)

Contra Bass	32
Open Diapason, wood	16
Violin	16
Open Diapason, metal	16
Octave	8
Twelfth	5⅓
Super Octave	4
Mixture	IV
Contra Bombarde, free reed	32
Bombarde	16
Trumpet	8
Clarion	4

The stops are grouped by soundboards, each subject to the control of a combination pedal, or ventil:

Swell to Great	Choir to Pedals
Swell to Great, Sub Octave	Great to Pedals
Swell to Great, Super Octave	Choir to Great
Swell to Pedals	Sforzando pedal (Great to swell)
Swell to Choir	Tremulant (Swell)
Solo to Great	3 Combination Pedals (ventils) to Great
Solo to Choir	and Pedal
Great Super Octave	2 Combination Pedals (ventils) to Swell
Solo to Pedals	1 Combination Pedal (ventil) to Choir

All couplers excepting those associated with the Solo Organ acted upon by individual pedals.

Although the organ had been ready for the 1857 Festival, it was not at that time entirely complete. Macfarren makes it clear that a few stops of the Choir and Solo organs 'not essential to the present orchestral and solo duties of the instrument, nor forming part of the original design and which time now makes it absolutely imperative to complete are at present omitted and will take their distinctive positions as soon as opportunity permits'.[12] Some of these changes were made in 1871, when the *The Musical World* itemizes the following: to the Choir, 2 harmonic flutes, voix celeste, orchestral oboe, clarinet; to the Great, grand cornet of large scale and trompette harmonique, with strengthening of 16' and 8' fluework, to the Swell, vox humana; to the Solo, flute octaviante, corno di bassetto; to the pedal, 32' contra bombarde on high pressure. Of these additions *The Musical World* comments that 'the organ may now take its place with the largest and best organs, while, from the nature of the building in which it stands, it is not exceeded by any'. But further changes must have taken place, because in autumn 1882 a series of recitals by visiting players is advertised on the 'Grand Organ, reconstructed by Gray and Davison', and including a specification. But, though it includes the 1871 additions, it is not clear in what other respects the instrument was changed.

The final completion of the organ gave the signal for a new emphasis on recitals at the Palace. The traditional responsibility for functional music before and after the Saturday concerts and on other occasions had been in the hands of the resident organist. There were three during the high period of the Palace music. James Coward[13] from the opening till his sudden death in January 1880; Alfred J. Eyre[14] from 1880 to 1894; Walter Hedgcock[15] from 1894 till the early years of the new century. All were organists to the Handel Festival, Coward establishing his connection through the Sacred Harmonic Society, for which he played during the period. The list of organists closely associated with the Palace must also include the name of Alfred Hollins, who played regularly and left a vivid recollection of practising in the auditorium at the only time when the building was free – 6 a.m. – if not entirely quiet.[16] Hollins was the most distinguished of the many blind musicians who attended the Royal Normal College for the Blind situated in Upper Norwood, close to the Palace, where it had been established by its founder, Dr Francis Joseph Campbell,[17] a progressive educationalist, specifically to avail its students of the opportunity of attending the Saturday concerts: free entry was arranged for the students from early on.[18] The fame of the instrument and the building drew players from far and wide, names remembered today, and those forgotten. The first outstanding player was John Stainer. He had close contacts with the Palace through his teaching at the School of Arts, Science and Literature from 1874. The doyen of British organists, W. T. Best of St George's Hall, Liverpool, came in the '70s, and by the 1882 series, the weekly list from 21 October to 16 December comprises the following names: Frederick Bridge (Westminster Abbey), Charles Pearce (Glasgow), W. E. Gladstone (London), W. S. Hoyte (London), W. T. Best (Liverpool), E. H. Turpin (London), Walter Parratt (Windsor), Mullineux (Bolton), C. H. Lloyd (Oxford).

Programme patterns for these Saturday events appear to have been established early on and show consistency: six items which generally include a transcription from an oratorio or opera, and composed organ music and extemporization, the whole patterned to begin and end with a celebratory piece, and to alternate internally larger and more intimate pieces. Although the programme is essentially popular, there is a discernible development over the years reflecting changing taste: towards modern French music on the one hand, and the Baroque, through J. S. Bach, on the other.

The programme from 1865 by Coward is entirely of transcriptions, save for one extempore item: from Schumann's *Paradise and the Peri*, Meyerbeer's *Les Huguenots*, Mozart's *Don Giovanni*, and Beethoven's *Egmont* Overture, with an Arne song. 1868 is similar, with a chorus from *Solomon*, the March from *Le Prophète* as well as the Mozart, a Haydn air and a march from *Egmont*. By 1877, the *Don Giovanni* item is still present, with a selection from Mendelssohn's *Hymn of Praise*; but the rest is more idiomatic, with an Andante for organ by Smart, the Toccata, Adagio and Fugue of J. S. Bach and *Grand Chœur* by Lemmens. The programme with which Eyre reopened the organ in 1882 shows the same repertory remaining for a big occasion, with twelve items, beginning with the *Euryanthe* Overture and ending with the 'Halleluiah Chorus'; the Mendelssohn D minor Sonata is the most modern organ piece. But when Pearce and Lloyd came later in the series, the newer repertory began to establish itself, Pearce including the D major Prelude and Fugue of Bach as well as a rare example of programme notes on the organ pieces; Lloyd includes a sonata by Rheinberger, a composer to become much more prominent in later years.

Despite the strength of the native tradition, the ultimate sign of

From Four till Five o'clock, in Alhambra Court,

THE CRYSTAL PALACE MILITARY BAND.

BANDMASTER—MR. CHARLES GODFREY, JUN.

1. OVERTURE, "The Armourer" ... ... *Lortzing.*
2. GAVOTTE, "The Rajah" ... ... *Rabottini.*
3. INCIDENTAL MUSIC to Henry VIII. ... ... *Sullivan.*
   1. Introduction. 2. King Henry's Song. 3. Graceful Dance.
4. VALSE, "Nid d'Amour" ... ... *Waldteufel.*
5. POLKA, "The Tin Gee-gee" ... ... *Karl Kaps.*

After Concert,

ORGAN RECITAL

BY MR. WALTER W. HEDGCOCK.

OVERTURE in D ... ... *J. Kinross.*
PRÉLUDE DU DÉLUGE... ... ... *St.-Saëns.*
SONATA in D minor, No. 4 ... ... *Guilmant.*
   Allegro assai, Andante, Menuetto, Finale
AIR, "My heart ever faithful" ... ... *Bach.*
MARCHE PONTIFICALE ... ... *De la Tombelle.*

Six o'clock, on Great Stage,

VARIETY SHOW

ATROY, American Juggler and Equilibrist.

THE ELLIOTT FAMILY, Male and Female Acrobats.

KELLY AND ASHBY, Chinese Grotesques.

MDLLE. EMMY, Canine Wonders.

MISS BEATRICE HAROLD, Character Dancer.

THE CRYSTAL PALACE MILITARY BAND.
Bandmaster—MR. CHARLES GODFREY, Jun.

Seats on Great Orchestra, Free.
Chairs in Front of Great Stage, Sixpence.

After Variety Show,

ORGAN RECITAL

BY MR. WALTER W. HEDGCOCK.

FANTASIA in F ... ... *Best.*
BENEDICTUS ... . *Mackenzie.*
SELECTION, "Carmen" ... ... *Bizet.*
   Including : Prelude, Habanera, Seguedille, Entr'acte (to Act II.),
   The Flower Song, Duet, March, and Final Chorus.
IMPERIAL MARCH ... ... *Sullivan.*

16 A typical supporting programme for the afternoon and early evening of a
Saturday in the 1895-6 season.

the status of the institution was the patronage of the foreign player. Guilmant and LeJeune were distinguished French visitors: but an Austrian visitor fared less well. Bruckner played at the Crystal Palace immediately after his Albert Hall performance in August 1871. His visit was under the auspices of a German trade connection which also brought other German players to London. At the Palace his appearance was part of a National German Festival on 21 August: the Festival included a concert of exclusively German music in the Concert Room conducted by Manns. His programme was of five items: Mendelssohn's F minor Sonata, Bach's 'Fugue in E major', and three improvisations, two of his own, and one based on the 'Halleluiah Chorus'. But he got a bad press at the Albert Hall, where he played the same programme as at the Palace, *The Musical World* thinking little of his improvisations.[19]

Over the years, the Handel Organ became 'one of the busiest organs in the country'. And, like the Palace itself, it began to show signs of wear in the early years of the twentieth century. The opportunity for renovation and innovation came with the decision to invest in the refurbishment and modernization of the Palace after the First War. The ambitious plans included a complete rebuild of the organ. The work was undertaken by the firm of Walker and Sons which had absorbed that of Gray and Davison. The change was of tonal design as well as mechanics, in view of the great changes that had come over organ design and performance since the original conception.

The rebuild involved a complete reconstruction and modernization of the instrument, involving new soundboards, new console, tubular-pneumatic action, selective pistons.[20] The existing tracker action was replaced by tubular pneumatic and new soundboards. A modern Discus electrical blower was installed. The instrument remained one of the largest in the country, boasting five miles of lead piping for the pneumatic action and 3,714 pipes. Several new registers were installed to substitute for others discarded. The old stops were thoroughly renovated and overhauled. There were hardly any changes in the overall numbers of stops, save on the Great, which was reduced by four. But some change in the character of the foundation tone emerged. The distinctive reeds were largely retained, complete on the Pedals, and with small changes on the Great and Swell: for example, there was now no echo tromba on the Swell. The diapason section on the Great was rearranged to replace the 16' open diapason with three 8' diapasons; the celeste and furniture stops were discarded. But the most notable feature was the increase in the accessories made possible by the new action, to bring the instrument under much lighter and quicker control for large scale works. It is ironical that after all the expense and time, the instrument should have been completed only when the great festivals and choral activities were rapidly drawing to a close. But the instrument played its final part in the death of the Palace, its bellows reputedly heaving with the draught of air caused by the fire.[21] The new specification is given in Table 2.

Table 2. *The Crystal Palace Handel Festival Organ, entirely rebuilt by J. W. Walker and Sons, 1920*

Great Organ (C-c⁴)	
Double Open Diapason	16
Open Diapason Large	8
Open Diapason Medium	8
Open Diapason Small	8
Harmonic Flute	8
Wald Flute	8
Quint	5⅓
Principal	4
Flute	4
Twelfth	2⅔
Fifteenth	2
Mixture	4 ranks
Double Trumpet	16
Posaune	8
Harmonic Trumpet	8
Clarion	4
Swell Organ (C-c⁴)	
Bourdon	16
Open Diapason	8
Gamba	8
Voix Celeste (tenor C)	8
Concert Flute	8
Octave	4
Flute	4
Twelfth	2⅔
Fifteenth	2
Flageolet Harmonic	2
Mixture	4 ranks
Contra Fagotto	16
Cornopean	8
Oboe	8

Table 2 *continued*

Clarion	4
Vox Humana	8
Tremulant	

Choir Organ (C-c⁴)
Contra Gamba	16
Lieblich Bourdon	16
Gamba	8
Salicional	8
Vox Angelica (tenor C)	8
Clarinet Flute	8
Harmonic Flute	4
Claribel Flute	4
Octave Flute	2
Harmonic Piccolo	2
Clarinet	8
Orchestral Oboe	8
Tremulant	

Solo Organ (CC-c⁴) (separate swell box for nos 2 and 6)
Open Diapason Large	8
Harmonic Flute	8
Harmonic Flute	4
Tromba	8
Clarion	4
Cornetto di Bassetto	8

Pedal Organ (C-f¹)
Double Open Diapason	32
Open Diapason, wood	16
Open Diapason, metal	16
Bourdon	16
Gamba (from Choir)	16
Quint	16⅔
Principal	8
Violoncello	8
Octave	8
Flute	8
Contra Bombarde	32
Trombone, metal	16
Ophicleide, wood	16
Trumpet	8

Couplers
Great to Pedal
Swell to Pedal
Choir to Pedal
Solo to Pedal
Swell to Great

Table 2 *continued*

Swell to Choir
Solo to Great
Swell Octave
Swell Sub Octave
Swell Unison Off
Solo Octave
Solo Sub Octave
Solo Unison Off
Great Pistons to Pedal Combinations

Accessories
Adjustable Combination Pistons to Great
Adjustable Combination Pistons to Swell
Adjustable Combination Pistons to Choir
Adjustable Combination Pistons to Solo
Adjustable Combination Piston, controlling Combinations over whole organ
Adjustable Combination Pedals to Pedal Organ
Combination Pedals to Swell Organ, duplicating Swell Pistons
Double Acting Pedal controlling Great to Pedal Coupler
Double Acting Pedal controlling Swell to Great Coupler
Double Acting Piston controlling Swell Tremulant
Double Acting Piston controlling Choir Tremulant

THE CONCERT ROOM ORGAN

The organ which was installed with the completion of the Concert
Room in 1868 was also built by Walker. Its function was both to
participate in choral music and to play solo or in concertos.
Although the repertory suggests it had no extensive role in either
capacity, it was a substantial instrument which must have been used
for the organ teaching which is advertised for the School of Arts
from the time of its installation. Its specification is reproduced in
Table 3 as it appeared in the programme of the first Saturday
concert for the 1868–9 season:

Table 3. *The Concert Room Organ of the Crystal Palace*
J. W. Walker and Sons [1868]

Great Organ (CC-C in Alto)	
Double Diapason, metal	16
Open Diapason, metal	8
Bell Diapason, metal	8

Table 3 *continued*

Hohl Flute (tenor C, wood, continued by Stop'd Bass)	8
Stop'd Diapason, wood	8
Principal, metal	4
Flute Harmonic (tenor C, metal, wood bass)	4
Flageolet Harmonic, metal	2
Twelfth and Fifteenth Mixture, metal	IV
Double Trumpet, metal and wood	16
Posaune	16
Spare Slide	8

Swell Organ (CC-C in Alto)

Double Diapason, metal and wood	16
Open Diapason, metal	8
Spare Slide for Horn Diapason	8
Stopp'd Diapason, metal and wood	8
Principal, metal	4
Wald Flute, wood	4
Piccolo, metal	2
Twelfth and Fifteenth, metal	2⅔ and 2
Mixture, 5 ranks, metal	
Spare Slide for Contra Fagotto	16
Cornopean, metal	8
Orchestral Oboe, metal	8
Clarion, metal	4

Choir Organ (CC-C in Alto)

Keraulophone, metal	8
Dulciana (Tenor C, metal, continued by Lieblich)	8
Lieblich Gedackt (Tenor C, metal, wood bass)	8
Flute Harmonic, metal	4
Concert Flute, wood	4
Flageolet, wood	2
Bassoon Bass, metal	8
Clarionette, metal	8

Pedal Organ (CCC-F Tenor)

Open Diapason, wood	16
Open Diapason, metal	16
Bourdon, wood	16
Octave, wood	8
Tromba, wood	16
Posaune, metal	8
Spare	
Spare	
Spare	

Couplers
Swell to Great
Swell super to Great

Table 3 *continued*

Swell sub to Great
Great super Octave
Great to Pedal
Swell to Pedal
Choir to Pedal

Accessories
Three Composition Pedals to Great Organ acting also on pedal
Three Composition Pedals to Swell Organ
Tremulant to Swell
Tremulant to Choir

The Pneumatic Lever is applied to Great Organ Manual, and Couplers.

PART 5

The broader educational dimension

CHAPTER II

Exhibitions; the School of Art, Science and Literature; the Theatre

EXHIBITIONS

If the orchestral concerts and great choral festivals of the Crystal Palace claim the first attention of musicians, they were only part of a much broader musical life. The enlightened programming at the Palace did marvels for the musical advancement of the cultivated classes of London – and frequently beyond – but it can have affected the musical awareness of the vast potential working-class audience hardly at all, for obvious reasons of expense and time: Saturday was a working day and travelling was costly.[1] Yet if the broader criterion of the social significance of music-making is placed before the essentially aesthetic, then the educational achievement of the Palace appears in an even stronger perspective: for it was intimately associated with the new massed meetings of the burgeoning movements for educational and social reform, in which the development of musical literacy was a key factor. Such meetings played a role in ordinary lives which was vital, and to which the Palace lent a special character, making it a focus for young and old. But before turning to these mammoth undertakings, the most immediate outgrowth of the Palace's own residential music may first be considered: the opportunities for the class of society who had leisured access to the institution, provided through the School of Arts, Science and Literature, which appeared by 1860, and the Theatre of 1868, which had a significant musical role. A direct link exists to the original role of the 'exhibition' facility, which existed at both buildings not only in the static sense of display, but also in the animated sense, since some of the musical performances were first termed 'exhibitions'.[2]

The exhibition dimension was the one tangible link between the Crystal Palace at Hyde Park and that at Sydenham. But its musical possibilities were determined by the very different purposes of the two buildings: the latter assigned to domestic rather than commercial activity. At its opening, only one permanent musical exhibition existed at Sydenham: that of the Court of Musical Instruments, which included, in addition to its permanent illustrative decoration, busts of composers and some instruments – 'pianos, harps, drums and stringed instruments' – chosen to reflect the educational and historical ethos of the exhibits at the Palace as a whole.[3] No description is given of paintings or engravings, though the display facilities apparently existed for them and they were presumably taken up over the years.

But there was no opportunity for the extensive display of modern musical instruments in use, the feature which had dominated the musical contents of the Great Exhibition at Hyde Park (though a suggestion was made that organs should be exhibited during the first year,[4] and instruments offered as prizes were on exhibit prior to competition finals). The natural focus for any exhibition at Sydenham came rather from the special character of the Palace's developing musical life: from the backgrounds to the works performed and which were already discussed in the printed programmes. Many of the significant orchestral and choral performances were accompanied by exhibitions, to which the audience was directed through the programme. The Nave and Centre Transept offered plenty of space for the location of these, and they appeared from the early years, through the period of Saturday concerts, and intermittently beyond. The very opening of the building prompted Novello to mount a display stand for the opening ceremony. For the Handel Commemoration Festival of 1859 an exhibition of Handelian relics was held in the Court of Musical Instruments throughout, including the autograph scores of the featured works, *Messiah, Israel in Egypt*, the *Dettingen Te Deum* and *Acis and Galatea*. There were also letters, personal ornaments and portraits of the composer, together with a harpsichord whose keys were hollowed through use. In the middle of the Court stood the Roubilac statue of Handel.[5] For the Rossini Festival of 1 May 1868, the programme directed the attention of the audience to the 'bust of Rossini and the photographs of his monument and of the house in which he was born in Pessaro, autographs, portraits and other objects connected with the dead composer placed in the Centre Transept' on that day. Contemporary representations for display have already been mentioned in the performing context (the detailed model of the Handel Festival displayed in the building during the 1862 event[6] and the statue of Mendelssohn erected for the 1860 Mendelssohn Festival).[7] Exhibitions naturally reached their greatest educational focus in relation to the 'novelties' of the Saturday concerts and, occasionally, Handel Festivals. The Schubert discoveries were an obvious attraction. The performance of Barnett's completion of the Symphony in E (No. 7) was the occasion for the display both of the autograph score and the score of the transcription being performed. When the Handel Festival gave the composer's setting of 'Gloria Patri' on Selection Day in 1892, the manuscript from which the parts had been taken was also placed on display.[8]

As the century drew to its close, and a very great sense of its own history descended upon the Palace, the occasion of Queen Victoria's diamond jubilee in 1894 offered the chance to review some significant musical connections in the Imperial Victorian Exhibition reviewed in detail in *The Musical Times*:[9]

Here, under the same glass roof which covered the Great Exhibition of 1851 have been gathered various specimens of the arts and crafts of the world which will be sure to attract many visitors to the Palace during the next few months. The music section is limited in the Egyptian Court, and though somewhat limited in extent has several points of interest. The principal exhibit is the collection of the late Sir Michael Costa, kindly lent by Madame Raphael Costa ... Of interest is the MS of a libretto for a cantata on the subject of Prometheus and Pandora written by the great Duke of Wellington (and) probably dating from the Iron Duke's College Days ... From Costa to Manns is a natural step and in a large case the visitor will find a large collection of testimonials presented to the veteran conductor who has held sway over the music of the Palace for nearly the whole of its history. Sir George Grove is very naturally an exhibitor. He has works by S. Wesley, Beethoven and Mendelssohn, the autograph of the full score of Sir Alexander MacKenzie's breezy overture Rule Britannia rightly being prominent. By permission of the Queen, Messrs John Broadwood exhibit the grand pianoforte from the Red Drawing Room of Windsor Castle. This instrument is in a splendid state of preservation, although it has been much played since the Great Exhibition of 1851 and was then made by the Prince Consort for Her Majesty's use.

But these associations only hinted at the musical connections of the Palace which are manifest in the materials loaned for the International Music Exhibition, held there in July–November 1900: a 'Loan Collection of Musical Instruments of all countries illustrating the progress and advance of musical art ... not only during the past one hundred years, but from the earliest times and in different parts of the world, in order that, by comparison, an idea might be readily gathered of the musical standpoint of today'. The introduction to the extensive and detailed catalogue[10] points out not only how unique the exhibition is in England, but how it transcends those 'Great Musical Exhibitions that have taken place during the last thirty years' on the Continent, especially in adopting the classification which is borrowed from that used by the curator of the Brussels Conservatoire. In hosting the exhibition, the Crystal Palace placed itself symbolically at the head of musical concerns for the country. Its 'Honorary Committee of Advice' lists around one hundred of the most prominent musical names in England, composers, performers and scholars, most with special Palace associations, not least Arthur Sullivan as Chairman: but also including names not formerly especially associated with the Palace, such as Otto Goldschmidt, founder and conductor of the Bach Choir, and Arthur Chappell, founder of the Monday Popular Concerts at St James's Hall. Younger names show the continuing relevance of the Palace in 1900: W. W. Cobbett, A. J. Fuller Maitland and, most important of all, Francis W. Galpin, obviously the leading spirit, who wrote the foreword, and whose loaned items constitute the largest proportion of the whole by far.

Though the Palace's musical status was without par, one notes in the publicity quoted from *The Standard* in the exhibition catalogue – as from comments contained in it – how late was the appearance of exhibitions of musical items reflecting an interest in musical scholarship, relative to those for the other arts. For the contents of this exhibition were no more than had been provided in the various Courts of Fine Arts at the Palace from the very beginning, when music was represented with seemingly few instruments (though many busts and some portraits of composers).The catalogue reads:

even to those who possess little or no knowledge of the history of music, the collection can hardly fail to prove interesting, if only from its comprehensiveness and the many curious instruments that are shown. No more agreeable or efficient way of acquiring knowledge exists than by object lessons, and in these the Exhibition is remarkably rich.

In fact, visitors were offered more than the objects themselves. Three lectures are advertised in connection with the exhibition, two speakers having close Palace associations: Edgar Jacques on keyboard instruments 'with illustrations on Harpsichord, Pianoforte and Organ by Herr J. H. Bonawitz', recalls Bonawitz's historical recitals, given likewise in the lecture room of the School of Arts, south wing; while W. H. Cumming's interest in the choral repertory, already manifest in his contributions to the repertory of Selection Day at the Handel Festivals, is reflected in his title 'Historical Songs, Glees and Part Songs'. But Francis Galpin's contribution sounds a new note, in having no obvious connection with the musical provision of the School of Art: 'Some Notes on the gentle art of horn blowing'. Indeed, this exhibition shows the Palace's musical provision intersecting with the newly developing study of musical instruments, in which Galpin would be such a conspicuous name, and his text is markedly more technical than the others.

For of the 8 sections A–H, fully six were devoted to musical instruments. But the emphasis was still European, only one of these (G) being given to popular Instruments of other countries. The first five European sections were of 'sonorous substances', 'vibrating membranes', 'wind instruments', 'stringed instruments', 'automatic instruments'. Only in the sixth category, 'popular instruments of other countries' do items loaned by the Crystal Palace Company itself come into play: presumably, some of them from the original Court of Musical Instruments, since they seem to relate to the general description first given of its contents: from China, urheen, yankin (dulcimer), chapan, pepa, kin; from Burma, plan (or shan); from Africa, three sizes of kaffir drum. But within the fourth section, 'stringed instruments', pianos and violins offer some remarkable items. Of the seventeen keyboard instruments, from a sixteenth-century clavichord up to a modern cottage piano, three had special association with the repertory of the Palace: an Erard grand piano selected by Liszt in 1840, a Broadwood played by Chopin in his 1848 London tour and an Erard used by Rubinstein at his first Philharmonic appearance in 1857. The violins include the 'Hellier Stradivarius' of 1679.[11] Direct Crystal Palace connections become closer in the final two classes. Class G, 'musical accessories', includes items of interest about performers, whether bringing vivid dramatic associations to mind – the dagger used by Patti in *Ernani*, the pistol used by Tietjens in *Fidelio* – or special events – the baton used by Spohr at the first performance of *The Fall of Babylon*, or a more intimate object of musical activity – Meyerbeer's inkstand.

But it is with the final class H, 'musical literature and portraits', that the Palace's many musical associations become clearest – both in the items it owned itself and presumably kept, at some stage at least, on display, and those relating to its musical life – the music and the individuals associated with it. Most of the twenty busts listed are of performers or composers in its own period (which also enables the likely identity of the original displays to be deduced). The twenty-three portraits and engravings include several of Beethoven, one of Brahms, of the Schubert circle, and of Liszt (the last photograph before his death) as well as of English figures – Macfarren, Curwen and Thomas Wingham (notable because of his early death). Although there is a portrait of Grove, the exhibition is conspicuous in making no reference to, loan from, or exhibit of materials associated with, August Manns himself. The most intimate Palace connections are through the autograph manuscript (and printed) material: ninety items. Of musical scores, all are restricted to composers who had performances through the Palace: notably of Sullivan, who loaned ten items, including the full scores of *The Mikado*, *The Golden Legend*, *Cox and Box*; and of Barnett, who lent the score of *The Ancient Mariner*. More significant are the autograph letters. Grove loans two letters of Beethoven, Jacobi one of Berlioz: others are of Spohr, Mendelssohn, Verdi, Tchaikovsky. Of composers who had visited, Saint-Saëns, Gounod; and of performers, Costa, Mario, Jenny Lind, Clara Schumann and others.

THE SCHOOL OF ART, SCIENCE AND LITERATURE: THE ROLE OF MUSIC

Generous provision for the needs of the enquiring patrons of the Crystal Palace had been part of its original complement of facilities. There was a fine library on the first floor and a reading room near the Byzantine Court which kept the daily papers and boasted its own headed notepaper with last posting and arrival times for London to keep writers in closest touch with correspondents, and enhance its sense of leisurely permanence for the visitor (who was most likely the leisured local resident). Although much was destroyed in the fire of 1866, the facilities were replaced. It was inevitable that the wealth of developing cultural provision would soon demand some more formal and social expression. The School of Art, Science and Literature was instituted in the 1859–60 season and quickly grew to establish an extensive provision by the end of the first decade. Though it is difficult to chart its progress after the discontinuation of the regular Saturday concerts by 1904, it was flourishing as never before by early years of the new century, when new facilities were opened in the south wing. Though the original facilities were within the main building, the first advertisements make it clear that they were 'strictly private'. Although the precise location of the School is not clear, members of one class were instructed in 1861 that entrance was from the railway or by the Queen's Apartments, Rockhills entrance.[12] Information was available (from the literary department near the reading room and the Byzantine Court, where 'names can be received and prospectus with every information obtained from the Literary Department'. Much is made in advertisements of 1900 of the new facilities in the south wing, with a suite of rooms and a lecture room, partly intended to give relief from noise, though, as will emerge, the music section soon came to share these facilities.

Typical of the time, the School was structured in two divisions: ladies' and gentlemen's; but the overwhelming majority of advertisements are for the classes for ladies. Classes for gentlemen were limited mostly to the School of Engineering, and this school was housed in a separate building on the perimeter of the site on Anerley Hill.[13] By the beginning of the second full decade, in the 1871–2 season, the ladies were offered a wide variety of subjects, of which music, by then the biggest area, constituted about a third; the other subjects included art (listed as water colours and sketching, figure drawing and modelling, painting in oils); English language and literature; the literature of other nations, especially French, German and Italian; history (English, European and Biblical); Sciences (zoology, botany, chemistry, physical geography, maths and arithmetic); and finally wood carving and dressmaking. Subsequently, classes in cookery were held. Classes were described from the first as 'of the highest class and at moderate terms'. Evidence of the seriousness of the activity is provided by the examination provision. The Crystal Palace School was a centre for the examinations of the Oxford and Cambridge Syndicate. Although professional training is advertised for the women, the School of Engineering advertises that it 'Offers a full professional training'. But there must have been some greater liaison, since the 1900 advertisements describe the school as of art, science, music and literature.

The first mention of music in the advertisements for the School appear in the Saturday programmes for the 1860–1 season. They are

CRYSTAL PALACE SCHOOL OF ART, SCIENCE, AND LITERATURE.—LADIES' DIVISION.

SIXTEENTH SESSION, 1875–6.

Course of Instruction in Music.

Teachers :

SIR JULIUS BENEDICT,   HERR ERNST PAUER,
MR. E. PROUT, B.A.,   DR. JOHN STAINER, M.A.,
SIGNOR RIZZELLI,   MDME. ST. GERMAINE.

THE Course consists of at least one year's regular instruction, that is, during one whole Session of the School, extending through thirty-six weeks of work, and comprises the following

SUBJECTS :—

*1. PIANOFORTE PLAYING.—Private Lessons.
2. EXPLANATORY DEMONSTRATIONS OF MUSIC.
3. HARMONY AND COMPOSITION.
*4. SINGING.—Private Lessons.
5. SINGING. CLASS TEACHING. READING AT SIGHT.

A Student can select either 1 or 4 as the initial object of her studies to be taken with Nos. 2, 3, and 5 at the following fee :—

Course, allowing choice of either of the Teachers for
the Pianoforte or for Singing £35
Course, without right of choice as to Teachers . . £28

If the Student elect to take both 1 and 4, a proportionate addition to the above fee will be made.

Once a month such Students as may be recommended for proficiency by the Teacher may take their Lessons as part of a performance with Strings (Duets, Trios, Quartets). In such case an extra fee of £3 3s. per Course must be paid, or *pro rata* for the number of performances.

Students to have privilege of admission, for purposes of study, to the private rehearsals of Classical Music by the Crystal Palace Orchestra.

Students who have regularly attended at least one Course may be recommended by the Teacher for examination, with the view of winning a Certificate ; such Certificate to be endorsed as of first, second, or third grade by each Teacher under whom the Pupil has studied for each subject respectively.

Students can inscribe their names only in the Office of the Crystal Palace Company's School of Art, Science, and Literature, next the Reading Room, North End.

By order of the Committee,
F. K. J. SHENTON,
Superintendent Literary Department.

17 An advertisement in a Saturday Concert programme for the classes in music held in the School of Arts, Science and Literature during the 1875–6 season.

for choral classes (a ladies' singing class and an evening choir, presumably mixed), for individual piano instruction with two teachers listed, and in dancing. By 1863 a ballad singing class is added. By 1871, no less than fourteen classes are advertised: now with several classes in singing, which include part-singing and choir practice. In addition to the piano classes, which now have five teachers, and the dancing class, harp tuition is now offered. But most notable is the introduction of theory tuition, in the form of classes in harmony and transposition. The advertisements were also used to show vacancies available with individual teachers. With the exception of the evening choir on Tuesdays, lessons were during the day, not as yet including Saturdays. With the programmes for the season 1875–6, music is given its own advertisement, headed 'Course of Instruction in Music'. This clarifies both the types of courses available and the teaching staff, which continue in the pattern already described. One point of special interest is a new kind of class that goes beyond the provisions of normal individual tuition: 'Explanatory Demonstrations of Music' are advertised, that is, offering instruction in analysis as well as performing technique, though this seems to have been through duet playing of transcriptions. 'Historical Demonstrations', showing the growth of repertory, are first given in 1875 by Ernst Pauer,[14] a leading authority on the subject at the time, who gave a series of six lectures, three on technique and three on composers. These were followed by H. G. Ernst's 'Demonstration in the Higher Art of Playing'. But the fullest description is of a class given in 1879 by Julius Benedict. Already in 1874 he had given a lecture on 'the characteristics of national melodies and their influence on the development of music'. But in 1879 he gave a series which throws much clearer light on the detail of the activity as well as stressing the vital background connection with the Saturday concerts, the essential adjunct to the music in the School.

Described as a 'Class for the Cultivation of Pianoforte Performance and particularly the practice and study of the classical music selected for performance at the ensuing Saturday Concerts of the Crystal Palace', it met for twelve Thursdays at a total fee of £2. 2s. The meeting was at 11 a.m., though the advertisement shows a second identical class being recruited for 1.00 p.m. Students could, if they wished, present themselves for examination at the end of the series, conducted 'in private by examiners of eminence, who may award a certificate for knowledge of the works studied, and for proficiency in performance'. Performance was the basis of the class, 'pursued with or under the immediate tuition of the master'. Since all the listed works were orchestral, these performances would, again, have been of transcriptions. The first meeting of each month was devoted entirely to such performances, when students could bring friends (ladies only) through their own purchase of a ticket at 1s. Students were admitted to the gallery (of the concert room) for the private concert rehearsals 'during the pleasure of the Directors'. The works listed for 'analysis, practice and performance' represented a remarkably advanced repertory: as well as four by Beethoven, symphonies by Mozart, Haydn, Schubert, Schumann, Berlioz, Raff; and the 'Ländliche Hochzeit' Symphony of Goldmark and First Symphony of Brahms were very new; the latter first performed in England and published only months before.

The institution of a School of Music as such within the larger School of Arts, Science and Literature was to be anticipated, and first mention is made of it in the advertisements for 1880–1, though no formal opening is described nor separate accommodation indicated. Despite the intention of the School of Art to have independent facilities in the south wing, music is soon associated with it. By 1901, music students appear to be under the aegis of the Registrar of the School of Art, south wing, suggesting that art and music are now grouped together locationally and in organization. It must have been a wonderful ambience for a school, and certainly stuck in the memory of Samuel Coleridge-Taylor when he taught there in the early years of the century. 'The view from the Crystal Palace Towers is famous, but one does not realize that the classrooms of the School of Art and Music, perched as they are in the loftiest building on the loftiest hill in the south of London, command a range of country unsurpassed in England.'[15]

With the formation of the School of Music as such, a more competitive environment may have ensued. Examinations had already been available though the Joint Syndicate of Oxford and Cambridge Universities. The award of a scholarship in music gained press attention in 1884, though with the suggestion that this was not the first, and also indicating the social status of the pupils, since the winner's address – Lawrie Park, Sydenham (Miss Florence E. Brooker) – was in a fashionable part of the nearby locality, adjacent to the grounds.[16] The examiners were Arthur O'Leary, E. J. Hopkins, George Grove and August Manns.

By 1900 the music operation had significantly expanded. In addition to the existing instrumental classes, there were now classes in violin, cello and ensemble; on the 'theoretical side', in composition and orchestration. And reflective of this growing interest in ensemble and composition, the lecture room of the school was now host to its own concerts. In January–March 1901 a series of chamber music concerts is given by artists of the calibre of Fanny Davies, Gabriele Wietrowetz, Krause, William Hurlstone and the Wietrowetz Quartet; tickets were 4s., including admission to the Palace after 8.00 p.m., since the concerts began at 8.30. Moreover there were now end-of-term students' concerts, as on 19 December 1900, at 3.30, to which 'past and present students and their friends are invited', tickets admitting to the Palace and the concert by application to the Registrar. Student works were included. The now well established tradition of the historical recital also reflected a developing musical culture. Pauer's historical keyboard recitals from 1875 had been for piano, including 'specimens of Bach, Haydn, Mozart, Beethoven, Schubert, Weber, Mendelssohn, Schumann'. But from 29 January 1901, Bonawitz gave a series of historical recitals on organ and piano, with repertory stretching from Paumann, Schlick, Cabezon and Palestrina (on the organ), through Bull, Froberger, Scarlatti and Handel (specified as harpsichord music, though apparently played on the piano), to piano music from Haydn to Liszt. Tickets were 1s. 6d. (music students half price). From the early years of the new century, advertisements for the School suggest that it was flourishing as never before.

As with the public performance of music at the Palace, so the aim of the management was clearly to provide the best in instruction at the School: this came naturally through individuals already associated with the concerts, but quickly involved other distinguished musicians as well as newly emerging talent. Grove clearly had a strong hand in the appointments, though doubtless many opinions were available and he would have sought them, not least those of Manns. There was a steady expansion through the first decade. In the first year of the School, the choral tuition, both in the day and on Wednesday evenings, was in the hands of Henry Leslie. Manuel Garcia took the solo singing class, and the two piano teachers were Julius Benedict and Lindsay Sloper. The dancing class, which appeared in 1861, was taken by Mr L. d'Eqville, and the ballad singing class of 1863 by Arthur Sullivan. With the opening of the concert room organ in 1867, the first organ teacher was John Stainer. By 1869–70 James Coward, the Palace organist, was responsible for the part-singing class, while Ebenezer Prout has joined the piano staff. These names continue largely unchanged through the 1870s. A significant addition is J. F. Bridge, who came in 1876 on the recommendation of Stainer to teach organ and theory.[17] In the same period Sullivan was also still connected with the School, not only as a piano teacher but as Professor of Theory, Harmony and Transposition.

By 1880, there are new names with Palace connections as well as the old guard: Prout, Benedict, Stainer, Bridge as theorists and writers; Pauer, Rizelli, Sloper, Garcia, St Germaine as performers; Frederick Cliffe, Gustav Ernst, Henry Blower as composers and singers. But by 1900, the complement had significantly changed with a new generation, though it still reflected connections with Palace music: singers were Blower, Lloyd, Marriott, Musson; pianists, L. Bonwitz, Cooke, Webbe, George, Douglas, Davies, Eyre; organist, Eyre; violinist, Aves; cellist, Renard. And just as Sullivan had had a role in theory teaching in his early life, so another aspiring composer, Samuel Coleridge Taylor, took a leading role, likewise relying on it for income. He taught from about 1898 till his death in 1912 as Professor of Theory, Harmony and Orchestration.

THE ROYAL COLLEGE OF MUSIC CONNECTION

Some of these teachers also taught at the Royal College of Music, where, for one, Coleridge Taylor had been a student (of Stanford). Surveying the early beginnings of the College, its strong links to the Crystal Palace become clear. If the Royal Academy of Music, founded in 1834, had provided some of the most prominent players during the early years of the Palace's concert life, the Palace now in its turn provided the new institution in South Kensington with some of its senior figures, reconnecting the Palace with the neighbourhood of its origins in Hyde Park. For the National Training School, founded in 1873, and the Royal College which succeeded it in 1882, were established in the new museum quarter of London, which was founded on the exhibits of the Great Exhibition. Indeed, the very first plans by Prince Albert for a National Training School went back to the year of the Palace's opening, 1854. Grove, as senior figure of the Crystal Palace, was to be the first Director of the College. Sullivan, as its brightest young star, was the first Director of the National Training School. And other staff were in common. Of the ten first professors at the College, Ernst Pauer and J. F. Bridge taught at the Palace and most had connections with it: Stanford, Parry, Holmes, Taylor, Visetti, Goldschmidt. Grove continued to take his RCM pupils to the concerts, which remained the outstanding venue for regular orchestral music till the nineties, and his pleasure in it is vividly recalled by Bennett.[18]

THE THEATRE

The creation of the Theatre represented the third of the major adaptations of the Palace facilities for performance purposes. It complemented the concert hall in finding its location on the facing, north side of the centre transept to the garden front. Though to a lesser extent than that of the concert room, its construction was in response to an emerging need: the final completion of the concert room stage in 1868 had quickly made it the focus for dramatic musical performances. These must be dated from the spring of 1869, from press notification of the 'great and novel attraction' of 'operas to be performed on the complete and most commodious stage which was last year erected in the Concert Hall ... the series commencing at the termination of the Whitsuntide Amusements'.[19] The works presented were Wallace's *Lurline* and *Maritana*, given by a company apparently created at the Palace, since it bears no name, and its director, George Perren, is unrecorded on the London stage. The success of these[20] showed that, as in other musical activities, the Palace acted as a training ground for aspiring performers, some of whom would play a part in the later activities of the Theatre.

The Operas in English have taken so firm a hold on the public as to enable many of our established vocalists to present themselves, in turn, as the heroines of some of the most popular lyrical works. Miss Blanche Cole has made so excellent an impression as to cause Mr Vining to secure her for the Galatea at the Princess's Theatre. Miss Hersee gave six performances before her departure for America and Miss Arabella Smythe has also been cordially welcomed. Of the future of Miss. Edith Wynne, who made her first appearance in Wallace's opera *Maritana* we can entertain no doubt: she is a thoroughly trained vocalist and possesses a very good knowledge of stage effect.[21]

The marked success was an obvious spur to the creation of proper facilities for musical drama, and the Theatre was first termed the Opera Theatre. A Saturday concert programme for summer 1869 notes that 'the great success of the afternoon operas will be resumed on the north side of the Centre Transept as soon as the new stage and appointments can be got ready'. This had happened by the autumn when the first season began, visitors to the orchestral concerts being eagerly encouraged in the programme to come and view. A later description shows it as 'enclosed from the main building (with) eight entrances or exits ... galleries at the sides and rear, and ... accommodation for some 1950 spectators ... the stage 59 feet by 28 feet.[22] It thus complemented the Concert Room in every sense, the galleries being those of the main building, likewise screened off, with a staging of roughly the same area, leaving audience accommodation of slightly less. In the course of its life, it would be used for many purposes: for drama – which came to take a larger role than any musical performances there – for lectures of many kinds, dramatic readings, as well as numerous entertainments of a more limited scope than those that took place in the Centre Transept, and it was variously named accordingly: Lecture Theatre, Opera Theatre, even Opera House. By 1911 it was the Variety Theatre, probably having assumed this name in the 1890s, when operatic performances declined in favour of lighter entertainments.

Despite the ample facilities for large-scale production, the Crystal Palace was never a promising location for an opera house, since it lacked the metropolitan status which was essential for the audiences of the various opera companies, and it never seems to have been part of any of the recurrent plans to create a national opera. It served a different purpose, drawing on its natural catchment of a suburban matinee audience. The first decade or so shows the genuine attempt to create regular audiences for varied operatic and operetta forms. Though it did not maintain this momentum, it still provided a useful venue for occasional works on tour or in second performances. Visiting companies were the key, despite the attempt to establish a Palace-based company in the early years. The two strongest draws for its audience were the provision of operas in English, both native and in translation, and the appearance of London Italian opera performers on stage (rather than in concert, as for the opera concerts, which had by now reached their greatest popularity). 'Opera in English' encompassed a wide range, from traditional smaller-scale ballad works of the English mid-century, through standard European operas in translation to opera and operetta in English in the stricter sense. The dominance of this title in the advertising shows its initial attraction to patrons. Not until 1879 is there opera in Italian, and it seems that German and French opera was never given in the native tongue. As well as varieties of dramatic music, the role of music can also be traced in incidental music to spoken stage drama, and also a wide variety of entertainments in which it had a part, some of which spilled into the Centre Transept as a more appropriate location.

'Opera in English'

Whether the works performed were of the native tradition or in translation, they were clearly intended for a popular audience; indeed at the end of the second season, the advertisement is of 'Crystal Palace Shilling Operas'. Like the two works with which the operatic performances had earlier begun, 'Opera in English' opened the New Stage (or Theatre) on Monday, 25 October 1869, with an English work, Balfe's *The Rose of Castile*, to extensive advance publicity in the concert programme. The Company was under the same direction, that of George Perren, with the full orchestra conducted by Manns, though none of the names previously noted reappear: the advertised names are now Connell, Cottee, Corri, Richard Temple, Ainsley Cooke, Annie Goodall and F. Lancia.

Reviews from the *Morning Post* quoted for advertisement in the Saturday programmes of October show the theatre not only encouraging but demarcating an audience, one of some musical discernment but not as elevated as that of the now 'world famous' Saturday orchestral concerts: 'If anyone doubts the effect of pure melody – united with subtle yet sensible words – upon an audience now accustomed somewhat to classical music of high degree ... let that person go to hear soloists at the Crystal Palace.' The two existing repertory works, *Lurline* and *Maritana*, remained, returning in later November. On 8 November came Dibden's double bill, *The Quaker* and *The Waterman*. And now the advertising can be seen to set about creating a tradition: thus, for the next performance, *The Rose of Castile* is described as a 'favourite opera', and likewise for the repeat of the Dibden works. They ran till December and were to recur regularly over the next ten years, *The Rose of Castile* till 1875. Other works were soon added to alternate with them. The second season introduced *The Bohemian Girl* and Benedict's *Lily of Killarney*, both recurring regularly over the next decade. The season 1872–3 introduced Macfarren's *Robin Hood*, and Charles Defell's *The Corsair*.

Until the middle 1870s there are therefore seven works of the English ballad tradition in repertory, all very well known from previous productions elsewhere. But despite their initial popularity, few held the Crystal Palace stage thereafter,[23] and their place is taken by, on the one hand, Italian opera (whether in the original or translation), and on the other, by a variety of light operas given in English. But the venue remained open with potential for English opera and in later years occasional new works would find a staging there. Benedict's *Grazielle*, an oratorio, was staged as an opera in 1888; in 1892, Granville Bantock's *Cadmon*, premiered earlier in that year, received a second performance; and as late as 1931, Martin Shaw's *The Thorn of Avalon* appeared on this stage.[24]

Although the theatre opened with an English opera, at least some of the potential Crystal Palace audience would have been more familiar with Italian opera, albeit most likely in single numbers, through the long-established Italian opera concerts. From the start 'Opera in English' had offered Italian opera in translation. During the first season, Perren's company gave two Italian operas: Verdi's *Il Trovatore* (translated as *The Gipsy's Vengeance*) and Bellini's *La Sonnambula*. They would remain until the 1873–4 season. The repertory broadens quickly in the second season, adding Donizetti's *Lucia di Lammermoor*, Auber's *Fra Diavolo* and Flotow's *Martha*, as well as two German operas, Beethoven's *Fidelio* and Weber's *Der Freischütz* 1872–3 offers Auber's *Crown Diamonds* and Mozart's *Don Giovanni*, and between 1873 and 1876 appear Donizetti's *The Daughter of the Regiment*, as well as *Der Freischütz* and *Il Trovatore*; *Le Domino Noir*, *Un Ballo in Maschera*, *Fra Diavolo*, *Don Giovanni*, and *The Barber of Seville*.

The seasons never covered the same extensive period as the Saturday concerts; but they gradually take up more of the year towards 1875, when the seeming disappearance of the regular company curtails the productions; the visiting companies which now appear give only one or two performances of a work on tour. When the theatre began, in 1869, the first season was of several performances per week through October and November; for the following year of twenty performances on alternate Tuesdays and Thursdays. By 1872–3, there are two series, November–December and March–June, with twelve performances from 1 May on alternate Tuesdays and Thursdays until June (with Whitsun intervals).

From 1876, personnel becomes more fluid, and repertory likewise. Perren's principal, Richard Temple, now appears as producer, and Perren's name disappears, while that of Rose Hersee appears in the production of Cimarosa's *Il matrimonio segreto*. The orchestra is still conducted by Manns, though in the following year Alfred Cellier is advertised. 1878 witnessed the first appearance of Carl Rosa[25] as an opera director at the Palace; his performances included Nicolai's *The Merry Wives of Windsor* and Wagner's *The Flying Dutchman*. In 1883 he produced *The Bohemian Girl* as well as Thomas's *Mignon*. Significantly higher seat prices indicate the appeal of these later productions to a different audience from that of Perren's Shilling Operas, with numbered stalls at 5s. and 2s. 6d. and only unnumbered at 1s. Although regular performances of standard operas decline, there remain occasional works of interest in this category. Outstanding is a performance in 1897 of Humperdinck's new opera *Königskinder*, given in English as *The Children of the King*. A whole page is devoted to advertising the work's West End reception at the Royal Court Theatre, which suggests the difficulty of gaining an audience for such a novelty by this time. An aspect of opera presentation that relates to other musical developments at the Palace is the advertisement of Evening Operas in May 1882, with the *Lily of Killarney* produced by Blanche Cole, with Manns directing: tickets were here not at as high a level as for the Rosa productions: 3s. 6d. and 2s. 6d.

Italian opera

By the end of the decade, the Crystal Palace audience was obviously thought ready for the best quality Italian opera, direct from the Royal Italian Opera, Covent Garden, and the respective managements were confident of filling the seats. In 1879 is advertised the 'first Series of Italian Operas that has ever taken place at the Crystal Palace': a list of nine operas from which six 'will be selected' for performance on Wednesday afternoons – likewise 'selected artists' from the listed troupe of thirty-eight singers, conducted by Visceni. The season was to run through May and June. In fact, only three appear to have been given, from the final advertisements: *Don Giovanni*, *Fra Diavolo* and *Martha*. Italian opera was to remain a rare occurrence, though of comparable quality when it came. The Royal Italian Opera is again advertised in 1890–1, though now for a single performance on Tuesday 25 November at 3.00 p.m. This had particularly powerful advertising, commending the production from Covent Garden featuring Giulia and Sofia Ravogli. Not only star singers but acclaimed new works made an appearance at the Crystal Palace. In the following season, 1891–2, Lago's Royal Italian Opera Company from the Shaftesbury Theatre appeared in Mascagni's *Cavaliera Rusticana* which 'has been playing to crowded houses in the West End'. And in 1894, another Covent Garden conductor, Augustus Harris, now with another company, the Drury Lane Italian Opera Company, gave *Cavaliera Rusticana* and *Pagliacci*.

Operetta; comic opera, vaudeville etc.

In addition to the many varieties of opera, vaudeville and even burlesque coexisted with it in the theatre almost from the first. The second season of Perren's 'Operas in English', 1870–1, with the Crystal Palace orchestra under Manns, gave Offenbach's *The Rose of Auvergne* and *The Forester's Daughter*. 1873–4 saw Tamplin's *Fleurette* and Suppe's *Galatea* by the John Hollingshead Company for one performance. In 1876–7 appeared Alfred Cellier's *The Spectre Knight*. From 1880, successive touring companies appear, usually in one or two performances only, of a new entertainment going quickly on tour. In October 1880, for example, Alice Barth's Comic Opera Company gave *Les Noces de Jeunette*, with English words (*The Runaway Match*) by William Grist and music by Victor Masse (followed by the Garden Scene from Gounod's *Faust*); in 1882, Planché's vaudeville *The Loan of a Lover* was given with Frederick Corder's *A Storm in a Teacup* by Alice Barth's Ballad Operatic Company: works of this kind continued regularly through the 1880s, with occasional repetitions of the more effective ones; prices ranged between 2s. 6d. and 1s.

The association of the Palace with the great popularity of Gilbert and Sullivan is not as immediate as might be anticipated. The Savoy Theatre productions come in regular sequence from the early 1890s with *The Mikado* and *Iolanthe* by the d'Oyly Carte Company under Manns in 1891–2, *The Mikado*, with the Savoy Company under Manns in 1895–6, and *The Pirates of Penzance* and *Trial by Jury* by the d'Oyly Carte Repertory Opera Company in 1899–1900. The wide spread of advertised prices, greater than previously, indicates the broad appeal of the works, from 5s. reserved stalls, to 1s. un-numbered and unreserved.

REHEARSING FOR THE PANTOMIME AT THE CRYSTAL PALACE.—SEE PAGE 622.

18 A rehearsal for the Christmas pantomime of 1868, 'Harlequin Little Boy Blue ...'.

Music for plays and other entertainments

As with the variety of its musical drama, the Crystal Palace theatre found a place for music in entertainments of all kinds, from the classic stage repertory to the most popular burlesque. At least two Shakespearean performances included incidental music. In the 1873–4 season, a production of *Macbeth* was given with the music of Matthew Locke, and in the 1876–7 season a production of *The Merry Wives of Windsor* featured Sullivan's music. In December 1876, Mendelssohn's music for Sophocles' tragedy *Antigone* was given in the production by Augustus Harris with great publicity: the chorus was under the direction of Henry Gadsby, and the orchestra was conducted by Manns. The seat pricing was at the higher level: at 3s. 6d. and 2s. 6d.

But this was not the limit of Manns's wider activity with his orchestra. Even in events of a very popular nature they were likely to find themselves involved. The longest-running work advertised in the Crystal Palace programmes is the 'extravagant farce' *Bluebeard*, which ran for years after the opening of the Theatre in 1869; it featured fifteen soloists, Emily Soldene among them, and full orchestra and chorus under Manns. And every Christmas the Palace ran a pantomime for the two weeks before and into the New Year, which had begun before the creation of the Theatre with productions of *Ali Baba and the Forty Thieves* produced by Meyer Lutz in 1866. *Illustrated London News* showed the rehearsal of *Harlequin Little Boy Blue and Little Bo Peep who lost her Sheep* in December 1868, with Pantaloon, Harlequin and Colombine leading the action.[26] Others in the first decade were *Jack and Jill* or *Dame Nature's Art* in 1871–2 and *Little Miss Muffet* in 1872–3. Manns was totally involved in the productions. Of *Miss Muffet*, Wyndham recalls 'the genial musician directing his band accompaniment to the evolutions of the ballet dancers as energetically and wholeheartedly as he devoted himself to the works of the great masters', despite his feeling that this kind of musical task was beneath him.[27] Nor was this all: as well as playing a pre-pantomime programme at 12.30 p.m. in the Centre Transept, he was required to provide orchestral support for the regular performances on the high wire by Blondin. As with every other aspect of Crystal Palace music, the variety was endless.

CHAPTER 12

The great popular festivals

THE CHORAL MOVEMENT IN EDUCATION

The Crystal Palace was soon recognized as an ideal venue for the massed meetings that came to epitomize the public image of the great movements for educational and social reform which gathered momentum after the mid-nineteenth century. The musical accommodation offered by the Handel Auditorium, the accessible grounds and national rail connections, to say nothing of the unique scale of the building, its exhibits, and its lofty prospect over the country beyond, gave the Palace both a character and a suitability for popular meetings which was never rivalled. Its first association with such events is in connection with school music.

The early years of the Crystal Palace coincided with accelerating improvements in the national education system. By 1870 the first national Elementary Education Act (the Forster Act[1]) provided a local education resource for all children: the (local) board schools. Hitherto education had been in the hands either of endowing institutions, such as the British and Foreign Bible Society or the Church of England,[2] or of charitable institutions; but for many children, Sunday Schools remained the only providers, offering not only religious instruction, but instruction in reading and writing. The development of the Sunday School movement[3] was the key to the popular development of choral music and meant that many children became part of the new interest in singing, not least massed singing, whether by rote or by the spreading *sol-fa* methods. Tonic *sol fa* had early and vital connections with the Palace. But before turning to the influence of the Crystal Palace on a new tradition, its connections with an old tradition, soon to disappear, claim attention: the public performances of the 'charity children'.

THE CHARITY SCHOOLS

The annual singing of the children of the charity schools at St Paul's Cathedral represented one of the oldest traditions of public musical performance in London, tracing its history back to 1704; the meetings were to last until 1877, apparently declining as a consequence of the effects of the 1870 Education Act.[4] These performances, which were regarded as a special event in the musical year and attracted fashionable audiences, could be profoundly affecting, as leading European musicians of entirely different epochs bore witness. Haydn, present at St Paul's in June 1792, on his first visit to London was 'moved to tears' by the singing of some 6,000 children.[5] Berlioz, in London for the judging at the Great Exhibition, attended the June 1851 performance, where, from the organ loft, he was able to experience the effect of 'All People that on Earth do dwell' sung under the dome by the 6,000 children (on raised benches): his addition of a *ripieno* part for 600 children's voices to the, as yet unperformed, Te Deum, was attributed to the experience.[6] The association of the new Crystal Palace in suburban Sydenham with this tradition extended over three years, 1858–60: firstly, as an addition to the regular St Paul's meetings, because the Handel Orchestra could accommodate more than the metropolitan cathedral, and latterly, in 1860, as an alternative venue, since the cathedral was under repair.[7]

The figures given in the press for the meeting on 4 August 1858 show that 4,600 children took part. With the teachers, church beadles and others, the total numbers were around 5,000.[8] They arrived from all over London at the Crystal Palace (Lower) station via London Bridge between 8.00 a.m and 10.00 a. m. Some had already been breakfasted by their parishes, Castle Bayard and St Magnus for example. They were duly seated on the Great Orchestra and by 11.00 a.m. the rehearsal took place. This was attended by about 5,000 visitors, many of whom must have been the upwards of 4,000 parents and near-relations who had been offered special seats, including the railway journey return at £1 'which were mostly taken up': they were seated in the main transept and in the galleries adjacent to it. But the traditional audience obviously remained loyal, since no less than 27,000 persons attended.[9]

Between the rehearsal and the regular performance refreshments were provided for the children in the North Wing, which is just now provided with preparations for the forthcoming great poultry show. The comestibles consisted of good substantial sandwiches and the beverage of wholesome unintoxicating milk and water. These were supplied in the old picture gallery, whence the juvenile 'convives' on receiving their rations, passed through the doors connecting to the terraces. This very indispensable ceremonial passed off without the least disturbance.[10]

After this the children were free to roam around the grounds, which they did fully, till recalled for the performance proper. This was scheduled for 3.00, but the Handel Orchestra was filled from 2.30 till about 3.30. Their disposition and appearance drew a lot of comment. Many observers were impressed by their good looks – their fresh, ruddy complexions, and lively, intelligent features, strongly indicative of 'the bodily as well as mental care and culture bestowed upon them'. The girls were situated in the centre, the boys to the sides and behind. There were also boys around the back of the gallery at the organ level. A particular feature was the raised dais in the centre, which housed Distin's monster drum and the choir of Norton Folgate School. The obbligato trumpet player – Mr Haupt, the principal trumpet player of the Saturday Orchestra – was hidden among the organ pipes behind the organ console.[11]

The girls occupied the whole of the lower part of the gigantic Handel orchestra; and the immense display of white pinafores and caps, relieved with minor accessories of frocks of different colours, told to great advantage. The girls of the Norton Folgate School occupied the stage (erected for the monster drum) in the centre of the Orchestra, a position for which their brilliant scarlet dresses admirably fitted them. The seats immediately below them were occupied by the girls belonging to Raine's Charity the charity which gives £100 dowry to deserving scholars on their marriage to husbands of approved character, and the girls of St Pancras occupied the front row.[12]

The programme notes for the performance made it clear that the singing of the children was not intended as a musical display, but rather as a performance of simple psalmody. The programme was in two parts:

Part 1 Voluntary on the organ; Old 100th Psalm, Martin Luther; 113th Psalm (Anniversary), Garthony; Chorale Luther's Hymn.

Part 2 Voluntary on the organ; 119th Psalm (London New), Dr Croft; 104th Psalm (Hannover), Handel or Croft; The National Anthem, John Bull

But, for *The Times*

MEETING OF THE METROPOLITAN CHARITY SCHOOL CHILDREN AT THE CRYSTAL PALACE

19 The 'charity children' perform in 1859.

it was, nevertheless, a musical display for all that – and of its kind magnificent. Singing in unison is the most simple and unpretending form of musical execution, but if not abused it is also the most imposing. The selection yesterday was happily concise: and at the conclusion of the six psalm tones – which were delivered by the thousands of young, fresh, sonorous voices with a precision and unanimity nothing short of astonishing, the prevalent feeling among the vast assembled crowd must have been that as many more might have been listened to without satiety ... Of the psalm tones the favourite was, of course, the glorious Old Hundreth – 'All People that on Earth do Dwell' – which, if impressive and sublime in St Paul's Cathedral, was positively transcendent in the Crystal Palace. The utmost effect was produced by the contrast of the girls' and boys' voices in alternate verses, and their subsequent combination, materially enhanced by (the) judicious management of the organ – the only medium of accompaniment, except in Luther's hymn, where the trumpet part was played on the instrument indicated[13]

The concert concluded with the National Anthem. The *Morning Star* commented that

the last was so splendidly sung that an encore was irresistible – in fact the audience could not restrain their enthusiasm until the anthem had been sung through once. They broke out in the middle of the second verse, at the words 'And make them fall' which were delivered 'staccato', and with an energy and precision that older singers might have envied. The effect was thrilling in the extreme ... After the concert the children gambolled about in the grounds and enjoyed themselves heartily.[14]

In addition to the appeal of their performance, the attraction of the Charity Children for the press may have rested on the knowledge that they were those least likely to have the chance of a visit to the Crystal Palace. Certainly their performances appear to have overshadowed the meetings of the National and Endowed Schools, which took place on 8 May 1858. This meeting clearly had a higher social status, with attendance by the Queen and Prince Albert and the Queen of Portugal, and with a charity as the object of its proceeds; the music was directed by G. W. Martin with the Palace organist Brownsmith.[15] Yet another such event took place in June, with 5,000 singers of the Metropolitan Schools Choral Society directed by John Hullah,[16] with E. J. Hopkins at the organ.[17] Hullah was by now the chief government inspector in music and these events had many rehearsals and much support, receiving regular press notice for years after.[18]

The tonic sol fa *meetings, competitions and festivals*

Despite Hullah's status in the educational establishment, his importance was to be eroded in the development of the popular choral movement, notably in the emergence of sight singing according to *sol fa* methods. His 'fixed doh' system of sight reading, based on a French model and employed by him since 1840,[19] was destined to be outshone by the 'movable doh' system of John Curwen, his greatest contemporary in the field of choral education.[20] Curwen's work had begun in 1841 when, as a young Congregationalist minister, he first introduced *sol fa* training to his Sunday School. Quickly realizing the profound limitations of a fixed-doh in the face of the musical realities of transposition and modulation, Curwen had quickly responded to the *Scheme to render Psalmody Congregational* published by Sarah Glover,[21] and published his own lessons in singing in the *Independent Magazine* in 1842. His methods soon attracted national attention in philanthropic and temperance circles and when, in 1852, he published a series of articles in Cassell's *Popular Educator*, he had, through the enthusiasm it evoked, a national movement on his hands. In 1853 he founded the Tonic *Sol Fa* Association and in 1865 resigned his Ministry. The Curwen publishing house appeared in 1863, and in 1869 the Tonic *Sol Fa* College was founded. Tonic *Sol Fa* was never free from controversy, partly because of the snobbish attitude to the method's limitations by musically well-educated traditionalists, and partly because of the excessive claims of its adherents. None the less it continued to play a vital role in music education, providing a key to the opening up of numerous standard works to a new audience unfamiliar with instrumental music and thus staff notation and played a major role in the raising of choral standards.[22] The Crystal Palace was central to the propagation of this musical message.

Despite the enthusiasm of its early followers, the task that lay before Curwen, like Hullah, in so radical an initiative in popular education, made the early years difficult, as is reflected in a letter to Curwen from Sarah Glover dated 20 April 1858.[23] But she acknowledges the resistance still to be overcome only in the course of welcoming the massively beneficial effect of the recently held first Crystal Palace *Sol Fa* meeting on 2 September 1857, commenting that the applause it 'so deservedly elicited may ... be considered ...

a brilliant exception to the common course of events'. The meeting had been prompted by a very successful juvenile meeting at the Exeter Hall on 24 June 1857, by the Tonic *Sol Fa* Association. The suggestion of using the newly freely available Handel Auditorium at the Palace was quickly made and a concert of 3,000 children announced. Reports show London Bridge Station overwhelmed for a considerable time on the heavily rainy morning of the event, with many attempting to sell their tickets at a discount and giving up the journey in despair. By the end of the day, 30,000 people had been at Sydenham – its largest audience so far, and, in the words of one of the papers 'it was left for an almost unknown institution to draw a larger concourse of persons than has ever been attracted in this country to listen to a musical performance. Curwen was of the view that 'every newspaper published in the English language contained some account, original or quoted, of the doings of the 3,000 chil-dren'.[24] Other festivals followed similar lines in 1858, 1859 and 1860, the last with 3,500 juveniles and 1,000 tenors and basses in support.

The competitive aspect of the *sol fa* method was quickly grasped and its progressive dimension emphasized by its adoption by the adult choral community, the numbers of which would rival those of children and juveniles in later massed meetings. The first Crystal Palace *Sol Fa* Competition took place in October 1860 and involved five choirs, from Staffordshire, Finsbury, West Riding, Brighton and Edinburgh, with West Riding as winners. The prize was 'a beauti-fully embroidered banner, crimson, purple and orange'.[25] The choirs were given £5 each for expenses. Twenty-one thousand people were present.

On 17 June 1863, more than 22,000 people attended. Large numbers of ministers of all religions were noted in the audience. Curwen also noted the presence of 'that more serious and earnest class of society which does not commonly now make its appearance at the Crystal Palace'.[26] But traditional resistance was slow to yield. Only in 1871 did the veteran educationalist and composer George Macfarren seem to publicly acknowledge its value. He reported in the *Cornhill Magazine* of a Crystal Palace occasion:

A piece of music which had been composed for the occasion and had not yet been seen by human eyes, save for those of the writer and the printers, was handed out to the members of the chorus there present, and then before an audience furnished at the same time with copies to test the accuracy of the performance, 4,500 singers sang it at first sight in a manner to fulfil the highest requirements of the severest judges.[27]

A musician of comparable status, John Stainer,[28] was similarly slow in public acknowledgement, admitting a familiarity with the method only in *c.* 1876 in the course of an endorsement, saying that, whereas staff notation was most effective for location on chromatic instruments of large compass, *sol fa* was best for the 'relationship of scale sounds', when a singer 'wants bearings'. The context of this endorsement, a pamphlet with many similar comments titled *Tonic Sol Fa in the Church of England*[29] suggests how important was the support of the established church in the acceptance of the method, support necessary for Curwen to project the range and importance of his method to the widest audience.

The steady development of the movement was to lead to the first of a long series of annual *Sol Fa* Festivals from 1874 into the twentieth century, preceded, in 1871, by a concert of 5,000 voices of the Tonic *Sol Fa* Association conducted by Messrs Sarll and Proudman,[30] with the Palace organist Coward in support. With the 1874 Festival the movement was put on a major national footing, 3,000 child singers taking part with tenors and basses in support. The audience is now specified precisely at 29,573. Just how popular these meetings were to become and how they spanned the age-range is clear from the Jubilee Festival held on Saturday 18 July 1891. This day at the Palace involved 20,000 singers in three concerts – morning, afternoon and evening – with solo vocalists, three organists and three conductors (with a Book of Words of the three concerts). In the morning 5,000 juveniles gave an exhibition of singing by hand signs, with hymns and glees, and including participation by the Juvenile Orchestra. In the afternoon, 4000 provincial singers sang with full orchestral accompaniment, the proceedings including 'the ear test' as the central event. In the evening, 3,000 metropolitan singers performed, in this case the sight reading being of a 'four part example'. The public performance of these tests represented the focal moment of such meetings, in demonstrating to vast audiences the effectiveness of the *sol fa* method, as previously verified by Macfarren in 1871.

The Sunday School movement

Although the Sunday School movement dated from the later eighteenth century,[31] providing the cradle for educational development, including the the Tonic *Sol Fa* movement, major public festivals seem to have developed momentum only in the later nineteenth century, though they lasted well into the twentieth, the movement remaining an essential fixture in church life across denominations. The London Sunday School Choir was founded in 1871 with the intent to 'promote and improve part-singing amongst Sunday School Teachers and Scholars and to cultivate Christian Unity amongst Sunday School Workers of all Denominations'. The meeting at the Crystal Palace on 9 June 1875 featured a Grand Concert with 5,000 voices. By the twentieth century it had a well-established and broader-based musical organization, whose committee included, as well as the leading musician of the Sunday School movement, Carey Bonner, the doyen of Anglican church musicians and educators, Walford Davies.[32] The Sunday School Festival of 2 June 1923, at the Palace revealed an elaborate organization with two choirs – a Junior as well as Senior Festival Choir (maximum age seventeen) – and the London Sunday School Orchestra. The programme fell into two parts, with a familiar sequence of Sunday School hymns and choruses in unison and two parts, both sacred and secular. Preparation was through a programme book (published by Novello), which provided instructions for the performance as well as the printed music. The Notice to Conductors shows the importance of the preparatory work in making the event a success. As well as the need to 'watch the baton . . . for the success of the concert depends upon it'; it required that for the performance all words be sung 'by heart' and that singers attend at least three practices under their local conductor and three under their district conductor. And in stressing first of all that every choir should have 'at least forty per cent of alto singers' it shows the emphasis placed on the balance for the effectivenss of the two-part pieces. A visual aspect was also a feature of the event, with the children required to 'have a clean white handkerchief for the Drill'.

COMPETITIVE MEETINGS AND FESTIVALS

The national music meetings

If the choral festivals inevitably contained some element of the competitive, this was incidental to their purpose. But it was inevitable that, with growing musical literacy and the rising performance standards it engendered, competition would soon come to play its part, and the Crystal Palace would offer an ideal context. The competitive spirit finds its most famous manifestation in the brass band movement, which focussed the attention of its many participants on the Palace first, but briefly, in 1860–3, and then permanently from 1900, when its name became synonymous with the now National Championships, held annually at the Palace from 1900 till 1936. But competition had found a broader outlet in the interim in a long-forgotten movement initiated by the musical impresario Thomas Willert Beale (1824–94) in the early 1870s: the 'National Music Meetings'. Since these meetings reflect a new consciousness of national musical standards, their association with the Palace represents another landmark in its musical history.

Indeed, previous musical associations were not without influence on Beale's concept itself. He notes his plan as being based on that of the 'Orpheonistes in France' as well as on the trials of skill at the National Eisteddfod in Wales. But he claimed his approach as 'more educational in its tendency than either, owing to the practical knowledge of music it enforces'.[33] His plans were published in the London press on 1 January 1872 and an impressive list of sponsors announced. His purpose was 'to show vocalists especially what they are expected to know and be able to sing before they have any right to claim proficiency in the art': for this reason he 'made it compulsory on those taking part in the meetings to study certain selections of pieces representative of the best music in their respective branches of composition, the selection being made by the most competent authorities on the subject'. All competitors were required to have mastery of a given number of pieces and to perform them if required. The singers, for example, had to know these works: Handel, 'The many rend the skies'; Bach, *I wrestle and pray* (Motet); Cherubini 'Dies Irae' (C minor Requiem); Beethoven 'Halleluiah' (*Mount of Olives*); Mendelssohn 'See what love' (*St Paul*) and 'Come with Torches' (*Walpurgisnacht*).[34]

The classes contested were as follows:

I   Choral societies not exceeding 500;
II   Choral societies not exceeding 200:
III   Choral societies for men's voices:
VI   Military bands not exceeding forty performers;
VIa   Other military bands;
VII   Bands of volunteer regiments;
VIII-XI   Solo singers: soprano, alto, tenor, bass.

Response to Beale's initiative in the musical press was immediate.

In gaining the support and assistance of the Crystal Palace authorities, Mr Beale succeeded in placing the scheme beyond the possibility of failure. For every reason the Crystal Palace was the most advantageous locale. No institution in our day has done as much towards the spreading of knowledge of music in all its varied branches, from the highest classical composition, performed by its unrivalled band, to the simple part song of the children's meetings ... and the completeness with which every detail was carried out once more justified the confidence placed in this great centre of Art.[35]

The Crystal Palace management had been responsible for 'the practical realization' of the meetings with Beale, who observed that they were 'entirely consistent with the original object of the Crystal Palace [and were] essentially educational and progressive in their tendency'.[36] At the presentation of prizes, the Chairman, Thomas Hughes, stressed that the 'Directors of the Crystal Palace Company believe that these trials

will do good service to Art: and will tend to elevate the standard of taste by a means familiar and always attractive to the public: and will establish a test of merit such as did not hitherto exist ... while those who come and hear ... will have the opportunity of comparing their opinions with those of the judges ... thus both competitors and hearers derive benefit from the competitive performances. Moreover ... a practical knowledge of the compositions of the greatest masters is acquired by all who enter the lists, whether they win prizes or not.[37]

This commitment was emphasized in both the prizes and the patronage. The prizes were attractive: in Class I, The Challenge Trophy; Class II, £100; Classes III-VII, £50; Classes VIII-XI, £30, making a total of £420 distributed, in addition to the cup. The judges included some of the most eminent musicians of the time, apparently chosen by the competitors:[38] for the choral classes Benedict, Barnby, Sullivan, Hatton, Leslie, Henry Smart; for the bands Godfrey sen., Randegger, Cusins and Rimbault, as well as some of the above; for the singers, Arditti, Benedict, Barnby, Wylde, Sullivan. Response was quick, and numbers of competitors had to be reduced in some classes by preliminary trials which, like the finals, took place in the Handel Orchestra with the judges on a raised dais in the front.

Beale recalls the preliminary hearings which

took place in the board room of the Palace, the Candidates being collected in groups in the Egyptian Court, waiting their turn. Six singers only were to compete in each class in public, and to decide upon these was the object of the private hearings – a severe ordeal for judges and performers, and certainly instructive to the latter. Sometimes a candidate having sung several of the pieces selected was sent for again, so close was the struggle for superiority, and sometimes, I fear too often, after singing a few bars, the fate of a candidate was decided in the minds of the judges.[39]

Yet, although Beale claims that entries were numerous, and many distinguished ensembles participated, some with existing Crystal Palace connections, not all classes were equally strongly contested. The Challenge Shield in Class I went to the South Wales Choral Union, without challenge, while the competition offered to the Tonic *Sol Fa* Association Choir, which won Class II, was considered inadequate, *The Musical Times* regretting the non-appearance of Yorkshire choirs which would 'have made short work of the small and somewhat tricky reading of the £100 prize choir'. Of the military bands, Class VI went to the Royal Engineers, VIa to the Thirty-Third Regiment (Duke of Wellington's), VII to St George's Rifles, the latter also without competition, particularly regrettable since, for one critic, 'hardly two instruments were in tune with each other'.[40] In the vocal classes the aims were achieved in at least one notable case, the soprano prize going to Anna Williams, later prominent in Palace music. But in choral activity it was the diplomas offered for sight-singing and general musical proficiency which elicited the greatest press response, with the Brixton Choral Union and the Bristol Choral Society reading pieces by Barnby and Smart at sight.

Hopes were high for the following year as the 1872 address promised 'to embrace circles and interests at present untouched', as well as to introduce organizational improvements:

the National Music Meetings have already brought forward four new singers who were a few days ago comparatively unknown [and] have also been the means of bringing singers from Bristol and South Wales and of giving some four or five hundred singers in the last-named musical part of the Kingdom, an opportunity of displaying their fresh and vigorous voices in a new and untried locality. The impulse which may thus be given to music in remote districts of the country and through it to culture and refinement in the best sense of the words is, though an indirect, by no means an unimportant or undesirable result to be anticipated . . .[41]

The changes involved the addition of a class for church and chapel choirs, while the military bands yielded to a brass band class as well as one for juvenile wind bands and a solo trumpet class. Standards were now considered much better and there was a good competition for the Grand Challenge Prize, though it still went to the South Wales Choral Union, with the Tonic *Sol Fa* Association, now competing in this, largest, class, coming second. But the dominance of the *Sol Fa* movement in the smaller class continued with the Stepney *Sol Fah* Association as winners. Of church and chapel choirs, St Nicholas Liverpool came out winners, and the brass band class was won by the Royal Artillery Band, Woolwich.[42] Plans for the following year in 1874 involved subdividing the single voice classes into two competitions and

removing the restrictions which have hitherto limited the candidates to those who have not received or fulfilled public engagements more than twelve months previous to the competitions. This limitation had always appeared an unwise one, considering that public singers of the second class, and not merely promising pupils, are the persons who require recognition and encouragement (since) there are many . . . who spend their whole life in the constant and vain endeavour to gain an adequate recognition. Hitherto pupils . . . have competed for and received prizes. In the future it is to be hoped singers will take their place.[43]

But no meetings actually happened in this year because of the Handel Festival, which dominated proceedings in May and June during every third year. The meetings in 1875 again covered four days in July, with a fifth for presentation. But, though reflecting in its bias the greater emphasis on solo singing, reports also reveal the diminishing scope of the enterprise: three days are given to singers (sopranos, altos, tenors and basses) with the fourth comprising the brass bands, choral societies and certificates for merit. And the scope for competition was now drastically different: only two choral societies competed in the Handel Orchestra, a prize of £100 going to the Liverpool Representative Choir, with no mention of the Challenge

Cup; and of the three brass bands, Carrow Works (Norwich) won. In contrast, eleven solo sopranos were selected to compete for a prize of £25, likewise altos or mezzos, five tenors and eight baritones or basses for the same sum each. Certificates were given again in sight-singing and for all 'having been selected to compete' through success in the preliminary examination. Prizes were given by no less an eminence than Jenny Lind Goldschmidt.[44] But the fact that the winners and runners-up were students from the Royal Academy of Music confirms that the national aspect of the undertaking was as limited as the scope of classes. The imbalance of representation revealed in the first year had not been overcome. This may explain the failure which Beale recalls to come to an arrangement for the continuation of the meetings at the Palace; the original agreement had been for three meetings only. We next read of the widespread acceptance by many distinguished Professors of Beale's invitation to join the Council of Musicians for the forthcoming series of Meetings 'to be held in the provinces', 'including some names very familiar at the Palace'. After this, no meetings are associated with it.[45]

The brass band movement

For all its ambitions, one notes the lack of any concerted instrumental activity outside banding in the National Meetings. Orchestral activity, whether or not for competitive prizes, was to be part of the twentieth century, and the Crystal Palace plays a relatively small part in it, other more appropriate venues having become by then available.[46] But for brass banding, the Palace offered the natural locale. Though first associated specifically with the industrial centres of the north, the brass band movement established a remarkable link in 1860–3 through association with Enderby Jackson. Though the phase was to be short-lived, it revealed another facet of the musical potentialities of the Palace, which would be explored more fully when it became the permanent home of the National Championships first held in 1900,[47] which made London rather than Manchester, Belle Vue, the natural focus for competition.[48]

Jackson (1827–1903) was brought up in the north of England, where banding was deeply embedded in the community, part of a reforming movement aimed at countering the evil effects of rapid industrialization, with strong employer support. Organized meetings and competitions were long a tradition by mid-century, which, by 1853, focussed on Belle Vue stadium at Manchester. But new interest developed around 1860 with the inception of the army volunteer movement, which raised no less than 130,000 men between May 1859 and June 1860, and in turn gave the stimulus to the creation or revival of many bands as a consequence. Jackson's ambition was for a national brass movement, which required contact with London. But the reputation of banding was not good: for all the skill of its participants, it had low social standing and thus low status in the musical hierarchy, not least as manifest in the emerging musical life of the Crystal Palace. Then there were the practicalities of bringing players such a distance. The Palace was the only remotely feasible venue in 1860, in view of the popular character of so many of its activities. But as far as music was concerned, Jackson still had to overcome the reservations of a management which, if go-ahead, was also aware of its growing association with high quality choral and orchestral performance. He had to persuade. Drawing on his previous experience, he offered the Palace a handbell-ringing contest to show his organizational capacity, with twelve teams from eleven towns in the north.[49] They obviously satisfied the Directors, who gave permission for a contest in 1859, the apparent success of which opened the door for competitive banding at the Palace in 1860.

The festivals 1860–3

The plan was for two contests: the Great National Contest on the first day, 10 July, open to all 'Amateur, Yeomanry, and Rifle Corps Bands', and the 'Sydenham Amateur Contest' for all amateur bands that had not won a prize over £20 in the preceding year. The eligible bands would be permitted to enter both contests, but the first day's winners and runners-up would be excluded from the second day. Admission price for the first day was greater in view of its greater competitive importance, 2s. 6d.; for the second day, 1s. per head. The unprecedented scope of the undertaking is clear from the prizes offered, generous for the times. For the National the winners would receive £40, a silver cup and an E♭ contra-bass (Value 35 guineas) The second-placed would win £25, the third, fourth and fifth, £15, £10 and £5 respectively. On the second day, the first prize was £30 with silver cup and a complete set of Boosey's *Brass Band Journal*, the remaining prizes, £20, £15, £10 and £5. And there were prizes for individuals: for the soprano cornet player and the best over-all bass player over the two days. The instruments were given by the manufacturers and traders.

In his preparation, Jackson spared no pains to ensure the success of the venture. To generate enthusiasm and thus encourage supporting audiences for the bands, he paraded them through their towns and cities prior to the event, drawing on the success of this ploy in previous contests; and he arranged subsidized transport.[50] His calculations had been correct. The entry list was quite unprecedented – over forty bands for the first day and seventy for the second. Precise numbers are difficult to confirm since some bands must have entered for both contests and are counted twice, as can be deduced from the newspaper reports of the numbers present. Both *The Times* and *The Telegraph* for 11 July describe 1,200 musicians in the massed band for the first day; since the limit was on eighteen performers for each band, this indicated at least sixty-six bands for the two days.[51] These were vast numbers and posed great organizational problems. Of the composition of the entry, two features stand out: first the proportion of north to south, second the influence of the volunteer or army bands.

The first day's proceedings began at 10.00 a.m. on the Tuesday morning. The forty-or-so contestants were split into six groups, each of which played out a preliminary round at a different point in the grounds. In each tent there were three judges who had to take out two bands from each platform for the final. At 3.00 in the afternoon, the united bands gave a concert on the Handel Orchestra accompanied by the organ and 'Distin's Drum' (famed from the Handel Festival). The effect was sensational: for the first time, the great organ was almost drowned by the combined 'brass tempest'. Jackson conducted with 'wonderful vigour and precision'. After this the twelve winners from the morning mounted the stage one by one and played their pieces. The first day's winners were Black Dyke Mills. The audience for the following day was even greater: 22,000. And the effect was even more astounding, with three encores for 'Rule Britannia', the 'Wedding March' and the National Anthem. The winners were Cyfarthfla. In the judgement of *The Times* for the following day, 12 July 'for a first event of this kind the effect was quite extraordinary' and Jackson even found himself congratulated by Charles Godfrey sen., the oldest bandmaster in the country.[52]

This unreserved success ensured the future of the brass band meetings at the Crystal Palace. It also gave a focus for the national movement. Just as had been observed of a winning Welsh choir in the National Music Meetings, so a winning Welsh band was seen as contributing to a national context for the competition – and likewise for the Palace. And from the point of view of its Directors, the financial aspect – ever one of its preoccupations – was also an unreserved success. Jackson claimed to have spent £1,900, 15s. 6d. on prize money and gifts, subsidies to the railway companies, judges' fees, printing, publicity and postage, including in his accounts the uninformative entry '£800 allowed for two days ordinary takings at the Crystal Palace'. Setting against the income raised by admissions, reserved seats and programme sales, the Crystal Palace Company took two-thirds of the profit and Jackson one third 'over expenses'.[53]

But the contest was not destined to establish itself at this stage, although the following year's meetings, on 23 and 25 July 1861, maintained the momentum. The massed concert on the first day was equally impressive; indeed, though Yorkshire again won – Saltaire and Marriners' – there was a much better southern representation, with eight bands from London and southern counties, included a band drawn from the employees of Distin. Despite heavy rain on the second day, the arrangements held well. As the *Guardian* recorded: 'no adjournment took place from the terrace to the interior ... many of the pieces were thus performed in the midst of driving rain, the musicians being wholly unsheltered ...'[54] But the entry had been much smaller: twenty-eight only, allowing for duplication, compared with sixty to seventy in the previous year. In the following year, 1862, one day was therefore considered adequate, twenty-six ensembles contesting for the prize taken by Chesterfield. In 1863, only twenty-one competed, though forty-four were advertised, the twelve finalists now including several southern bands. But this was to be the last of Jackson's events at the Palace. Whether through the trend towards declining entries, through his interest and energies now going elsewhere, or through the failure of his planned special French event at the Palace, which for some reason was opposed by English officials, he now abandoned the band competition in 1864 to become involved in theatrical and music-hall speculation. Events may have been influenced by the death in 1864 of Robert Bowley, the first general manager of the Palace, who had promised that the contests would not be entrusted to anyone else as long as he, Bowley, lived. Since he died in this year, Jackson was probably not able to make sufficiently advantageous financial arrangements with the Palace.[55]

Though Jackson's initiative had made a remarkable incursion into the emerging character of Crystal Palace music, it did not affect the strong continuity of banding in the north: on the contrary, there is considerable suggestion of resentment from the traditional centres towards the new venue in the south. Though various proposals were made in following years for special brass events, the Palace was not to encourage brass contests for many years. Belle Vue reasserted itself as a focal centre. For many years to come, brass bands would be heard only in the context of religious meetings, though their sonic effect would be equally powerful.

The national championships: 1900–1936

The second, and now permanent, phase of the Crystal Palace's involvement with the brass movement was associated with the efforts of another remarkable individual, though now one not previously associated with the band movement. John Henry Iles (1871–1951) had come across the achievements of bands almost by accident, attending a festival at Belle Vue and being overwhelmed by the striking discrepancy between the high professional standards of the players and their lowly amateur status and circumstances. Inspired with admiration for what he heard, Iles wished to achieve something for the players, and formed a strong identity with them. He was to remain a father-figure of banding for the rest of his life, even when he had ceased direct involvement with the contests. Like Jackson, London became the natural focus of his ambitious plans for the bandsmen: but not at first the Crystal Palace, which, in the forty years since 1860, had gained immeasurably in its national cultural status. Iles would have to do much to prepare for a successful festival there. Above all he needed friends in high places. No better connection could be imagined than with Arthur Sullivan, the now knighted leading English composer of the day, pre-eminently associated with the Palace over the years, and now one of its directors. Iles invited Sullivan to conduct the massed bands in Sullivan's own arrangement of Kipling's patriotic and popular poem *The Absent-Minded Beggar* in a concert at the Albert Hall on 20 January 1900, before an audience of 10,000 people, with a brass orchestra of 250 with organ, and vocal soloist, Bertha Flotow. The effect was overwhelming, not least in directing the audience's attention to the qualities of the players themselves. Sullivan was instantly moved by their skill and wished to help their musical cause.[56]

The first National Championship took place on 27 July 1900. The plans were laid with Sullivan's help, and the test piece was a Sullivan potpourri.[57] A trophy, apparently the Challenge Cup of the National Music Meetings, long resident in the vaults of the Palace, was retrieved at Sullivan's insistence to become The Thousand-Guinea Trophy. From this moment, the North and Belle Vue could no longer regard banding as their province: it had gained a new focus with a prestigious national event. Iles's organization of the first year was very impressive: he devised a 'stepping-stone' competition with graded concerts to enable each band to compete at its appropriate level. Twenty-nine bands entered for the three sections: not as many as in 1860, but a start. Though from the north, the winners – Denton Original (conducted by Alexander Owen) were unfancied, and the result caused some unpleasant scenes when the losers walked out.[58] Though the Championship had been well supported and successful in gaining national credibility – the unruly behaviour and far from comprehensive press coverage (the Belle Vue supporting press almost ignoring it) showed that the banding movement still had a long way to go to musical respectability.[59]

The next few years were to remain a challenge while Iles sought to establish the contest on firm foundations to overcome resistance. In 1901 only twenty-seven bands entered and some northern names were pointedly absent. In 1902 Iles announced that area competitions would be held, so that entry to the Championship proper would be by invitation only. This decision was very unpopular, denying second-class bands the right to compete directly with the 'cracks' and in some areas it had to be abandoned. But ninety bands had competed (twenty-one in the first section) and this represented a positive achievement for Iles, the basis of the establishment of the Crystal Palaceas comparable with Belle Vue. Iles insisted that the first section bands now wear uniform.[60] In the years up to the first World War, its status was steadily to grow, with the gradual expansion of numbers. In 1903 there were 117 entrants; by 1908 five grades existed (five sections for brass, reed and concert bands). In 1910, 200 entered, only 160 being accepted. After the War, yet another new grade system would be introduced, though entrance took some time to pick up: in the first year, 1920, only 120 bands entered.

But more than the increasing numbers and classes, and the daunting organizational factors that accompanied them, the future of the band movement as a serious vehicle for performance rested on the renewal of the repertory. The rapid expansion since 1900 had been based on a foundation of musical material which was increasingly outdated: essentially medleys of popular operatic tunes and the like, something much more appropriate to the entertainment offered daily by the Palace's resident military than to high level competition. With such repertory, the serious musical world and the press would continue to regard brass music with disdain. Iles again showed his foresight. He commissioned new music from native composers. The first fruit was Percy Fletcher's tone poem *Labour and Love* of 1913, the title reflecting the background of so many bands in the growing force of the Salvation Army, whose motto it was. The contest also included a special concert of British music by Elgar, Bantock, Holst and Ireland. For the following year Cyril Jenkins wrote *Coriolanus*, though the War intervened to prevent any Championship or performance in 1914. During the War the Palace was requisitioned by the Admiralty and was not immediately free for use thereafter. Only in 1920 was Jenkins's work played as the Test Piece for the resumed Championships, when 120 entered (though twenty-five were prevented from competing through the miners' strike. By now a new grading system had been introduced and standards continued to rise, with some bands dominating: St Hilda Colliery won in 1920, 1921, 1924, 1926. A symptom of the new interest in repertory is the rise of the specialist composer. Percy Fletcher appears again in 1926. In 1923 and 1924 Henry Geehl's *Oliver Cromwell* and *On the Cornish Coast* appear, the former another work in succession to *Labour and Love* as a milestone in the expansion of the musical scope of works for band.

The foundation being laid for commissioned new works by English composers was bound to have its effects. From the late 1920s a new phase in repertory performed at the Palace is apparent, through the responses of a number of established and younger composers who provided a sequence of new and ambitious test pieces for the annual Championship which were destined to have far-reaching effects into the future. The crucial year was 1928, in which the first concert devoted entirely to English works for band took place: the works by Elgar, Holst and Ireland. It was also the year of Holst's *A Moorside Suite*, given on 29 September, the first test piece by a leading composer outside the movement. In 1930 came Elgar's *Severn Suite*, completed in April especially for the Championships. The following year saw a piece by Hubert Bath, the symphony *Freedom*, then, in 1932, another work destined to go with the Holst and Elgar as standard repertory for the future: Ireland's *A Downland Suite*. Two years later Ireland had another Championship commission: *Comedy Overture*. In the meantime, Granville Bantock made his appearance with the tone poem *Prometheus Unbound*. Finally in 1936 came the last commission to be heard at the Palace played by the then premier band, Fodens: Arthur Bliss wrote a piece of pageantry called *Kenilworth*, inspired by the 1575 celebrations for Queen Elizabeth held there, and described as 'nine minutes of rather ordinary, 'popular stuff' by *The Musical Times*, which went on to say: 'The band played with rich tone and natty rhythm, except in "Passing By", where the old pausey, dragging style was adopted. I hope Mr Bliss heard his work'.[61] He did, for, as was usual, the composer was also an adjudicator:

It was those first shattering chords which made me jump. They were definitely exciting, so exact was the precision, so brilliant the tone, so irresistible the rhythm. There are few times in a composer's life when the actual performance comes up to the ideal dreamed of, but I can truthfully say that last Saturday was such an occasion. The mastery of technique and the musical understanding were alike superb.[62]

The destruction of the Palace within only weeks of this performance was a massive shock to the banding movement. But the sentiment expressed in the *British Bandsman* was one of affection and appreciation for the building which had helped to define the modern movement:

Brave old Palace! though you have stirred thousands and thousands of memories this night, and a great multitude of people will miss you, we shall feel that your end was such as you would have wished for yourself. Truly you went out in a blaze of light.[63]

Festivals seasonal, religious, imperial and social

With consideration of the great national and international celebratory festivals the subject of Crystal Palace music comes full circle. For whatever their purpose – from the annual celebration of season to the extended celebrations of Empire – music played a central role.

In following broadly similar programme patterns (sometimes bearing more than a passing resemblance to the Selection programmes of the Handel Festivals) the music throws light on the essential appeal of all these great occasions: the reassuring repetition of the familiar to stimulate a collective sense. However wide the sources of the selections of choruses, hymns, arias, sacred solos and instrumental items, they always had a familiar national or religious quality, according to the tradition relevant to the particular event, and the Crystal Palace setting gave them the stamp of national expression in the era before broadcasting. A representative survey highlights the main subjects of national celebration and social concern as well as their characteristic musical content. First to attract attention are the seasonal festivals of Harvest and Good Friday; the day of the former was variable, not fixed in the religious calendar like Good Friday; though Sunday observance prevented an Easter event, Easter Monday was a special day at the Palace and in addition Ash Wednesday also received musical recognition. Since the Palace was closed over Christmas, musical activity took a different form in longer-running entertainments before and after. Of the movements for social reform, the meetings of the temperance movement and the Salvation Army dominate. With the new century, an increasing recognition of Britain's power in the world reflects itself in international and imperial Festivals, though after the First War, a marked change of emphasis reflects new approaches to social issues through the Co-operative and Fellowship movements.

Harvest, Good Friday, Ash Wednesday, Easter Monday
The traditional religious celebration of Harvest Festival found an ideal context for expression at the Palace: the ambience was perfect for the most advantageous display of flowers and fruit, to complement the pervasive greenery within the glass structure. The first festivals appear in the 1860s, when a date in mid-October, usually midweek, is set aside for a celebration involving display acts and fireworks, for example on 11 October 1869, the appearance of Blondin and Etharo. [64] By 1875 a pattern had become established. Celebration was still a midweek event, held this year on Wednesday, 20 October, but now as the culmination of a series of Harvest Fetes, known collectively as the Golden Grain Festival. It is advertised as involving 4,000 trained performers, though the review had only 'upwards of 2,000 in the choir', [65] with the Crystal Palace orchestra under Manns, James Coward, the Palace organist, and the

band of the Scottish Fusiliers; Joseph Barnby also conducted some choral pieces. The programme fell into two parts. Part 1 was devoted to religious music and began with the Introduction and Allegro from Mendelssohn's *Reformation* Symphony and the March from *Athalie* by the orchestra. Four choral hymns included the Reformation chorale, sung as 'Rejoice today with one accord', the others being 'Come ye thankful people, come', 'Now thank we all our God' and the Old 100th, audience participation being invited. Goss's 'I will magnify' and Barnby's 'O Lord how manifold' were the Harvest anthems, conducted by Barnby; Blanche Cole[66] sang 'With verdure clad' from Haydn's *Creation* and Coward played a movement from Handel's Fourth Organ Concerto. The second part comprised 'All among the barley', the trio and chorus 'Thus nature ever kind' from *The Seasons*, the Vintage Song from Mendelssohn's Loreley and 'O the pleasure of the plains' from Handel's *Acis and Galatea*. The orchestra played Suppe's overture *Poet and Peasant* and the March from Gounod's *Reine de Saba*. The programme ended with 'God bless the Prince of Wales' and the National Anthem. Some items were re-demanded, and such was the success that the entire programme was repeated the following week.

No comparable spring festival existed at the Palace, but rather individual days were recognized, both bank holiday, special Shilling Days, Good Friday and Easter Day, as well as Ash Wednesday, which, as a working day, had an evening concert. Good Friday attracts attention from early on. On 4 April 1857, the doors are advertised to open from 1.00 p.m. till sunset, with trains running at short intervals throughout the afternoon. By 30 April 1860, two concerts are advertised. Though the printed programme acknowledged the day with black print and edging, the musical fare was hardly in accordance. The performers were three soloists from the Royal Italian Opera and two principals from the Palace Band, which performed under Manns. The programme at 1.00 was of six popular orchestral items, two opera overtures, Mendelssohn's Wedding March, a Waltz and Galop, and a selection from Verdi's *Rigoletto*. The vocal and instrumental concert at 3.00 was of twelve items, some more extended, including Beethoven's overture Leonora No. 2 (though in second rather than final or first position in the sequence), Weber's *Concertino* for clarinet and orchestra, the scherzo from Mendelssohn's Octet, popular Verdi arias, ballads and airs and a piano solo.

By the 1870s the event had become more solemn as well as

growing in scope, establishing a pattern of programme and repertory which remained constant for many years. Good Friday, 14 April 1874, again offered two concerts during the day. The first, at 3.00 p.m., the 'Grand Sacred Concert', featured Rossini's *Stabat Mater*, and selections from Oratorios: the four soloists were leading names familiar from the Handel Festivals (Lemmens-Sherrington, Patey, Lloyd, Foli), the orchestra that of the Company under Manns, with support from the bands of the Royal Horse Guards, the Scots Fusiliers and the Royal Artillery and with a chorus of a thousand voices under Manns and Coward. The evening concert at 7.30 p.m. was given in the 'Opera House' by the 'celebrated Hague's Minstrels', with 'comprehensive selections from Messiah, Elijah and other oratorios'. At various times of the day 'special selections' were played by military bands. Excursion trains are advertised throughout the day. Things had hardly changed by 1910, when *The Musical Times* commented that 'the custom of attending sacred concerts on that day showed no diminution in popularity ... (in) a popular programme, part of which could scarcely have been avoided'.[67] In the afternoon, again Rossini's *Stabat Mater*, with a miscellaneous second part, though now the London Symphony Orchestra is the assisting orchestra. The Evening Concert is given by the Band of the Coldstream Guards with organist and piano, all under the direction of Walter Hedgcock, now the Director of the Palace music, to an enormous gathering. From the 1870s also appear concerts of Sacred Music on the evening of Ash Wednesday with a suitable choral work as the centrepiece of a mixed programme. In 1875, it is Beethoven's *Mount of Olaves*. In 1881, the last movement of *The Light of the World* balances a Handel organ concerto, the *Largo*, instrumental movements by Mendelssohn and other concerted pieces and songs, with four soloists, organ, cornet soloist, and orchestra under Manns. Seats were 2s. 6d., 1s. and 6d. Easter Monday for this year has a Great Ballad and Military Concert, with four soloists, the Bands of the Scots Guards and Royal Engineers and the Crystal Palace orchestra under Manns.

Temperance movements and the Salvation Army
Prior to the appearance of the Salvation Army, the spearhead of social reform was provided by the various organizations that comprised the temperance movement.[68] Direct in its attack on the manifest evils of alcoholism, it was non-conformist in religion and

independent in music, with its own musical literature, strongly influenced by the *Sol Fa* movement. Items ranged from simple unison songs to short cantatas with moralizing texts, and much of the music was only ever published in *sol fa* notation, the Curwen house having an apparent monopoly in the field.[69] As with the Sunday School and other meetings, a special book of music and words, with *sol fa*, was published for the day, and choirs were required to prepare in detail and, as in one case, to sing 'with only slight reference to books and considerable attention to the baton', juniors being required to sing from memory. The context of the music-making was similar. All were attached to fetes held in the building and grounds. In some cases there were several concerts on the day. An early festival is that of the National Temperance League, which held its annual fete at the Palace on Tuesday 3 September 1867, with the Band of Hope. The Band of Hope held its own meeting on 13 July 1880, with three concerts, morning, afternoon and evening, the first of fifteen items, the last of twelve, essentially a sequence of hymns, varied with hymn-anthems or patriotic songs; the shorter afternoon concert included the chorus 'To Thee, great Lord' from Rossini's *Moses in Egypt*, and ended with the Halleluiah Chorus from *Messiah*. For the National Fete of the Independent Order of Grand Templars on 8 July 1884, there was a good deal more variety, with solo voices in the hymns and anthems and a wider variety of composed music. It comprised fifteen items, only two by composers whose names are known from the broader nonconformist repertory: Carey Bonner and Josiah Booth. Elsewhere, compositions are drawn from the wide range of temperance literature, with only two items from the standard hymn literature: the imagery stresses the pastoral, as in Stainer's 'The Flowers of England', Martin's 'Beautiful Flowers' and 'Bells of long ago', though marching songs provide a strong contrast where necessary, and dominate the evening programme for soloists and choir, where they also involve whistling.

The Salvation Army assumed its name in 1885, having been founded in 1865 as the Salvation Mission. Addressing itself to broader social concerns than the temperance movement, its more distinctly militant style and its vast and international administration captured a broader base of support which has lasted till the present day.[70] In music too its achievements were to be lasting. To the limited musical scope of the temperance music it brought more solo

UNITED KINGDOM BAND OF HOPE UNION.

Selection of Pieces.

TO BE SUNG AT THE

CRYSTAL PALACE FÊTE,

TUESDAY, JULY 13th, 1880.

AFTERNOON CONCERT.

Members of the Choir must not expect that the practice at the Rehearsals will be sufficient to perfect them in their respective parts. Daily practice at home should be bestowed on the pieces.

Junior Members of the Choir must bear in mind that they are required to commit the words to memory.

All Singers should be sufficiently familiar with the words and music as to be able to sing with only slight reference to the books and considerable attention to the *bâton*.

LONDON:

UNITED KINGDOM BAND OF HOPE UNION,

4, LUDGATE HILL, E.C.

20 The cover of the programme book for the concert at the Fete of the United Kingdom Band of Hope Union on 13 July 1880.

items, emphasis on high instrumental standards, a much wider repertory, and public events the organization of which was without previous parallel. Of all the institutions that used the Palace, none explored its potential further than the Salvation Army. Indeed, the decision to book the Palace for a special event was, as in the case of the *sol fa* meeting of 1857, to be a key moment in the development of the movement itself, through the emphasis which would then be placed on the role of music in the largest-scale context. After several years of successful field days at the Alexandra Palace, the movement's founder, William Booth,[71] decided to celebrate the first twenty-five years with an all-day event at the Crystal Palace in 1890, in which a musical festival – 'the Battle of Song' – would be a major feature. A later account recalls

The huge [o]rchestra was a phalanx of faces. Around the conductor on the lower seats were the massed string bands ... Next in ascending order were the members of the Household Troops and Home Office bands... Behind the bands were ranged the first company of singers, 500 in number, each carrying a tambourine, the sight and sound of which in action was likened by Herbert Booth to 'the rattle and glitter of a steel-clad battalion doing musical drill'. Up and beyond these were the main body of singers – to the left 1200 male officers, each man wearing a red jersey and carrying in his hand a fluttering flag. On the right there was a corresponding company of female officers, each ... robed in the sombre uniform of bonnet and dark blue, and each holding one of the many coloured pennants. Above the great chorus, fringing the semi-chorus at the top, was the junior chorus. 500 girls ranged above the women and 500 boys above the men. Each youngster held a flag, making another brilliant scene of colour.

At a signal from Herbert Booth, [the organist] struck the keys of the Grand Organ, and the women singers removed their sashes, then their bonnets, and suddenly the sashes were seen to stretch out into broad folds of pure white, the colourful effect strongly contrasting with the flame red jerseys of the men. The audience of some 15,000 people sat spellbound as, in response to his conductor's baton, that mighty chorus thundered forth Herbert Booth's music to William Pearson's 'God is keeping his soldiers fighting ... but we are sure to have the victory.[72]

If the Crystal Palace was used to vast musical effects, such a spectacle has never been seen: only the visual impact of the Charity Children in 1858–9 offered a parallel, and the contrast in the musical presentation mirrored the major changes in social attitudes as in musical ones. A leading preacher exclaimed to an interviewer 'Man, the Army is made, but it will have to go wary and not lose its head and become great in its own conceit'.[73] The event marked the end of the Army's years of establishment, a fact symbolized in the approaching death of the 'Army Mother', Catherine Booth, wife of the founder: her 'last message' was emblazoned in giant letters on a banner spanning the nave.[74] On 19 October 1890, 10,000 would brave dreadful weather to attend her memorial service at the Palace, led by a choir of 3,000.[75]

As with the first Handel Festivals, the practicalities of transporting so many people to South London made the event highly visible. A vivid description of the journey from central London survives through the recollections of a veteran bandsman from the Regent Hall corps in Oxford Street.

We travelled in several horse-drawn wagonettes, the proprietor himself riding in that containing the band. The horses had red, white and blue rosettes on the harness and our driver had a tri-coloured rosette on his whip. A few weeks earlier I had taken up the G trombone and it was an eerie experience for me when we moved off en route for the Palace, for it was the first time I had played with the band mounted. We started off with 'Jesus is mine forever', which got played along Regent St and across Picadilly Circus. When we got to Herne Hill we began to overtake Salvationist comrades of all sorts, some on foot, others in different types of vehicles. When going up the rise at Dulwich Wood Park, we had to disembark to relieve the strain upon the horses.[76]

The success of the event prompted even greater musical plans for the following year, which featured what was advertised as 'the biggest band in the world' comprising 10,000 of brass, concertina and tambourines, the individual bands selected to represent geographical areas of the British Isles: Belfast, Kilmarnock, Pentre, London (Clapton), South Shields, Northampton, Bristol, Brighton, Norwich. A special Tambourine Band also took part. The effect was now described as 'far more stupendous and magnificent than had ever been known before, and we see how by the grace of God, a vast force of music is spreading all over the country to bear on the wings of music the message of salvation'.[77]

Large-scale musical performance had now become an indispensable part of the meetings. Within several years the Songsters would become a regular feature. In 1894, attenders of the Second International Congress would experience a 'tornado of Halleluiah music' and impressive performances by the International Headquarters Band and the Staff Band of the Swedish Army.[78] Band performances reached new heights in 1895 with the appointment of the seventeen-

21 'The Great Welcome to the General'. The Salvation Army Meeting of 16 March 1896, as pictured in *The Warcry* of 21 March 1896.

year-old Alfred Punchard as conductor of the Chalk Farm Band, which he directed to great effect at the Palace meeting of that year.[79] The Palace had become the 'home' of the movement, with the General marking his return from a mission in South Africa with a meeting on 16 April 1896 with 20,000 people in attendance.

With the twentieth century, celebrations were on such a scale that several venues were taken together. The Third International Congress of 1904 involved the Royal Albert Hall, the Exeter Hall and an International Congress Hall, specially erected in the Strand, as well as the Crystal Palace. The meeting on 5 July attracted 70,000 people and seems to have exceeded all previous events, for the organization of the day used the facilities to the maximum: Centre Transept, Concert Room, Theatre, King's Rooms, various courts and parts of the nave, Upper and Lower Terrace, and the rest of the grounds, set aside for about six different locations. It consisted of a continuous sequence of events throughout the day, others taking place simultaneously in the grounds. Those attending were given the most detailed explanation of why they were there. The programme of events explained the sequence of events for the participants in the utmost detail, running to about six sides of the programme. The musical events punctuated the day and were of wide variety. They began with a brass band assembly and parade to the central transept from the Upper Terrace at 9.00. At 9.30 a special combination of vocal and instrumental music was offered by the International Staff Songsters in the concert hall. At 12.15 an open air brass festival was available in the Polo Ground. At 2.30 in the Transept, a gigantic brass band festival (at which the performance of the National Staff Band of the USA in cowboy costume caused a sensation): At 5.00 a grand march past of the troops and salute on the Lower Terrace, and, finally, at 7.30 in the Transept. a great festival of song by a choir and massed bands of orchestra of 4,000.[80]

Continuing associations with the Palace in the following years culminated in the First International Festival of 1914, which reflected the rapid spread of music in the international salvationist movement; singing brigades came from Switzerland, Finland, Holland, Denmark and Norway and coloured vocalists from America, as well as the International Staff Songsters, to perform in the Great Thanksgiving Service. Staff bands came from Sweden and Germany, and corps bands from the USA (Flint, Michigan) and Canada (Peterborough, Ontario).[81] The association continued after the reopening of the Palace in 1920, with celebrations of the Diamond Jubilee in 1925, the Founder's Celebration in 1929, and annual meetings in which band performance was a major feature, notably the Coventry Band in 1931 and 1932.[82] The final meeting was a 'Solemn Assembly' in 1934. A measure of the importance of the Palace to the Salvation Army is the fact that it is the only organization that returned there after the destruction of the building: 50,000 celebrated the centenary in the sports stadium in 1965.[83]

National and imperial festivals

By the turn of the century, the Crystal Palace had an unrivalled status as a venue for major meetings expressive of national pride. Significantly larger than the Albert Hall, it had as yet no rival in the metropolis. The growing sense of both imperial power and international relationship led to meetings in which the music of British composers associated with the Palace was conspicuous. One of the first of the new century was the Grand British and American Peace Concert, held on 5 July 1902 at 3.00 p.m. in commemoration of the South African War. It involved the Handel Festival Choir, the band of the Coldstream Guards and soloists including Albani, Santley, Clara Butt, David Bispham and Ella Russell, conducted by Frederick Cowen with Walter Hedgcock at the organ. The musical programme was framed with choral items featuring composers especially associated with the Palace: Sullivan and Cowen. It began with a selection from Sullivan's Te Deum with full forces, recalling in the programme, for its audience, the work's first performance at the Palace in 1872, in celebration of the recovery of the Prince of Wales from illness; Sullivan appears again with the chorus 'Song of Peace' ('sink and scatter, clouds of war'). Cowen's item was the Coronation March for the Handel Festival Orchestra and the Band of the Coldstream Guards, while the entire complement returned at the close for 'The Star Spangled Banner' and 'Rule, Britannia'; the seventeen other items explored the themes of war and peace through songs, arias and choruses from a wide range of sources: everything from Schumann's song 'The two Grenadiers' to Beethoven's chorus 'Creation's Hymn', and from American negro songs to English ballads, with Tchaikovsky's *1812* Overture as an orchestral contrast: pieces obviously chosen for their variety, familiarity and effectiveness.

But it was the British Empire which naturally inspired the largest events. Already in 1904, a South African Festival had taken place, in which Samuel Coleridge Taylor (who had strong links with the Palace) had conducted. The first Empire Festival was held in May–July 1910, an extended event of unparalleled scope which represented every corner of the Empire through exhibitions and displays, involving extensive prefabricated buildings in the grounds. The musical provision included nine weekly concerts, each devoted to a different country. The Empire Choir was of 400 voices, trained and conducted by Sir Charles Harriss.[84] In 1911 the festival ran from May to July, with Coleridge Taylor again conducting a South African concert. The programme of the final concert had much greater musical scope than the Anglo-American concert of 1902. It comprised thirteen items, choral and orchestral, with solo vocal participation. The repertory is entirely by native English composers, almost all of the present or preceding generation, and many associated with the Palace. New patriotic works are prominent, two given their first performances as winners in Harriss's Empire Chorus Competition: Percy Fletcher's patriotic chorus 'For Empire and King' and Cuthbert Harris's chorus 'For Empire and Motherland'. The older generation of composers was well represented: Elgar frames the programme with his arrangement of the National Anthem and the Epilogue and March 'It comes from the misty ages', providing the fourth item, and the solo and chorus 'Land of Hope and Glory' given by Clara Butt and the choir; Sullivan provided the Choral Epilogue from *The Golden Legend*, J. B. Dykes the recessional 'God of our Fathers', Parry the 'Orestes' March from *Hypatia*, and MacKenzie the 'Britannia' Overture, the latter composers conducting their own works: the programme was completed with an unnamed orchestral piece conducted by Henry Wood, and another solo from Clara Butt. Only a Purcell chorus 'Come if you dare' stood apart in style.

By the post-war years, imperial celebrations had shifted to the metropolis, chiefly to the newly built Wembley Exhibition Centre, which hosted the British Empire Exhibition in 1924–5.[85] At the Palace the imperial theme was tentatively continued in a competitive musical context through the British Empire Eisteddfod in September 1924 – though its poor organization shows waning interest, and the authorities refused the use of the Palace for the event in the following year. More characteristic of the post-war activities at the Palace were the festivals inspired by the newer movements towards social equality and international cooperation. Oldest of these was the socialist movement.

Already, on 22 August 1908, the twenty-first National Co-operative Festival[86] had used the Crystal Palace and concluded with a concert: The Great Adult Concert featured ten items for choir and orchestra. These also placed emphasis on new English composers, and suggests a relatively specialist musical direction, which was in the hands of Allen Gill. The music was almost entirely part songs and choruses. With older composers providing the anchor – Mendelssohn's 'O Great is the Depth' from *St Paul* as the final item and Prout's setting of Psalm 100 'O be joyful in the Lord' – the prevailing mood of the intervening items is pastoral and reflective, with two works by the young Thomas Dunhill and one by the assistant conductor Frank Idle representing the newer generation. The music was printed in a special programme published by the National Cooperative Festival Society. Meetings of associated socialist organizations would continue till the demise of the Palace, making full use of the grounds for the new 'music and movement' open air events.

The National Brotherhood Festival[87] of 12 June 1920 was a more elaborate event. The organization was by the London Brotherhood Federation, part of the Brotherhoods, Sisterhoods and Kindred Societies. Again, the organization published its own programme, with words and music in staff and *sol fa* notation. The event featured the Festival Choir and Organ. There were now fifteen items, though with heavier reliance on the traditional choral literature: Rossini ('To Thee, Great Lord' from *Moses*), Mendelssohn ('How lovely are the Messengers' from *St Paul*), Handel ('Sing unto the Lord' from *Judas Maccabeus*); Haydn ('O be joyful' from the 'First Mass'), the programme beginning with the hymn 'O God our Help in Ages Past'. But one still notes a pastoral element, suggesting a newer ethos of open air and recreation which the Palace offered to organizations reflecting the new spiritual aspirations of a suburban patronage, aspirations giving a new relevance to the Palace in its post-war life: English glees and part songs made wide demands on the singers, with some bold imitative subjects which would have stretched the *sol-fa*-ists beyond their familiar patterns. Again, new compositions are a part of the programme, on this occasion 'A Song of Peace', specially composed for the event by W. T. Deane to words by J. G. Whittier, was performed.

Though the life of the Palace was destroyed by the fire, such open-air social activities represent the link from the past to the post-war era. For the events held in the International Athletics Stadium (built on the area of the south west fountain basin) and elsewhere in the grounds, have made great use of music, whether for religious meetings, for pop festivals, or open-air symphony concerts: the vast numbers that attend these and the sporting events serve to retain for new generations the great sense of a focal and lofty location which was always the special quality of the unique site on the top of the Sydenham Hills.

APPENDIX I

The Handel Festivals selection day programmes and repertory, 1857–1923

SELECTION DAY PROGRAMMES FOR THE FESTIVALS OF
1859 AND 1862

1859: The Great [Second] Handel Commemoration Festival: 20, 22 and 24 June

(Novello, Rudersdorff, Dolby, Lemmens-Sherrington, Reeves, Belletti, Weiss, Formes, Costa, Brownsmith)

Part 1
Dettingen Te Deum

Part 2

Belshazzar:	Recit.	'Rejoice, my countrymen'
	Aria:	'Thus saith the Lord'
	Chorus:	'Sing, O ye Heavens'
Saul:	Chorus:	'Envy! eldest-born of Hell'
	Orchestra:	Dead March
Samson:	Chorus:	'Fix'd in his everlasting seat'
	Aria:	'Return, O God of Hosts'
	Chorus:	'To dust his glory they would tread'
	Aria:	'Let the bright Seraphim'
Judas Maccabeus:	Chorus:	'O father, whose almighty pow'r'
	Recit.:	'My arms, against this Gorgias I will go'
	Aria:	'Sound an alarm'
	Aria:	'From mighty Kings'
	Duet:	'O! never, never bow we down'
Joshua:	Trio and Chorus:	'See the conquering hero comes'

1862: First Great Triennial (Third) Handel Festival (23, 25, 27 June)

(Tietiens, Rudersdorff, Lemmens-Sherrington, Parepa, Sainton-Dolby, Reeves, Weiss, Belletti, Costa, Brownsmith)

215

Part 1
Dettingen Te Deum: Chorus: 'We praise thee, O God'
                                     'All the earth doth worship thee'

Samson: Aria: 'Return O God of Hosts'
                       Chorus: 'To dust his glory they would tread'
                       Aria: 'Let the bright Seraphim'
                       Chorus: 'Let their celestial concerts'
                       Aria: 'Honour and arms'

Judas Maccabeus: Chorus: 'Grant a leader bold and brave'
                       Aria: 'Sound an alarm'

Saul: Chorus: 'Envy, eldest born of hell'
                       Orchestra: Dead March

Ode for St Cecilia's Air: 'As from the power of sacred lays'
Day: Chorus: 'The dead shall live'

Part 2
Hercules: Chorus: 'Tyrants now no more shall dread'
Alexander's Feast: Aria: 'Revenge, Timotheus cries'
Solomon: Chorus: 'May no rash intruder' ('Nightingale
                                     Chorus')
Acis and Galatea: Aria: 'Hush ye pretty warbling choir'
                       Aria: 'Where shall I seek the charming fair'
                       Chorus: 'Happy we'
L'Allegro: Aria and Chorus: 'Haste ye, nymph'

Part 3
Samson: Overture
Deborah: Chorus (Double): 'Immortal Lord'
Solomon: Chorus (Double): 'From the censer curling rise'
                                       'Praise the Lord with harp and
                                       tongue'
                                       'Music spread thy voice around'
                                       'Draw the tear'
Joshua: Air: 'O! had I Jubal's lyre'
                       Chorus: 'See the conquering hero comes'

The Repertory of Selection Day 1859–1923

Works drawn upon (including entire instrumental works) in order of their
introduction, in the periods of Costa, Manns, Cowen and Wood.

1859–80 (Costa)

Dettingen Te Deum; *Belshazzar*; *Saul*; *Samson*; *Judas Maccabeus*; *Joshua*; *Ode for St Cecilia's Day*; *Hercules*; *Alexander's Feast*; *Solomon*; *Acis and Galatea*; *L'Allegro*; *Deborah*; Coronation Anthem 'Zadok the Priest'; *La Resurrezione*; *Theodora*; *Occasional Oratorio*; *Rinaldo*; *Semele*; Organ Concerto No. 1 in G minor (W. T. Best); *Orlando*; *Alcina*; *Ezio*; *Il Pensieroso*; *Athalia*; *Susanna*; *Utrecht Jubilate*; Organ Concerto No. 4 in F (W. T. Best): Coronation Anthem 'The King shall rejoice': Organ Concerto No. 2 in B♭ (W. T. Best); *Joseph and his Brethren*; First Grand Concerto for Orchestra in G

1883–1900 (Manns)

Concerto for Double Orchestra in F; Organ Concerto in B♭ (Set 2, No. 3, W. T. Best): *Serse*; *Atalanta*; Violin Sonata in A; Organ Concerto No. 7 in B♭ (W. T. Best): *Almira*; *Alexander Balus*; *Ottone*; *Deidamia*; *The Triumph of Time and Truth*; *Gloria Patri*; *Rodelinda*; *Water Music*; *Giustino*; *Berenice*; *Gulio Cesare*; Chandos Anthem ' O Come, let us sing'; 'Minuet in D' from Concerto Grosso in D; 'Concerto in D' (Oboe Concerto No. 6); Bourrée in D minor (Oboe Concerto No. 5), *Sosarme*

1903–23 (Cowen)

Organ Concerto No. 4 (with original choral ending); Concerto Grosso No. 1: *Alessandro*.

1926 (Wood)

Admeto; *Tamerlano*; *Roderigo*; *Lotario;* Organ Concerto No. 10 (M. Dupré); *Xerxes*

Personnel of the Saturday Orchestra

A periodic listing of four seasons during the years 1856–1900

1856–7

First Violin	Viola	Flute	Cornet
Van Heddeghem	Stehling	Svendsen	Miller
Gravenstein	Lutgen	Hartman	
Watson	Reynolds	(piccolo)	*French Horn*
Wedmeyer	Roelandt		Eckhoff
Schmidt		*Oboe*	Stock
Kleine	*Cello*	Peisel	Keevill
Vogel	Daubert	Adam	Tetley
	W. F. Reed		
Second Violin	R. Reed	*Clarinet*	*Trumpet*
Collins	Webb	Pape	Blight
Chenery		Van Ufeln	Jacobs
Forster	*Double Bass*		
Van Hamme	Progatzky	*Bassoon*	*Trombone*
Humfress	Tettenborn	Almenrader	Nabich
Shargold	Wenkle	Gunniss	Reisland
			Tull
		Bombardon	Healey
		Lentge	
		Kettle Drum	
		Thompson	

1866–7*

First Violin	*Viola*	*Flute*	*Cornet*
Van Heddeghem	Stehling	Alfred Wells	Levy
Watson	Reynolds		Duhem
Vogel			
	Cello	*Oboe*	*Horn*
Second Violin	W. Reed	Crozier	Eckhoff
Collins			
	Double Bass	*Clarinet*	*Timpani*
	Biehl	Pape	Thompson
		George Webb	
		Bassoon	
		Hutchins	

* Incomplete listing based on a reconstruction given in Saxe Wyndham, *August Manns*, p. 89.

1885–6

First Violins	Violas	Flutes	Horns
C. Jung [Princ.]	H. Krause [Princ.]	A. Wells	W. Naldrett
H. Celis	R. Foghill	A. Tootill	R. Keevil
V. Collins	W. H. Hann		C. Clinton
W. H. Eayres	T. Lawrence	*Piccolo*	A. Stock
O. Manns	E. Lockwood	J. Wilcocke	
A. W. Payne	T. Reynolds		*Cornets*
F. Ralph	A. Stehling	*Clarinets*	L. W. Hardy
E. Roberts	W. W. Waud	G. A. Clinton	S. West
V. Schmidt	S. R. Webb	G. J. Webb	
A. Streather	A. Wright		*Trumpets*
W. Sutton		*Bass Clarinet*	MacGrath
A. Viercek		E. Augarde	Neuzerling
F. M. Wallace			
W. Wolthers			

Second Violins	Cellos	Oboes	Trombones
A. Reynolds	R. H. Reed	W. M. Malsch	W. T. Hadfield
[Princ.]	[Princ.]	A. Peisel	C. Geard
O. H. Barrett	J. Boatwright		A. J. Phasey
E. Deane	J. A. Brousil	*Cor Anglais*	
J. Earnshaw	P. Kleine	H. Smith	*Tuba*
E. Frewin	R. Melling		C. Andrews
J. W. Gunniss	C. Ould	*Bassoons*	
H. Lewis	W. F. Reed	W. Wotton	*Timpani*
J. Perry	E. Trust	T. Wotton	J. Smith
G. Schnitzler	E. Woolhouse		
J. Spelman		*ContraFagotto*	*Percussion*
J. W. Thirlwall	*Contra Bassos*	J. Hawes	C. Henderson
M. Vogel	H. Progatzky		
J. Weaver	B. Biehl		*Bass Drum*
J. B. Zerbini	A. Collins		W. Wilmore
	W. J. Griffiths		
	S. J. Jackeway		*Harps*
	E. Ould		E. Lockwood
	W. J. Strugnell		E. Deane
	J. H. Waud		
	J. P. Waud		

1899–1900

First Violins	Violas	Flutes	Horns
A. V. Belinski	O. Manns jnr.	E. R. Hudson	C. Clinton
[Princ.]	[Princ.]	[Princ.]	[Princ.]
C. J. Aves	J. Cruft	F. Seidel	R. Spencer
J. W. Breeden	E. Deane	J. Hayes	L. Carvelli
T. Carrington	M. Dolovitch		J. Colton
V. Fawcett	H. Krause	*Piccolo*	
R. Gray	T. Lawrence	J. Hayes	*Cornets*
J. Hayes	K. A. Stehling		L. W. Hardy
H. Lewis	F. A. Wirth	*Oboes*	J. C. Scotts
O. Manns	A. Wright	A. Robert	
E. Messais	Another	A. Hullaert	*Trumpets*
J. E. Platt		F. Montara	W. Morrow
G. Schmidt			J. Solomon
W. Sutton			
E. Wheldon			

Second Violins	Cellos	Cor Anglais	Trombones
H. Renard	M. Belinski	E. Dubrucq	F. A. Clink
[Princ.]	[Princ.]		H. Fawcett
De Beriot Green	J. Boatwright	*Clarinets*	M. May
J. Earnshaw	W. J. Claxton	C. Fawcett	
A. Fossati	R. Melling	[Princ.]	*Bass Tuba*
J. W. Gunnis	R. Paggi	W. F. Gregory	F. McConnell
H. D. Haarnack	C. N. Price	H. G. Chapman	
F. Hachenberger	R. H. Reed		*Timpani*
J. E. Hall	H. Trust	*D Clarinet*	J. A. Smith
T. A. Kelley	E. Woolhouse	J. Egerton	
W. B. Norris			*Percussion*
J. Ricketts	*Double Basses*	*Bass Clarinet*	J. Farren
S. J. Waud	W. H. Stewart	J. Park	A. White
	A. Collins		J. Schroeder
	A. Cooke	*Bassoons*	A. Smith
	W. Griffiths	J. Anderson	
	N. Morel	[Princ.]	*Harps*
	C. Stewart	E. Dubrucq	H. Fernbacher
	W. R. Streather	G. A. Day	E. Deane
	W. A. Satch		
	J. P. Waud	*Contra Fagotto*	
		W. Davis	

Works by non-British composers given first British performances in the Saturday concerts of the Crystal Palace

A selective listing of principal symphonic works, overtures and other orchestral items, concertos and choral works (based on the programme specification 'First Performance in England' and/or the evidence of the programme notes or other sources). Original titles are retained. Where the numbering of a work differs from current usage (for example, that of the Dvořák Symphonies), the current numbering is given in square brackets. The list excludes single movements of composite works and first concert performances of works, or parts of works, previously premiered elsewhere in England. An asterisk denotes a world premiere.

SYMPHONIES

1855–60

Schumann	Symphony No. 4 in D minor, 16 Feb. 1856
Schubert	Symphony No. 9 in C, 5 April 1856

1860–9

Gade	Symphony No. 4 in B♭, 14 March 1863
Mehul	Symphony in G minor, 8 March 1862
Brahms	Serenade in D major (movements 4–6), 25 April 1863
Schubert	Symphony No. 8 in B minor, 6 April 1867
Mendelssohn	Symphony No. 5 in D, *Reformation*, 6 Dec. 1867
Schubert	Symphony in C minor, *Tragic* (MS), 28 Feb. 1868
Schubert	Symphony No. 6 in C (MS), 21 Nov. 1868

1870–9

Hiller	*Symphonic Fantasia*, op. 127, 10 Feb. 1872
Mozart	Symphony in E♭ (1773), 7 Dec. 1872
Schubert	Symphony No. 5 in B flat, 1 Feb. 1873
Hiller	*Dramatic Fantasia*, 22 March 1873

Raff	Symphony in E♭, *Leonore*, op. 117, 14 Nov. 1874
Raff	Symphony No. 4 in G minor, op. 167, 6 Nov. 1875
Liszt	Symphonic Poem *Mazeppa*, 9 Dec. 1876
Saint-Saëns	Symphonic Poem *La Jeunesse d'Hercule*, 20 Oct. 1877
Schubert	Symphony No. 2 in B♭ (MS), 20 Oct. 1877*
Brahms	Symphony No. 2 in D major, op. 73, 5 Oct. 1878
Raff	Symphony No. 8 in A, *The Voice of Spring*, 15 Nov. 1879

1880–9

Raff	Symphony No. 10 in E minor *In Summer Time* 9 Oct. 1880
Schubert	Symphony No. 1 in D (MS), 5 Feb. 1881*
Schubert	Symphony No. 3 in D, 19 Feb. 1881*
Smetana	Symphonic Poem *Vltava*, 5 March 1881
Bandini	Symphonic Poem *Eleanore*, 12 March 1881
Liszt	Symphonic Poem *The Ideal (Die Ideale)*, 16 April 1881
Rubinstein	Symphony No. 5 in G minor *Russian*, op. 107, 21 May 1881
Dvořák	Symphony in D major [No. 6], 22 April 1882
Berlioz	Grand Symphony *Funebre et Triomphale*, 3 June 1882
Sgambati	Symphony in D (MS), 10 June 1882
Raff	Symphony No. 6 in D minor, op. 189, 21 Oct. 1882
Smetana	Symphonic Poem *Vysehrad'* 11 Nov. 1882
Schubert	Symphony No. 7 in E (real. Barnett) 5 May, 1883
Raff	Symphony No. 10 in F minor *Zur Herbstzeit* 20 Oct. 1883
Dvořák	Symphony F [No 5] (revised version) 7 April 1888

1890–9

| Sinding | Symphony in D minor, op. 121, 18 April 1896 |

1900–

Strauss R	Symphony in F minor, op. 12, 28 Nov. 1896
Strauss R.	Symphonic Poem, 'Till Eulenspiegel', 21 March 1896
Strauss R.	Symphonic Poem 'Also Sprach Zarathustra', 6 March 1897

OVERTURES AND OTHER ORCHESTRAL ITEMS

1860–

Glinka	Overture *A Life for the Tsar*, 3 Nov. 1860
Schubert	Overture *Alfonso and Estrella*, 3 Nov. 1866
Schubert	Entr'actes in B minor and B♭ major from the incidental music to *Rosamunde*, 10 Nov. 1866

Schubert	Overture *In the Italian Style* in C, 1 Dec. 1866
Schubert	'Ballo' in B minor-G major; Ballet Air in G from *Rosamunde* music, 16 March 1867
Volkmann	*Festival* Overture in F, op. 50, 3 Oct. 1868
Reinecke	Entr'acte from the opera *King Manfred*, 10 Oct. 1868
Schubert	Overture *Die beiden Freunden von Salamanka*, 9 Oct. 1869
Schumann	Overture 'Hermann and Dorothea', 10 April, 1869

1870–9

Gade	Overture 'Michaelangelo' 12 March, 1870
Mendelssohn	Overture *Die einsame Insel* (original version of *The Hebrides Overture*), 14 Oct. 1871
Haydn	Overture in D, 18 Nov. 1871
Brahms	*St Antoni Variations* 7 March 1873
Wagner	*Faust Overture*, 10 Oct. 1874
Brahms	Hungarian Dances Nos. 1–3, 31 Oct. 1874
Bazzani	Overture 'Saul' 17 Feb. 1877
Rubinstein	Overture *Dmitri Donskoi*, 16 Jan. 1875
Volkmann	Overture *Richard III*, 30 Oct. 1875
Tchaikovsky	Overture *Romeo and Juliet*, 4 Nov. 1876
Saint-Saëns	*La Jeunesse d'Hercule*, 20 Oct. 1877
Liszt	*Rhapsodie Hongroise* No. 4 in d/G, 8 Dec. 1877
Saint-Saëns	Ballet Music from *Samson and Delilah*, 16 Nov. 1878
Dvořák	Slavonic Dances (first set), 15 Feb. 1879
Reinecke	*Festival* Overture in C, op. 146, 12 April 1879

1880–9

Svendsen	*Norwegian Rhapsody* No. 4, op. 22, 13 March 1880
Praeger	Symphonic Prelude to Byron's *Manfred*, 17 April 1880
Svendsen	*The Carnaval at Paris*, op. 9, 16 Oct. 1880
Massenet	Orchestral Movements *La Vierge*, 30 Oct. 1880
Mozart	Serenade *Eine kleine Nachtmusik*, 6 Nov. 1880
Dvořák	Slavonic Dances (second set), 27 March 1880
Brahms	*Academic Festival Overture* and *Tragic Overture*, 30 April 1881
Wagner	'Carfreitags-Zauber' from *Parsifal*, 3 March 1883
Dvořák	*Notturno* for strings, 22 March 1884
Dvořák	*Scherzo Capriccioso*, 22 March 1884
Dvořák	Overture *Mein Heim*, 12 May 1883
Saint-Saëns	Ballet 'Fetes Populaires' from *Henry VIII*, 16 Feb. 1884
Smetana	*Lustspiel* (Comedy Overture), 18 Oct. 1884
Dvořák	Overture *In Nature's Realm*, 24 March 1885

Tchaikovsky *Capriccio Italien* 5 Dec. 1885
Delibes   Scènes de Ballet from *Le Roi s'amuse*, 20 Feb. 1886

1890–

Rimsky-Korsakoff 'Suite of Characteristic Dances' from *Mlada*,
                  10 Oct. 1896
Rimsky-Korsakoff *Capriccio Espagnole*, 8 April 1899
Berlioz   Overture *Rob Roy*, 24 Feb. 1900

CONCERTOS AND CONCERT PIECES

1860–

Piatti   Cello Concerto (Piatti), 20 Nov. 1869*

1870

Brahms   Piano Concerto in D minor (Baglehole), 9 March 1872
Rubinstein   Concerto in D minor (Hartvigson), 16 Nov. 1872
Piatti   Violin Concerto No. 2 (Piatti), 18 Jan. 1873
Grieg   Piano Concerto in A minor (Dannreuther), 18 April 1874
Tchaikovsky   Piano Concerto in B♭ minor (Dannreuther)
              11 March 1876
Raff   Cello Concerto (Piatti), 1 April 1876
Raff   Violin Concerto in B minor (Wilhelmj), 8 Dec. 1877
Lalo   Violin Concerto *Symphonie Espagnole*, op. 21 (Sarasate),
              30 March 1878
Brassin   Piano Concerto No. 1 in F, op. 22 (Brassin), 9 Nov. 1878
Rheinberger   Piano Concerto in A♭, op. 94 (Halle), 23 Nov. 1878
Brahms   Violin Concerto in D (Joachim), 22 Feb. 1879
Scharwenka   Piano Concerto in B♭ minor (Scharwenka),
              1 March, 1879
Saint-Saëns   Piano Concerto No. 3 in E♭, 6 Dec. 1879

1880

Goetz   Violin Concerto (MS) (Hermann), 13 March 1880
Bonawitz   Piano Concerto in A minor (Bonawitz), 30 Oct. 1880
Saint-Saëns   Cello Concerto (Hollmann), 27 Nov. 1880
Gernsheim   Violin Concerto in D (Sauret), 18 Dec. 1880
Brüll   Piano Concerto No.1 (Brüll), 12 Feb. 1881
Reinecke   *Concertstück* in G minor for piano and orchestra (Hopekirk),
              19 Feb. 1881
Rufer P.   Violin Concerto in D, op. 33 (Mayer), 16 April 1881

Brahms	Piano Concerto No. 2 in B♭ (Beringer), 14 Oct. 1882
Dvořák	Piano Concerto (Beringer), 13 Oct. 1883
Dupont	Piano Concerto in F minor (Frickenhaus), 15 Dec. 1883
Mozart	Concerto No. 5 in A (Joachim), 15 March 1884
Gade	Violin Concerto in D, op. 56, (Dunn), 13 Nov. 1886
Dvořák	Violin Concerto (Ondříček), 11 Feb. 1888

1890

| Rosenhain | Piano Concerto in D minor (Davies), 15 Feb. 1890 |
| Klengel | Cello Concerto No. 3 (Klengel), 25 Nov. 1893 |

1900

| Macdowell | Piano Concerto No. 2 in D minor, 7 April 1900 |
| Becker | Cello Concerto No. 3 in A, 9 March 1901 |

CHORAL AND DRAMATIC WORKS

1860–1890

Schubert	Offertorium *Salve Regina*, 1 Dec. 1866
Schubert	*The Song of Miriam* (orch. Lachner), 14 Nov. 1868
Schumann	*Festival Overture* for chorus and orchestra op. 123, 15 April 1876
Brahms	Cantata *Rinaldo*, 15 April 1876
Joachim	Scena 'Marfa' from Schiller's *Demetrius* for chorus and orchestra, 6 April 1878
Brahms	*Liebeslieder Waltzes* (2nd set), 5 May 1878
Verdi	*Ave Maria* for soprano and strings, 16 Oct. 1880
Rubinstein	*The Tower of Babel*, 11 June 1881
Berlioz	Lyrical Monodrama *Lelio, or The Return to Life* with chorus and solos, 29 Oct. 1881
Berlioz	*Grand Messe des Morts* for chorus and orchestra, 26 March 1883
Berlioz	Te Deum for chorus and orchestra, 18 April 1885
Berlioz	*Tristia* for chorus and orchestra: chorus No. 2
Dvořák	Mass in D for chorus and orchestra, 11 March 1893

Works by British composers given first performances in the Saturday concerts of the Crystal Palace

A selective listing of symphonic works, overtures and other orchestral items, concertos and concert pieces and choral works (based on the programme specification 'First performance in England' and/or the evidence of the programme notes or other sources).

SYMPHONIES AND SYMPHONIC WORKS

1860–9

Sullivan A.   Symphony in E (MS), 10 March 1866

1870–9

Gadsby H.   Symphony No. 2 in A (Larghetto and scherzo), 11 Feb. 1871

Holmes H.   Symphony No 1 in A (MS), 24 Feb. 1872

Wingham T.   Symphony No 2 in B♭ (MS), 23 March 1872

Cowen F. H.   Symphony No 2 in F (MS), 5 April 1873

Prout E.   Symphony No 1 in C, 28 Feb. 1874

Holmes A.   *Symphonie Dramatique* No. 1 in E 'Jeanne d'Arc', 27 Feb. 1875

Prout E.   Symphony in G minor, 1 Dec. 1877

1880–9

Praeger F.   Symphonic Prelude to Byron's *Manfred*, 17 April 1880

Wuerst R.   Serenade for Strings, 12 Nov. 1881

Leslie H.   Symphony in D minor, *Chivalry*, 17 Dec. 1881

Wingham T.   Symphony No 4 in D (MS), 28 April 1883

Prout E.   Symphony No 4 in D, 27 Feb. 1887

Bennett G. J.   Serenade in Symphonic Form, 12 March 1887

Gadsby H.	Festal Symphony in D (MS), 3 Nov. 1888
Praeger F.	Symphonic Prelude *Life and Love, Battle and Victory*, 7 Nov. 1888
Stanford C. V.	Symphony No 4 in F, 23 Feb. 1889
Cliffe F.	Symphony in C minor, 20 April 1889

1890–9

Smyth E.	Serenade, 26 April 1890
German E.	Symphony No. 2 in E, 13 Dec. 1890
Wallace W.	Symphonic Poem *The Passing of Beatrice*, 26 Nov. 1892
Pringle G.	Ballad *Durand*, 14 Oct. 1893
Davies H. Walford	Symphony No. 1 in D, 19 Oct. 1895
Wallace W.	Symphonic Poem *Amboss oder Hammer*, 17 Oct. 1896
Bedford H.	Symphonic Prologue *Kit Marlowe*, 19 March 1898
Wallace W.	Symphonic Poem *Sister Helen*, 25 Feb. 1899
Bell W. H.	Symphonic Prologue to Chaucer's *Canterbury Tales*, 30 April 1898
Bell W. H.	Symphonic Poem *The Pardoner's Tale*, 5 April 1899

1900

Bell W. H.	Symphony, *Walt Whitman*, 10 March 1900
Holbrooke J.	Symphonic Poem *The Raven*, 3 March 1900

OVERTURES AND OTHER ORCHESTRAL ITEMS

1860

Cusins W. H.	Scherzo 'Queen Mab', 21 Feb. 1863
Sullivan A.	Overture *The Sapphire Necklace* (revised version), 20 Oct. 1866

1870–9

Smith A. M.	Overture *Endymion* (MS), 18 Nov. 1871
Smart H.	Overture *King Rene's Daughter*, 23 Nov. 1872
Gadsby H.	Overture *Andromeda* (MS), 22 Feb. 1873
Pierson H. H.	Overture *As you like it*, 17 Jan. 1874
Cusins W. H.	Concert Overture *Love's Labour's Lost*, 9 Oct. 1875
Corder F.	Masque *The Triumph of Spring*, 8 Feb. 1879
Parry C. H. H.	Overture *Guillaume de Cabestanh, Troubadour*, 15 March 1879
Heap C. S.	Concert Overture, 22 Nov. 1879

1880–9

Smith A. M.	Overture *Jason*, 14 May 1881
Cowen F. H.	Characteristic Overture in C *Niagra*, 22 Oct. 1881
Cowen F. H.	Suite *In the Olden Time*, 17 March 1883
Thomas H.	Overture *Mountain, Lake and Moorland*, 17 Nov. 1883
Couldery C.	Concert Overture *Richard I*, 14 Feb. 1885
Corder F.	Overture in E minor, *Prospero*, 24 Oct. 1885
Bennett G. J.	Overture in B *Jugendträume*, 8 Oct. 1887
MacCunn H.	Overture *The Land of the Mountain and Flood*, 5 Nov. 1887
MacCunn H.	Overture *The Dowie Dens of Yarrow*, 13 Oct. 1888

1890

Couldery C. H.	*St Cecilia* for Organ, Harp, Violin and Orchestra
Couldery C. H.	Concert Overture *To the Memory of a Hero*, 8 Feb. 1890
Smyth E. M.	Overture *Anthony and Cleopatra*, 18 Oct. 1890
Drysdale L.	Concert Overture *Tam O'Shanter*, 24 Oct. 1891
German E.	Gipsy Suite, 20 Feb. 1892
Jones A. Barclay	Concert Overture in C minor, 22 Oct. 1892
Marshall Hall.	Concert Overture, 4 March 1893
Wallace V.	Orchestral Prelude *The Eumenides of Aeschylus*, 21 Oct. 1893
Couldery C. H.	Cradle Song for orchestra, 18 Nov. 1893
Hiles H.	Overture *Youth*, 28 Oct. 1893
Wallace W.	Overture *In Praise of Scottish Poesie*, 17 Nov. 1894
Macpherson S.	*Idyll: A Summer Day Dream*, 8 Dec. 1894
Marshall Hall	*An Idyll* for Orchestra, 25 Feb. 1895
D'Albert E.	Vorspiel *Der Rubin*, 22 Feb. 1896
Bunning H.	*Village Suite*, 4 April 1896
MacCunn. H.	Suite for Orchestra *Highland Memories, op. 30*, 13 March 1897
German E.	Suite *Romeo and Juliet*, 10 April 1897
Bunning H.	Dramatic Overture *Mistral*, 24 April 1897
Macfarren W.	Concert Overture *Othello* (MS), 10 Oct. 1897
Elgar E.	Three Dances *From The Bavarian Highlands*, 23 Oct. 1897
Vincent C.	Overture *The Wreck of the Hesperus*, 13 Nov. 1897
German E.	*Fantasia on March Themes* (revised version), 8 Oct. 1898
Couldery C. H.	*Trumpet Fantasia*, 15 Oct. 1898
Maclean C.	*Pageant March*, 22 Oct. 1898
Simpson F. J.	Concert Overture *Robert Bruce*, 2 Nov. 1898
Matras M.	*Esquisses Polonaises*, 10 Dec. 1898
Steggall R.	Suite No 1 in E, 19 April 1899

Appendix 3b

CONCERTOS, CONCERT PIECES ETC

1860–9

Sullivan A.   Cello Concerto (Piatti), 24 Nov. 1866

1870–9

Prout E.   Organ Concerto in E minor (Stainer), 19 Oct. 1872
Holmes H.   Concertino di bravura (Holmes), 18 Oct. 1873
Gadsby H.   Organ Concerto in F (MS), 21 Jan. 1874
Macfarren G. A.   Violin Concerto (MS), 3 April 1875
Gadsby H.   Violin Concerto in F (H. Holmes), 11 Dec. 1875

1880–9

Parry C. H.   Piano Concerto in F♯ (Dannreuther), 3 April 1880

1890–9

Bright D.   Piano Concerto (Bright), 28 March 1891
Ames J. C.   Piano Concerto in C minor, 13 April 1889

CHORAL AND DRAMATIC WORKS

1850–9

Sullivan A.   Music to Shakespeare's *The Tempest* (MS), 5 April 1862
Sullivan A.   *Festival Te Deum*, 1 March, 1873 (first concert performance of the work written for the Festival for the Recovery of the Prince of Wales at the Crystal Palace on 1 May 1872)
Holmes A.   Dramatic Symphony *Jeanne d'Arc* 27 Feb. 1875
Prout E.   Magnificat for solo, chorus and orchestra. 15 Jan. 1876
Gadsby.   Cantata *Columbus* for tenor and male voice chorus, 19 March 1881
MacCunn H.   Ballad *Lord Ullin's Daughter*, 18 Feb. 1888
MacCunn H.   *The Lay of the Last Minstrel*, op. 7, 16 Feb. 1889
Bunning H.   Scena *Ludovico il Moro* for baritone and orchestra, 27 Feb. 1892
Lidgley C. A.   Ballad *A Day Dream*, 15 Oct. 1892
Arnott A. D.   *Young Lochinvar* Ballad for Orchestra and chorus, 16 March 1895

Staged works with music performed in the theatre

A representative listing of operas, operettas, comic operas and vaudevilles performed from 1869–99, based on the information given in the advertisements in the programmes of the Saturday Concerts, supplemented by information from K. Ganzl, *British Musical Theatre*, 2 vols., London (Macmillan), 1986.

1869–70 *OPERA IN ENGLISH* (UNNAMED CRYSTAL PALACE COMPANY, GEORGE PERREN; CRYSTAL PALACE ORCHESTRA, MANNS; OCT.–DEC. 1869)

Balfe	*The Rose of Castile*
Dibdin	*The Quaker*; *The Waterman*
Wallace	*Maritana*
Verdi	*Il Trovatore* (*'The Gipsy's Vengeance'*)
Bellini	*La Sonnambula*
Wallace	*Lurline*

1870–1 *OPERA IN ENGLISH* (UNNAMED CRYSTAL PALACE COMPANY, DIRECTED BY GEORGE PERREN; CRYSTAL PALACE ORCHESTRA. MANNS: OCT.–DEC. 1870)

Barnett	*The Mountain Sylph*
Weber	*Der Freischütz*
Auber	*Le Domino Noir*
Beethoven	*Fidelio*
Offenbach	*The Rose of Auvergne*
Offenbach	*The Forester's Daughter*
Wallace	*Maritana*
Balfe	*The Bohemian Girl*
Verdi	*Il Trovatore*
Wallace	*Lurline*
Flotow	*Martha*

Auber   *Fra Diavolo*
Donizetti   *Lucia di Lammermoor*
Weber   *Der Freischütz*

CRYSTAL PALACE OPERAS IN ENGLISH (DIRECTED BY
JOHN RUSSELL; CRYSTAL PALACE ORCHESTRA AND CHORUS,
MANNS; 5 MARCH 1870)

Offenbach   *Barbe Bleue*

CRYSTAL PALACE SHILLING OPERAS (JOHN RUSSELL; CRYSTAL
PALACE ORCHESTRA AND CHORUS, MANNS; 13 APRIL 1871)

Benedict   *The Lily of Killarney*
Bellini   *La Sonnambula*

1872–3   CRYSTAL PALACE OPERAS IN ENGLISH (GEORGE
PERREN, WITH B. COLE; CRYSTAL PALACE ORCHESTRA AND
CHORUS, MANNS; NOV.–DEC. 1872)

Auber   *Crown Diamonds*
Macfarren   *Robin Hood*
Deffell   *The Corsair*

(31 March–9 June)

Auber   *Crown Diamonds*
Balfe   *The Rose of Castile*
Wallace   *Lurline*
Macfarren   *Robin Hood*
Mozart   *Don Giovanni*
Balfe   *Satanella*

1873–4   CRYSTAL PALACE OPERAS IN ENGLISH (GEORGE PERREN;
CRYSTAL PALACE ORCHESTRA, MANNS; OCT.–DEC. 1873)

Donizetti   *The Daughter of the Regiment*
Benedict   *The Lily of Killarney*
Weber   *Der Freischütz*
Verdi   *Il Trovatore*
Donizetti   *Lucretia Borgia*
Mozart   *Don Giovanni*

CRYSTAL PALACE OPERAS IN ENGLISH (GEORGE PERREN; CRYSTAL
PALACE ORCHESTRA, MANNS; MARCH–APRIL 1874)

Benedict	*The Lily of Killarney*
Wallace	*Maritana*
Tamplin	*Fleurette*
Suppé	*Galatea*

CRYSTAL PALACE THEATRE COMPANY (I. WILKINSON;
3 MARCH 1874)

Shakespeare/Locke: *Macbeth* (incidental music)

1875–6   CRYSTAL PALACE OPERAS IN ENGLISH (VERNON RIGBY;
CRYSTAL PALACE ORCHESTRA, MANNS; MAY–JUNE 1876)

Verdi	*Un Ballo in Maschera*
Auber	*Le Domino Noir*
Auber	*Fra Diavolo*
Balfe	*The Rose of Castile*

CRYSTAL PALACE OPERAS IN ENGLISH; SUMMER SERIES (CRYSTAL
PALACE ORCHESTRA AND CHORUS, MANNS; JUNE–JULY 1876)

Mozart	*Don Giovanni*
Balfe	*The Bohemian Girl*
Weber	*Der Freischütz*
Rossini	*Il Barbiere di Seviglia*
Auber	*Crown Diamonds*
Balfe	*Satanella*
Balfe	*The Rose of Castile*

1876–7   CRYSTAL PALACE OPERAS IN ENGLISH
(RICHARD TEMPLE, WITH R. HERSEE; CRYSTAL PALACE
ORCHESTRA, MANNS; APRIL 1876)

Cellier	*The Spectre Knight*
Sullivan/Burnand	*Cox and Box*
Shakespeare/Sullivan	'*The Merry Wives of Windsor* (incidental music)

AUGUSTUS HARRIS COMPANY (AUGUSTUS HARRIS; CRYSTAL
PALACE ORCHESTRA, MANNS; 12 DEC. 1876)

Sophocles/Mendelssohn   *Antigone* (incidental music)

1877–8 *CRYSTAL PALACE OPERAS IN ENGLISH*
(RICHARD TEMPLE; CRYSTAL PALACE ORCHESTRA, A. CELLIER OR
MANNS)

Cimarosa	*Il Matrimonio segreto*

1878–9 *CARL ROSA COMPANY* (CARL ROSA; MARCH–APRIL 1879)

Nicolai	*The Merry Wives of Windsor* (English text adapted from Mosenthal's version)
Wagner	*The Flying Dutchman*

CRYSTAL PALACE OPERAS IN ENGLISH (RICHARD TEMPLE, WITH
ROSE HERSEE; CRYSTAL PALACE ORCHESTRA, CELLIER)

Cimarosa	*Il matrimonio segreto*
Donizetti	*Don Pasquale*

ROYAL ITALIAN OPERA COMPANY (GYE; ORCHESTRA OF THE
ROYAL OPERA, VILANESI; MAY–JUNE 1879)

Mozart	*Don Giovanni*
Auber	*Fra Diavolo*
Flotow	*Martha*

1879–80 *HACKNEY CHORAL SOCIETY* (CRYSTAL PALACE
ORCHESTRA, PROUT; 20 DEC. 1879)

Prout	Dramatic Cantata *Hereward*

JOHN HOLLINGSHEAD COMPANY (JOHN HOLLINGSHEAD; CRYSTAL
PALACE ORCHESTRA/MANNS; 26 FEB. 1880)

Offenbach	*The Rose of Auvergne*
Lecocq	*The Rajah of Mysore*

1880–81 *THE ALICE BARTH COMIC OPERA COMPANY*
(ALICE BARTH; 18 OCT. 1880)

Mass	*Les Noces de Jeanette* (*The Runaway Match* tr. Grist)
Gounod	*The Garden Scene* from *Faust.*

1881–2 *THE GAIETY BURLESQUE DRAMAS* (MEYER LUTZ;
CRYSTAL PALACE ORCHESTRA, MANNS)

Lutz	*The Forty Thieves*

THE NATIONAL COMIC OPERA (MAY-JUNE 1882)

Stephens/Solomon   *Billie Taylor*

1882–3   ENGLISH OPERAS BY THE CARL ROSA COMPANY
(CRYSTAL PALACE ORCHESTRA, JOHN PEW; 21, 23 MARCH 1883)

Thomas   *Mignon*
Balfe   *The Bohemian Girl*

THE BALLAD OPERATIC COMPANY (ALICE BARTH; MAY 1883)

Planché   *The Loan of a Lover*
Corder   *A Storm in a Teacup*

1886–7   THE COMEDY THEATRE COMPANY (20 SEPT. 1886)

Bellamy/Pauston   *Erminee* (Comic Opera)

1887–8   THE GEORGE FOX COMPANY (GEORGE FOX; 20 SEPT. 1887)

Fox   *Macaire*
Parker/Hogarth *Gipsy Gabriel*

1888–9   CRYSTAL PALACE COMIC OPERAS (EMILY SOLDENE; OCT. 1888)

LeCocq   *La Fille de Madame Angot*
Offenbach   *Genevieve de Brabant*
Suppé   *Boccaccio*

THE PRINCE OF WALES COMPANY (NOV. 1888)

Stephenson/Cellier   *Dorothy*

THE ROYALTY THEATRE COMPANY (28 MAY 1889)

Broad/Parker   *Mignonette*

1889–90   THE LYRIC THEATRE COMPANY (J. H. LESLIE; 6 MARCH 1890)

Stephens   *The Red Hussar*

1890–1   *COVENT GARDEN OPERA COMPANY*

Verdi   *Il Trovatore*

1891–2   *THE ROYAL ITALIAN OPERA COMPANY* (SHAFTESBURY
THEATRE, LAGO; 3 NOV. 1891)

Mascagni   *Cavaliera Rusticana*

The D'Oyly Carte Company (Manns; 28 July 1892)

Sullivan   *The Mikado, Iolanthe*

1894–5   *THE DRURY LANE COMPANY* (A. HARRIS; CRYSTAL
PALACE ORCHESTRA, MANNS)

Mascagni   *Cavaliera Rusticana*
Leoncavallo *Pagliacci*

1895–6   *THE SAVOY THEATRE COMPANY* (CARTE;
CRYSTAL PALACE ORCHESTRA, MANNS; 28 NOV. 1895)

Sullivan   *The Mikado*

The Royal Court Theatre Company (16 Dec. 1895)

Humperdinck: *The Children of the King* (*Königskinder*)

1899   *THE REPERTORY OPERA COMPANY* (D'OYLY CARTE)

Sullivan   *The Pirates of Penzance*
Sullivan   *Trial by Jury*

APPENDIX 5

The Brass Band Championships

The Winning Bands

	The National Contest	The Sydenham Amateur Contest
1860	Black Dyke Mills	Cyfarthfa
1861	Saltaire	Marriner's, Keighley
1862	Chesterfield Rifle Corps	–
1863	Blandford	–

THE NATIONAL BRASS BAND CHAMPIONSHIPS 1900-36

Winning Bands and Set Pieces

1900	Denton Original, *Gems from Sullivan's Operas No. 1* (arr. J. Ord Hume)
1901	Lee Mount, *Gems from Sullivan's Operas No. 3* (arr. J. Ord Hume)
1902	Black Dyke Mills, *Hiawatha* (Coleridge Taylor, arr. C.Godfrey)
1903	Bess O' the Barn', *Die Meistersinger* (Wagner, arr. Shipley Douglas)
1904	Hebburn Colliery, *Gems of Mendelssohn* (arr. C.Godfrey)
1905	Irwell Springs, *Roland à Roncervaux* (Auguste Mermet)
1906	Wingates Temperance, *Gems of Chopin* (arr. W. Short)
1907	Wingates Temperance, *Gems of Schumann* (arr. W.Short)
1908	Irwell Springs, *Rienzi* (Wagner, arr. S. Cope)
1909	Shaw, Overture, *The Flying Dutchman* (Wagner)
1910	Foden's Motor Works, *Gems of Schubert* (arr.W. Rimmer)
1911	Crossfields (Perfection) Soap Works, *Les Huguenots* (Meyerbeer, arr. Rimmer)
1912	St Hilda Colliery, Overture, *William Tell* (Rossini)
1913	Irwell Springs, *Labour and Love* (Percy Fletcher)
1914–19	No Festivals
1920	St Hilda Colliery, *Coriolanus* (Cyril Jenkins)
1921	St Hilda Colliery, *Life Divine* (Cyril Jenkins)
1922	Horwich R M I, *Freedom* (Hubert Bath)

1923   Luton Red Cross, *Oliver Cromwell* (Henry Geehl)
1924   St Hilda Colliery, *On the Cornish Coast* (Henry Geehl)
1925   Marsden Colliery, *Joan of Arc* (Denis Wright)
1926   St Hilda Colliery, *An Epic Symphony* (Percy Fletcher)
1927   Carlisle St Stephens, *The White Rider* (Denis Wright)
1928   Black Dyke Mills, *A Moorside Suite* (Gustav Holst)
1929   Carlisle St Stephens, *Victory* (Cyril Jenkins)
1930   Foden's Motor Works, *Severn Suite* (Elgar)
1931   Wingate's Temperance, *Honour and Glory* (Hubert Bath)
1932   Foden's Motor Works, *A Downland Suite* (John Ireland)
1933   Foden's Motor Works, *Prometheus Unbound* (Granville Bantock)
1934   Foden's Motor Works, *Comedy Overture* (John Ireland)
1935   Munn and Felton's Works, *Pride of Race* (Kenneth A.Wright)
1936   Foden's Motor Works, *Kenilworth* (Arthur Bliss)

Notes

1 In 1866 a massive fire destroyed the north transept and wing, which were never replaced; accordingly, only the earlier illustrations show the building in its original form. The glow of the 1936 fire was reputedly visible on the south coast.

2 A. R. Warwick, *The Phoenix Suburb*, London (Blue Boar Press), 1972, p. 242.

3 Since the 1980s, systematic restoration of the stonework of the terraces has taken place, and the previous 'closed grounds' adjacent to the site of the building opened to the public. A museum now exists in the building of the former School of Engineering on Anerley Hill, created and staffed by the Crystal Palace Foundation, which publishes a regular newsletter and magazine documenting the history of the Palace, particularly in the twentieth century, through the recording of personal recollections (*Crystal Palace Matters*, London, Crystal Palace Foundation, 1984–90, and *New Crystal Palace Matters*, 1990–).

4 The nickname 'Crystal Palace' was first used in *Punch* (vol. 20, 1851, p. 111) in describing the building.

5 Because of the destruction, Baird's experiments (which took place in the South Tower) went to Alexandra Palace, which became the first site of British (BBC) transmission. Appropriately, however, the Crystal Palace north end is now the site of the BBC and ITV transmitters.

6 It was, for example, reported in *The Musical Times* vol. 77 no. 1126 (December, 1936), p. 1122 that MSS material of Handel was reputed to be among the losses.

7 The building and grounds were put up for auction in 1911 and a major descriptive catalogue describing the facilities at that time produced: *The Crystal Palace, Sydenham*, [Auction Catalogue], London, 1911. The Palace was then purchased for the nation in 1912.

8 The building initiated a fashion for such prefabricated structures in London and elsewhere, and many proposals were aired; the Alexandra Palace (1873) at Wood Green, North London, was, however, the only comparably hill-sited structure. Though it was smaller and of different design and appearance, it was just as vulnerable to damage by fire: first

in 1873, almost immediately after its opening, when the organ was destroyed, and again in 1944, as well as 1985, when the building was gutted and the organ again destroyed. Though the original organ in the Alexandra Palace was a particularly fine instrument by Willis (extended from the instrument built for the 1862 Exhibition, with J. Frederick Archer as its first organist), the subsequent performing history of the Palace was very mixed, though its musical life included some interesting initiatives. (See P. A. Scholes, ed., *The Mirror of Music*, 2 vols., London (Novello and Oxford University Press), pp. 199–200 and p. 32.

1   THE CRYSTAL PALACE AT HYDE PARK

1 For the pre-history of the Great Exhibition, see Patrick Beaver, *The Crystal Palace*, Chichester (Philimore), p. 11.
2 For the rejected designs, see Beaver, ibid., pp. 10–11.
3 See G. F. Chadwick, *The Works of Sir Joseph Paxton*, London (Architectural Press), 1981.
4 See A. Bird, *Paxton's Palace*, London (Cassell), 1976.
5 Great Exhibition, 1851: *Official Descriptive and Illustrative Catalogue*, 3 vols., and supp. vol., London, 1851.
6 The musical content of the Catalogue has been reprinted as *Musical Instruments in the 1851 Exhibition: a transcription of the entries of musical interest from the Official Illustrated Catalogue of the Great Exhibition of the Art and Industry of all Nations, with additional material from contemporary sources*, ed. P. and A. Mactaggart, Welwyn, Herts (Mac and Me Ltd), 1986.
7 See H. Macdonald, *Berlioz*, London (Dent), p. 53.
8 The recitals on Willis's largest organ were a particular attraction. See Scholes, ed., *The Mirror of Music*, vol. 2, p. 583.
9 See Beaver, *Crystal Palace*, pp. 33–46.
10 Ibid., pp. 35–42.
11 Ibid., p. 65.

2   THE CRYSTAL PALACE AT SYDENHAM

1 For the description and illustration of the building of the Sydenham Palace, see Beaver, *Crystal Palace*, pp. 69–104.
2 Samuel Phillips, *Guide to the Crystal Palace and Park*, London (Bradbury and Evans), 1854, p. 39.
3 The aquarium was claimed as the largest in the world at its construction.
4 The football stadium was created from one of the fountain basins of the original garden design, and was subsequently developed into the modern athletics stadium.
5 The stations and railways are discussed in C. T. Goode, *To the Crystal Palace*, Bracknell (Forge Books), 1984.
6 See Bibliography for studies of Sir George Grove.

7 C. L. Graves, *The Life of Sir George Grove*, London (Macmillan), 1903, pp. 45–7.
8 See Phillips, *Crystal Palace and Park*, p. 134.
9 Ibid.
10 For the role of the Palace band, see pp. 67–8, 74, 255, n. 4.
11 It is very clear from Bowley's account of the opening cermony that the Society felt that the musical provision had been inadequate and that the new, larger Palace was seen as the opportunity for larger scale performance, and, by implication, beyond: 'It was desired that music *should* take its proper place at the People's Palace. *It has done so!* Let us be careful that, in future times, on future occasions, it is not permitted to be *secondary*.' See: R. Bowley, *An Account of the Arrangements for the Opening of the Crystal Palace at Sydenham* (MS), London, Royal College of Music. See also p. 117 for subsequent attitudes to music at the Palace.
12 Ibid.
13 Graves, *Life of Sir George Grove*, p. 46.
14 Bowley, *Account of the Arrangements*.
15 See pp. 96–7.

3 THE HANDEL FESTIVALS, 1857–1926

1 These centenary and sesquicentenary celebrations were dated on the supposition that Handel was born on 23 February 1684, a mistake arising from calculation according to the old-style calendar, in which the year began on 25 March; this existed in England until 1752 when it was replaced by the new-style (Gregorian) calendar. Confusion also surrounded the date of Handel's death. See Grove's *Dictionary of Music and Musicians* (2nd edn), ed. J. A. Fuller Maitland, London (Macmillan) 1903, vol. 3, p. 290. The issues were clarified for Crystal Palace audiences in the programme of the 1862 festival. Interim large-scale performances were held in Westminster Abbey in the years 1784, –85, –86, –87, –91: ibid., vol. 2, p. 290. In 1834, a festival of oratorios by Handel was held there with royal and aristocratic patronage.
2 The major new choral festivals of the early nineteenth century were: Liverpool (in modern form from 1823); Manchester (1828, 1836); Birmingham (in modern form, 1834); Bradford (1853); Leeds (1858). See ibid., entries for towns and 'British Festivals' (vol. 3, p. 28).
3 The early history of the Society is given in: R. K. Bowley, *The Sacred Harmonic Society, A Thirty-Five Years' Retrospect*, London (Sacred Harmonic Society), 1867, the year of its 500th performance; also the article 'Sacred Harmonic Society' in Grove's Dictionary, vol. 4, p. 201.
4 See Scholes *The Mirror of Music*, vol. 1, p. 66, for the use of the term 'oratorio' in the early years of the Society. Early performances were never complete in the later sense. The first popular vocal score of *Messiah* (Novello, 1846) indicates Nos. 23, 36 and 48 as 'usually

omitted', and Nos. 49–52 as 'sometimes omitted', suggesting a general pre-existent tradition, that continued, at least in the Novello score used at the Crystal Palace. This was identical with the programme text, until the revised score by Prout of 1902, by which time the festival had already given, in 1900, the text 'complete'. Few participants had any idea of the range of performing possibilities emerging from contemporary documentation which would render the term 'complete' irrelevant. Public performance of the other works seems to have depended on the easy availability of the vocal scores, which did not appear in popular Novello editions until 1846. See Scholes, ibid.; also Vincent Novello, *A Short History of Cheap Music*, London (Novello, Ewer), 1887.

5 Julian Herbage, *Messiah*, London and New York (Max Parrish), 1948, p. 58, quotes Mendelssohn's gratification 'in hearing my work performed in so beautiful a manner ... The power of the choruses, – that large body of good and musical voices. – and the style in which they sang the whole of my music.

6 *The Musical Times*, 25/496, (1 June 1884), p. 321.

7 For discussion of social status of the Sacred Harmonic Society see W. Weber, *Music and the Middle Classes*, London (Croom Helm), 1975, pp. 102–4. Also E. D. Mackerness, *A Social History of English Music*, London (Routledge and Kegan Paul), 1964, pp. 178, 184.

8 Royal patronage arose as a gesture to Dissenters in view of their increasingly powerful political role. See Weber, *Music and the Middle Classes*, pp. 88 and 102; further Trevelyan, *English Social History*, London (Longmans Green), 1942, pp. 511–12.

9 Exeter Hall was never considered big enough for the Sacred Harmonic Society, which had advanced plans to create a bigger national hall in the 1840s. Exeter Hall was situated on the site of the present Strand Palace Hotel, Strand, London. The idea was originally that of Bowley (see *Grove's Dictionary* (2nd edn) 'Handel Festival', vol. 3, p. 290).

10 *The Musical Times*, 8/173 (July 1857), p. 71.

11 See 'Handel Festival' in *Grove's Dictionary* (2nd edn) vol. 2, pp. 290–1.

12 For example in *Programme of Arrangements*, 1859 p. 10 and 1862, p. 26.

13 The transformation of the transept area required only the removal of a few statues from their central position. The raised dais which can be seen in the pictures of the completed Orchestra must have had direct stage access, since it appears in modern photographs with exit signs. Exit from such a large performance area was clearly a major problem. See also note 41 on Hollins.

14 For discussion of the organ, see, pp. 145–50.

15 Herbage, *Messiah*, p. 62.

16 The Palace established the use of highest quality singers from the first, some native, some foreign, rapidly overcoming the kind of initial prejudice about the venue implicit in resistance of Madame Rudersdorff towards performing there (see p. 87). It soon became a required

professional venue for rising stars: Charles Santley first sang there in 1857, though only at the Handel Festival first in 1865.

17 *The Musical Times*, 8/171 (May 1857), p. 41.

18 Figures for performance given in *Programme of Arrangements*, 1862, p. 19.

19 Herbage, *Messiah*, p. 63.

20 *The Musical Times*, vol. 173 (July 1857), p. 74.

21 *The Times*, 29 July 1857.

22 *Programme of arrangements*, 1859.

23 Ibid., 1862.

24 *Illustrated London News*, vol. 34 no. / July, 1859.

25 The 1862 *Programme of Arrangements* claimed that 'most of the professors and amateurs in London' were participants.

26 Quoted in Herbage, *Messiah*, p. 64. Charlotte Dolby later married Prosper Sainton to become known as Madame Sainton-Dolby; Helen Sherrington married the Belgian organist Nicolas Lemmens to become known as Lemmens-Sherrington. The Guadagni version of 'But who may abide' for alto was subsequently incorporated into the Prout edition. For descriptions of Reeves's performances and others of the period to 1865, Bowley, *The Sacred Harmonic Society*, pp. 42–47.

27 The changes are clear from the seating plans illustrated in the *Programme of Arrangements* for 1859 and 1862. So great were the numbers involved that the chorus singers accessed the Orchestra by separate entrances, A,B,C,D.

28 *Programme of Arrangements* 1862, pp. 12–13.

29 Reaction to *Israel in Egypt* in 1857 had been so enthusiasic that the 1859 *Programme of Arrangements* stated that 'there was no possibility of omitting it'.

30 *The Musical World*, 37/28 (9 July 1859), pp. 440–1.

31 *The Musical Times*, 9/198 (August 1859), pp. 94–9.

32 The International Exhibition of 1862 (Royal Albert Hall and other local venues, May–September).

33 *Programme of Arrangements*, 1862, p. 8.

34 Ibid., p. 12.

35 *The Musical Times*, 10/232 (July 1862), p. 271.

36 *Illustrated London News*, 52, June 1868 (20 June, 1868) p. 614.

37 Ibid.

38 Printed sheets were distributed with the invitations by the Sacred Harmonic Society.

39 Described in *The Musical Times*, 71/1038 (August 1929), p. 737. See also Scholes (ed.) *The Mirror of Music*, vol. 1, pp. 180–1; Scholes also states that it was displayed in the South Transept. See also Part 4, p. 162–3.

40 The commentary in *The Musical Times* clearly lacks any perspective on the performance issues of an event which took place over seventy years earlier.

41 See Alfred Hollins, *A Blind Musician* Looks Back, London (Blackwood),

1936, p. 92, for recollections of the very adverse effects on hot days of the Festival.

42 *The Musical Times*, 9/199 (September 1859), p. 116.

43 *Programme of Arrangements*, 1862.

44 The Programme for 1871 lists no less than thirty-five agents selling tickets in the London area, and five in other cities – furthest being Liverpool and Manchester, in addition to the Exeter Hall and the Palace. This far exceeds the agency for any other musical activity advertised at the Palace.

45 Applications closed by 31 March from 1860 onwards.

46 For other ticket prices at comparable Crystal Palace events see p. 122–3 (Orchestral concerts), p. 134 (Opera concerts), p. 177–80 (Theatre performances).

47 The programme was expansively laid out: twenty-five generous-sized pages of high quality paper and print, with an introduction and background to the works performed. But the first, 1857, programme had much more detailed notes on the works by Macfarren, and a 'Popular Description' of the organ.

48 *Punch*: '19,200 sandwiches, 14,000 pies, 240 forequarters of lamb, 3052 lobster salads, 600 lettuces, 40,000 penny buns, 25,000 twopenny buns, 32,000 ices, 3,500 quarts of tea, coffees and chocolate'. These numbers naturally increased commensurately with the festival audiences. For some statistics from the 1906 Festival, see Scholes (ed.), *The Mirror of Music*, vol. 1, p. 179.

49 Graves, *Life of Sir George Grove*, pp. 124–5.

50 Ibid., p. 125.

51 Ibid.

52 Scholes (ed.), *Mirror of Music*, vol. 1, p. 68.

53 See article 'Additional Accompaniments' in P. A. Scholes, ed., *The Oxford Companion to Music*, Oxford (Oxford University Press), 1938, p. 16.

54 See Scholes (ed.), *Mirror of Music*, vol. 2, p.752. See also: Novello, *A Short History of Cheap Music*.

55 According to the model described in *The Musical Times* in 1929 (see pp. 44–5).

56 Quoted in Graves, *Life of Sir George Grove*, p. 35.

57 Henry Wood, *My Life of Music*, London (Gollanoz), 1938, p. 318.

58 *Illustrated London News*, 30, 27 June 1857, pp. 630–1. The 1857 Festival used 'Distin's Monster Drum' (a bass drum of seven foot diameter) and for the 1859 Festival 'some giant kettle drums, far exceeding any yet in use' were being made. In 1868, the 'monster tower drums' which had originally been used for the 1784 Handel celebration, were introduced. See Scholes (ed.), *The Mirror of Music*, vol. 1, p. 180.

59 For details of the Selection Day repertory 1859–1926 with soloists, see Appendix 1. Though not originating with the Handel Festivals at the Crystal Palace (see note 11) the inclusion of Selection Day placed an

emphasis on the wider repertory which points to the future, despite criticism of oratorio performance, for example by Shaw and John Ruskin; though the early items were familiar, the works drawn from expanded steadily and came to include many items from the Italian operas which, like many of the oratorios, still remained little known well into the twentieth century. See also notes 68 and 76.

60 See 'Sacred Harmonic Society', *Grove's Dictionary*, 2nd edn, vol. 4, pp. 201–3. See also, Bennett, *Forty Years of Music*, pp. 334ff.

61 Henry Saxe-Wyndham, *August Manns and the Saturday Concerts*, London/ New York (Walter Scott), 1908, p. 131.

62 Ibid.

63 Ibid., pp. 132–3.

64 Ibid., p. 133.

65 *The Musical Times*, 24/485 (July 1883), pp. 378.

66 Quoted in Scholes (ed.), *The Mirror of Music*, vol. 1, p. 180, note.

67 For Manns's other activities as a choral conductor see Saxe Wyndham, *August Manns*, p. 143.

68 Although the critic of *The Musical Times* complained (July 1880) that the notable additions to the repertory in the Selection Day programme of 1877 had not been maintained. See Appendix 1 for an indication of which works were new to the Selection Day repertory from 1880 onwards. In fact, the Selection Day drew regularly larger audiences than the other Days from the 1870s. The innovations of Manns's era were not maintained by Cowen, though significantly resumed in the single, final year under Wood (see Appendix 1).

69 The background of the 'Gloria Patri' setting is given in Saxe Wyndham, *August Manns*, p. 151.

70 Ibid., p. 158.

71 Stated in Scholes (ed.), *Mirror of Music*, vol. 1, p. 58.

72 *The Musical Times*, 38/653 (July 1897), p. 461.

73 *The Musical Times*, vol. 32/581 (July 1891) had already noted especially the quality and power of the voices of the midland and northern societies, though 'pecuriary reasons' opposed their recruitment in large numbers.

74 J. A. Fuller-Maitland, *A Doorkeeper of Music*, London (John Murray), 1902, p. 46.

75 *Shaw's Music*, vol. 2, pp. 381–3.

76 H. Wood, *My Life in Music*, London (Gollanz), 1938, p. 318; Wood, however, also made his own arrangements for Handel performances at the Palace and 'completely rescored *Messiah* and *Israel in Egypt*' for the Handel Festival of 3,000 performers: see Scholes (ed.), *The Oxford Companion to Music*. For Wood's selection programme, see Appendix 1.

77 See Scholes (ed.), *Mirror of Music*, vol. 1, p. 180, note.

78 *The Musical Times*, 44/725 (July 1903), p. 475.

79 *The Musical Times*, 50/797 (July 1909), p. 464.

80 *The Musical Times*, 64/965 (July 1923), p. 495. The arrangements for

modern symphony orchestra of Sir Hamilton Harty (1879–1941) were for many years the most widely performed and recorded versions: (*The Water Music* and *The Music for the Royal Fireworks*).

81 Thomas Beecham, *A Mingled Chime; Leaves from an Autobiography*, London (Hutchinson), 1973, p. 68.

82 For the growth of Bach performance see Scholes (ed.), *Mirror of Music*, vol. 1, pp. 69–74 and 181–2.

83 There is no reference to the Festival at all in the issue of *The Musical Times*, which would customarily have carried the review (vol. 70/1037 (July 1929)). The inclusion in the following, August, issue of the description of the model of the Festival (see note 39) may have been an attempt to compensate for the lack of any report, though its wording gives no indication that the festival no longer exists.

4 OTHER LARGE-SCALE CHORAL PERFORMANCES

1 *The Musical Times*, 12/ 269 (July 1865), p. 93.

2 Ibid., 9/208 (June 1860), p. 203. See Plate 11, p. 34.

3 A torchlight procession for the Schiller Commemoration of the previous year, 1859, is described in *The Musical Times*, 9/ 202, December 1859, p. 170 as 'after the national custom of the Germans'.

4 Ibid., 9/ 208 (June 1860), p. 287–8.

5 Ibid., 11/ 244 (June 1863), p. 64.

6 Ibid., 30/ 557 (July 1889), p. 408.

7 Ibid., 31/ 659 (July 1890), p. 406.

8 Ibid., 9/212 (October 1860), p. 356.

9 As advertised in a Saturday concert programme.

10 As advertised in a Saturday concert programme.

11 As described in the early programmes. The name changed in the 1907–8 season, part of a general change of name amongst the Non-conformist churches which reflects the growing centrality of the denominations of the dissenting tradition in religious life. 'Free Church' implied organization according to the principle of the 'gathered church' in which individuals were free to attend where they wished, unlike the episcopal organization of the Church of England. Thus the strong musical centres of this movement were much less to be predicted than those of the Church of England, which were customarily in the major cathedral or city churches; hence the fact that only one major city is noted as being represented in the festival choir. The Union continues to the present.

12 Eric H. Thiman (1900–75), the leading musician of the Congregationalist denomination, notable as Director of Music at the City Temple, Holborn Viaduct, London, the leading metropolitan Congregationalist church, from 1957 to 1975. Ernest Read (1879–1965): a leading figure in music education, especially in the development of orchestral music in

schools: he conducted the London Junior and London Senior Orchestras, and concerts for children which bore his name.

13 *The Musical Times*, 73/1069 (March 1932), p. 251.

14 Attributed to Henry VIII in the programme, now generally to John Mundy. Broadening taste in nonconformist music continues in the *Congregational Anthem Book* of 1958 (Novello).

15 The 'College of St Nicholas' hosted courses in the preparation of church music and the School conducted examinations for the Archbishop of Canterbury's Diploma in Church Music (ADCM). The School became the Royal School of Church Music in 1945.

16 *The Musical Times*, vol. 74/1087 (Sept 1933), pp. 833–4.

5   THE CONCERTS, ORCHESTRA AND CONDUCTOR

1 See, for example, the interview in *The Saturday Review*, 27 April 1895.

2 For the history of the Upper Norwood and Sydenham districts, see: Alan R Warwick, *The Phoenix Suburb*, London (Blue Boar), 1972. Many musicians lived in these localities, of whom the earliest important figure was Thomas Attwood (1765–1838). The Royal Normal College for the Blind was established at Upper Norwood specifically to avail its students of the Saturday concerts; see also Part 3, 'Instrumental Music', note 17.

3 Stated in Manns's Preface to Frederick Shinn, *Catalogue of the Principal Instrumental and Choral Works Performed at the Saturday Concerts* (October 1855–May 1895), London, Crystal Palace (Evans), 1986.

4 A point stressed by Manns: see Saxe Wyndham, *August Manns*, p. 36, note.

5 James W Davison (1813–85) was one of the most important writers on music of his generation; he succeeded G. A. Macfarren as editor of *The Musical World* in 1844 and was music critic of *The Times* from 1846 to 1878. He exerted constant pressure for the advancement of classical music in Britain: see his entry in *Groves Dictionary*, 1904, vol. 1, p. 672; for a recent biography see Charles Osborne, *The Music Monster*, London (Quartet), 1984.

6 However, as Davison comments that since 'the proprietors of *The Musical World*, Messrs Boosey, were not on good terms with the conductor' ... the criticism must be taken with a grain of salt: J. W. Davison, *From Mendelssohn to Wagner*, p. 185.

7 See Saxe Wyndham, *August Manns*, pp. 15–18; also the article 'August Manns' in *Grove's Dictionary*, second edn, 1904–22, vol. 3, p. 42.

8 Clearly Bowley's concerns noted connection with the musical provision for the opening ceremony were not universally shared (see Part 2 note 11, p. 241). A later comment by Grove indicates that no thought had been given to the 'provision of entertainments'. Only two applications had been received for the 'musical conductorship', one from Schallehn

and the other from a Herr Somers – 'two Germans without position and quite unknown'. Schallehn's appointment was by recommendation of 'a member of the royal family' (see Saxe Wyndham, *August Manns*, pp. 20–1, note). Schallehn next appears as conductor of the concerts of the Surrey Gardens in 1859 (see Scholes (ed.), *Mirror of Music*, p. 199. He later directed music at Royal Military School of Music, Kneller Hall.

9 Saxe Wyndham, *August Manns*, pp. 21–2.

10 Ibid., pp. 26–7.

11 Ibid., *August Manns*, p. 28.

12 Manns kept 'among his most valued possessions', according to Wyndham: Ibid., pp. 31–2.

13 Ibid.

14 Ibid., p. 36.

15 Ibid., p. 54.

16 Ibid., p. 88.

17 Manns's Preface to Shinn, *Catalogue*. See Plate for the location of this court within the building.

18 Ibid.

19 Ibid.

20 This is confirmed in Shinn, *A Retrospect and Appeal*, (p. 4). Wyndham states that the 'enclosure in the garden side of the Centre Transept' was in use by the Spring of 1856. *August Manns*, p. 38.

21 Letter to Grove, 4 June, 1863. See Graves, *Life of Sir George Grove*, p. 96.

22 The entry on Manns in *Grove's Dictionary*, 2nd edn (vol. 3 p. 42) confirms that 'through the exertions of Robert Bowley, then General Manager of the Crystal Palace, the Concert Room was enclosed and roofed in'. Since Bowley died in 1870, it seems likely that the roofing in must have coincided with this stage of completion in 1864.

23 Alfred Hollins, *A Blind Musician*, p. 102.

24 *The Crystal Palace Auction Catalogue*, 1911, p. 38.

25 The Concert Room seems to have held a larger audience in the early years, at least on the evidence of a diary entry by Clara Schumann for June 1865 who noted an audience of 4000, a point repeated by Joachim in a letter to Brahms of 7 September 1874. Unless this is a striking coincidence in inaccurate approximation, an explanation would seem to lie in very different seating arrangements and the availability of standing accommodation. See B. Litzmann, *Clara Schumann, ein Künstlerleben*, Leipzig (Breitkopf und Härtel), 1909, p. 181; and *Johannes Brahms Briefwechsel*, vol. 6, Berlin (Deutsche Brahms Gesellschaft, 1908), p. 91

26 Confirmed in Hollins, *A Blind Musician*, pp. 102–4.

27 Walker, 'An Orchestra of the past', p. 139.

28 Ibid. Ernest Walker grew up in Clapham, attended his first concert in 1880 and regularly attended the daily music, hence his detailed information.

29 This was thus the first full orchestral performance of the Saturday concerts.

30 Manns's Preface to Shinn, *Catalogue*.

31 The Hallé Concerts are almost exactly contemporary in date with those of the Crystal Palace (commencing 1857) as well as aspiring to common goals in the establishment of serious orchestral music; they grew from the Manchester Gentlemen's Concerts and had an existing management structure at Hallé's which did not require change of the order of that brought about at the Crystal Palace by Manns and Grove. See M. Kennedy, *The Halle Tradition, A Century of Music*, Manchester (University of Manchester Press), 1960, pp. 25 ff.

32 The stronger analogy is with the orchestras for public gardens or spas – for example, that of the Surrey Gardens (see A. Carse, *The Life of Jullien*, Cambridge (Heffer), 1951, pp. 52 ff), with which the Palace sometimes compared itself in its programmes. In estimating his own achievements, Manns drew special parallel with the influence on Dan Godfrey's work in the establishment of classical concerts at the Bournemouth Winter Gardens (see Saxe Wyndham, *August Manns*, p. 121).

33 There is a discrepancy in the recording of these numbers of extra players. In Shinn, *Catalogue*, Manns quotes 'four extra players from London'. Saxe Wyndham, *August Manns*, p. 36, citing an interview in the *Daily News* 19 June 1903, quotes him as saying 'about half a dozen': the later may reflect Manns's failing memory or simply indicate that the numbers varied according to the pieces performed in the early years. There is also some conflicting evidence as to the extent of the music performed on the first day, 20 October 1855. Although Saxe Wyndham (*August Manns*, p. 37) reproduces the first programme (the programme elsewhere recorded as the first, as, for example, in the article on Manns in *The Musical Times*, vol. 39/661 (1 March 1898) p. 156), he also reproduces in an appendix an alternative programme with a different first half of a more popular character, clearly for wind band (Saxe Wyndham, *August Manns*, pp. 233–4). This must indicate that the wind band programme was given entire as the band's normal performance on that day, and that the mixed half of the programme was an addition, an extension of it in a different and distinctive venue. This would confirm Manns's view of the difficulty of persuading the management to permit orchestral music.

34 Saxe Wyndham, *August Manns*, p. 36, note.

35 Grove's reference to the 'enlightened liberality of the Directors' still perhaps suggests a hint of reservation as to the claims of a symphony orchestra at the Palace (see *Grove's Dictionary*, 1st edn, 1879–89, vol. 3, p. 42).

36 See Appendix 2 for the complete personnel of the orchestra in 1856–7 and thereafter in selected years.

37 As mentioned in his letter of 21 July 1855 (see Saxe Wyndham, *August Manns*, p. 31).

38 Wyndham states that 'at this time [12 November 1866], the Directors of the Palace had been urged to afford their conductor some increase in the numerical strength of the orchestra', though he does not state by whom. Ibid., p. 82.

39 The numbers were not identical with those of the Philharmonic, to judge at least from the listing given for 1866. See British Library Loan Manuscript Collection 48 (The Philharmonic Society of London).

40 See Appendix 2.

41 Nettel discusses the importance of the status of membership of the Philharmonic Society for orchestral players (see R. Nettel, *The Orchestra in England: A Social History*, London (Cape), 1948, p. 207).

42 Given in Saxe Wyndham, *August Manns*, p. 89 on the basis of the recollections to Wyndham (*c.* 1908) of George Webb, second clarinet.

43 Ibid., p. 32.

44 The common players were Vogel (first violin), Svendsen (flute) and Keevil (horn).

45 On the evidence of Manns's letter of 14 March 1874 (see British Library Manuscript Loan Collection 48 (The Philharmonic Society of London)).

46 Walker, 'An orchestra of the past', p. 141.

47 Stanford, *Interludes*, p. 37.

48 Walker, 'An orchestra of the past', p. 142.

49 Ibid., p. 141.

50 Stanford, *Interludes*, p. 37.

51 Bennett, *Forty Years of Music*, p. 117.

52 Ibid., p. 118.

53 Stanford, *Interludes*, pp. 19–20.

54 Writing in 1894 (see *Shaw's Music*, vol. 3, p. 282).

55 W. Bache, *Brother Musicians*, London (Methuen), 1901, p. 255.

56 See, for example, his comment on a performance of the 'Jupiter' Symphony in 1891: *Shaw's Music*, vol. 2, p. 483.

57 Stanford, *Interludes*, p. 20.

58 Saxe Wyndham, *August Manns*, p. 201.

59 Ibid., p. 31.

60 Graves, *Life of Sir George Grove*, p. 97.

61 Saxe Wyndham, *August Manns*, p. 97.

62 Ibid., pp. 202 and 207.

6 PROGRAMMES, PERFORMERS, REPERTORY, PROGRAMME NOTES

1 Saxe Wyndham, *August Manns*, p. 35.

2 'Crystal Palace Concerts' in Riemann, *Dictionary of Music*, London (Reeves), n.d. (1890s), p. 173, claims that they were modelled on the programmes of the Gewandhaus at Leipzig.

3 Saxe Wyndham, *August Manns*, p. 37.

4 H. Sullivan and N. Flower, *Sir Arthur Sullivan*, London (Cassell), p. 73.
5 Quoted by Manns in an interview in *The Daily Graphic*, 31 October 1891.
6 Unpublished letter of 2 November 1885, from August Manns to the Philharmonic Society of London: British Library Manuscript Loan Collection 48 (Philharmonic Society).
7 John Francis Barnett (1837–98), later a prominent composer of orchestral and choral works, was subsequently to have close contacts with the orchestral concerts.
8 Henry Blagrove (1811–72), was a leading figure in musical circles on the continent as well as in London, where he had been prominent as an orchestral leader since the 1840s.
9 Ernst Pauer (1826–1904) was a leading piano pedagogue who had been resident in London since 1851 and was to play an important role in the educational work aspect of Palace music. See pp. 169–171.
10 Saxe Wyndham, *August Manns*, p. 47.
11 The identification in the programme of the Haydn symphonies other than the *London* Symphonies performed, was by reference to the edition used (Wullner or Rieter-Biedermann New Edition) or the Philharmonic Society 'Letter' designation.
12 The 'Concerto in D major' was given once in March 1894 by Becker; another Concerto 'in MS' was given by Popper in his 'own arrangement' in December 1894.
13 See Appendix 3a for a selective listing of works by non-British composers given their first British performance at the Crystal Palace.
14 Saxe Wyndham, *August Manns*, p. 46. Manns believed his 1856 performance to have been the first complete performance in England: the evidence supports him. The work was rehearsed by Mendelssohn with the Philharmonic, and by Wylde with the New Philharmonic, but not performed publicly otherwise until 1871 under Cusins at the Philharmonic. Like other challenging works, this symphony was given in incomplete form before its full performance on 5 April 1856.
15 See Grove's appendix to H. Kreissle von Hellborn, *The Life of Schubert*, tr. Coleridge, London, 1868, vol. 2, p. 298.
16 Ibid., p. 299.
17 In H. Kreissle von Hellborn, *Franz Schubert*, Vienna (Gerold), 1865. He recounts his visit to Vienna in his appendix to the English translation of Hellborn's biography: *The Life of Schubert*, tr. Coleridge, London (Longmans, Green), 1868, vol. 2, pp. 221–6.
18 Stated by Grave in Hellborn, tr. Coleridge, *The Life of Schubert*, p. 325, note. Manns recalls in the preface to Shinn, *Catalogue*, that application was actually made to the Palace by the Gesellschaft der Musikfreunde, Vienna, for a loan of the manuscript copies for performance purposes.
19 Bennett, *Forty Years of Music*, p. 340.
20 Barnett was informed by Grove that he had obtained the manuscript through Paul Mendelssohn, Felix Mendelssohn's brother, who had in

turn received it from Schubert's brother Ferdinand with a view to completion. See Barnett, *Musical Reminiscences and Impressions*, p. 313–19. It was published by Breitkopf und Härtel, but not included in any complete edition.

21 *The Musical Times*, 9/429 (November 1878), p. 599.

22 Stanford, *Pages from an Unwritten Diary*, pp. 173–4.

23 *The Musical Times*, (November, 1878), p. 598.

24 No systematic numbering of the Dvořák symphonies was used in the Palace programmes.

25 See John Clapham, *Antonin Dvořák, Musician and Craftsman*, London (Faber and Faber), 1966, p. 62.

26 Saxe Wyndham, *August Manns*, pp. 117–18.

27 The first performance in England of the the Prelude to *Parsifal* had taken place on 28 October 1882, even closer to the work's first performance on 26 July 1882.

28 Saxe Wyndham, *August Manns*, p. 137.

29 Mackenzie, *A Musician's Narrative*, p. 151.

30 Saxe Wyndham, *August Manns*, p. 126.

31 Ibid., pp. 108–9.

32 See Appendix 3b for a list of British works which received their first performance at the Crystal Palace.

33 A. J. Fuller-Maitland, *English Music in the Nineteenth Century*, London (Grant Richards), 1902, p. 145. This is one of the earliest mentions of this term, and thus particularly significant.

34 It was never again repeated and the score was destroyed in a fire; modern performances have been of a reconstruction based on the solo cello part and the piano score. See A. Jacobs, *Arthur Sullivan, Victorian Musician*, London (Oxford University Press), 1984, p. 42.

35 Stanford already had Crystal Palace connections through his family and had lived in Sydenham in his school years in the 1860s. See Stanford, *Unwritten Diary*, p. 82 ff.

36 The Symphony in B♭, written in 1876 and never published in Stanford's lifetime, was written for a competition for a British symphony organized by the Alexandra Palace, where it took second place to a symphony by one Frances Davenport, some of whose music was played at the Palace.

37 W. H. Reed, *Elgar as I Knew Him*, London (Gollancz), 1936, pp. 46–7.

38 See J. Northropp Moore, *Edward Elgar: A Creative Life*, Oxford (Oxford University Press), 1984, p. 79.

39 Ibid., p. 92.

40 Ibid., p. 99.

41 Elgar's interest in the work was later reflected in a lecture at Birmingham University, where he held the Professorship, is published in *A Future for British Music and other Lectures*, ed. P. M. Young, London (Dennis Dobson), 1966, pp. 99ff.

42 W. H. Reed, *Elgar* (2nd ed.), London, 1943 (Dent), p. 41.

43 J. Northropp Moore, *Edward Elgar*, pp. 218–9.
44 Ibid., p. 227. Though Manns envisaged a performance of *Gerontius*, only the 'Introduction and Closing Scene', were given, on 10 November 1900. See also ibid., p. 334.
45 E. Smyth, *Impressions that Remained*, London (Longmans, Green), 1919, vol. 1, p. 227.
46 Holbrooke describes Manns's reception of his work in Saxe Wyndham, *August Manns*, pp. 188–200
47 Graves, *Life of Sir George Grove*, p. 52.
48 Ibid.
49 Later expanded in his book *Beethoven and his Nine Symphonies*, London (Novello), 1895. His discussion of the project is noted in Graves, *Life of Sir George Grove*, p. 397.
50 Saxe Wyndham, *August Manns*, pp. 119–20.

7 THE CRYSTAL PALACE AND ITS AUDIENCE

1 Saxe Wyndham, *August Manns*, p. 35.
2 Jullien played at the Surrey Gardens from 1847; see Carse, *Life of Jullien*, p. 62.
3 See Davison, *Mendelssohn to Wagner*, p. 185.
4 Saxe Wyndham, *August Manns*, p. 35.
5 Ibid.
6 Bennett, *Forty Years of Music*, p. 337.
7 Ibid.
8 This passage is quoted intermittently in the Saturday programmes over the years.
9 Nettel, *The Orchestra in England*, p. 211; it is hardly possible to speak of a public: there were different audiences. Nettel's generalization is also reflected in his mistaken view that Manns's concerts took place on Saturday evenings; evening concerts only came in the later years and were never of the kind of the famous 'Saturdays', which took place in the afternoon, when most 'working men' were unavailable.
10 The term 'reunion' is indicative of the popular assumption of the social role of a concert; *The Musical World*, 44/10 (10 March, 1866), cover page advertisement.
11 Saxe Wyndham, *August Manns*, p. 54, confirms the fact that the 'now universal shilling' (*c.* 1909) did not apply in the early years at the Palace.
12 *Shaw's Music*, vol. 1, pp. 272–3.
13 Ibid., vol. 2, p. 709.

8 AFTER MANNS

1 See Saxe Wyndham, *August Manns*, p. 193.

2 The concerts of Newman's Queen's Hall Orchestra conducted by Henry Wood (1869–1944) had begun in 1895, the year after the opening of the hall, and continued, later taking his name, until the destruction of the hall through bombing in 1940. Although Wood was a successor of Manns in the sense of giving regular concerts which included new repertory, the context of the beginnings of his performances was quite different: they were given in a purpose-built hall in the centre of London for a musically literate audience. Saxe Wyndham (*August Manns*, p. 212) notes Manns's favourable view of the achievements of Dan Godfrey, analogous to his own in pioneering symphonic music in the concerts of the Winter Gardens, Bournemouth.

3 Saxe Wyndham, *August Manns*, p. 197.

4 *The Musical Times*, 41/ 693 (November 1900), p. 749.

5 Saxe Wyndham, *August Manns*, p. 197.

6 Ibid.

7 Ibid.

8 Despite his reputation at the Palace, Walter Hedgcock never seems to have attracted national attention as a performer.

9 *The Musical Times*, 43/ 711 (May 1902), p. 320.

10 *The Musical Times*, 62/ 939 (May 1921), p. 351.

11 *The Musical Times*, 65/ 981 (November 1924), p. 1003.

9 POPULAR CONCERTS

1 See Graves, *Life of Sir George Grove*, p. 123.

2 *The Musical World*, 34/21 (24 May 1856), p. 331.

3 *The Musical World*, 34/50 (13 December 1856), p. 794.

4 *The Musical Times*, 11/ 257 (July 1864), p. 323.

5 Programme of May 1868.

6 *The Musical World*, 34/21 (24 May 1856), p. 331.

7 *The Musical Times*, 9/198 (August 1859), p. 100.

8 Advertisement of May 1868.

9 For German Reed's initiative in concert performance of opera, see Grove's *Dictionary of Music and Musicians*, ed. J. Fuller Maitland, 1910, vol. 4, p. 43.

10 *The Musical Times*, 49/31 (August 1871), p. 488.

11 *The Musical Times*, 11/ 256 (June 1864), p. 306.

12 *The Musical Times*, 11/ 257 (July, 1864), p. 323.

13 *The Musical Times*, 14/319 (September 1869), p. 204.

14 *The Musical Times*, 16/376 (June 1874), p. 510.

15 *The Musical Times*, 16/ 378 (August 1874), p. 577.

16 *The Musical Times*, 17/ 388 (June 1875), p. 108.

17 For contemporary reaction to Benedict's Vocal Association and Leslie's Choir see H. R. Haweis, *Music and Morals*, London (Bogue), 1881.

18 See Scholes (ed.), *Mirror of Music*, vol. 1, p. 30.

19 *The Musical Times*, 9/198 (August 1859), p. 100.
20 *The Musical Times*, 9/ 209 (July 1860), p. 298. The Orpheonistes created such an impression that a picture of them appeared in *Illustrated London News* 36, 7 July, 1860, p. 12.
21 The activities of the Distin family are discussed in Scholes (ed.), *Mirror of Music*, vol. 2, pp. 816–17. John Distin, the senior member of the family, had long established an international reputation in the orchestration of music for brass and wind groups. For other associations of the Distin's with Palace musical activity, see p. 196.
22 *The Musical Times*, 11/ 246 (August 1863), p. 102.
23 *The Musical Times*, 16/ 376. (June 1874) p. 510.
24 *The Musical Times*, 11/ 255 (May 1864), p. 285.
25 Luigi Arditi, *My Reminiscences*, compiled and edited with introduction and notes by Baroness von Zedlitz, London (Skeffington), 1896, pp. 134–5.
26 *The Musical Times*, 11/ 255 (May 1864), p. 285.

10 SOLO INSTRUMENTAL MUSIC

1 St James's Hall was opened in 1859 by William Chappell for solo and chamber music on Monday evenings, and later on Saturday evenings; his concerts were titled Monday and Saturday Popular Concerts, or 'Pops'.
2 Oscar Beringer (1844–1922) was the first solo pianist of the Crystal Palace, see Saxe-Wyndham, *August Manns*, p. 50.
3 See pp. 156–7.
4 The constitution of the original band is described by Manns in his autobiographical sketch as of sixty-two brass instruments, one piccolo and one Eb clarinet; see Saxe-Wyndham, *August Manns*, p. 34.
5 See p. 140.
6 G. A. Macfarren in *Programme of Arrangements for the Handel Festival*, 1857.
7 See N. Thistlethwaite, *The Making of the Victorian Organ*, Cambridge (Cambridge University Press), 1990, p. 283.
8 Macfarren, in *Programme*, pp. 2–4
9 Thistlethwaite, *Victorian Organ*, p. 283.
10 See p. 196.
11 *The Musical World*, vol. 49/22 (June 1871), p. 340.
12 Macfarren, ibid., p. 4.
13 James Coward (1824–80), chorister of Westminster Abbey, first appointment at Lambeth Parish Church.
14 Alfred J. Eyre (1853–?) held the position concurrently with his appointment as organist of St John's, Upper Norwood. His premature retirement as the Palace organist was due to ill health.
15 Walter Hedgcock (1864–1932). See further pp. 130–2.
16 Hollins (1865–1942), initially a pianist, subsequently travelled to the

USA as an organist. A composer for the instrument, some of his music remains in the repertory. His many connections with the Palace are recounted in his *A Blind Musician*, pp. 30ff.

17 Dr F. J. Campbell: his interest in the Crystal Palace as a location for his College and its background are discussed in Scholes (ed.), *Mirror of Music*, p. 695 and Saxe Wyndham, *August Manns*, pp. 228–9.

18 Hollins, *A Blind Musician*, p. 92.

19 Bruckner was clearly a victim of anti-German feeling, to judge from the tone of the review in *The Musical World*, vol. 49/33 (August 1871), p. 528. The Fugue in E major was presumably the (single) fugue from 'Leichte Präludien und Fugen' (No. 20). Of other players noted at the Palace, Hollins admired the performances of Wigand: see Hollins, *A Blind Musician*, p. 282.

20 *Musical Opinion*, vol. 44/523 (April 1921), p. 612.

21 A. R. Warwick, *The Phoenix Suburb. A South London Social History*, 2nd edn, London (Blue Boar), 1973, p. 241. The Fire had broken out close to the organ, and even before its rapid spread was giving out 'the most strange groans', as was noted by a member of the Crystal Palace Amateur Orchestra which had been practising in the vicinity.

11 EXHIBITIONS; THE SCHOOL OF ART, SCIENCE AND
LITERATURE; THE THEATRE

1 Ironically, because of Sunday observance, the one day on which the public could make the maximum use of the Palace was a closed day: the audience had to come on a bank holiday, hence the special 'shilling days'.

2 See Mackerness, *A Social History of Music*, p. 184, for use of the word 'exhibition' in relation to the public choral and orchestral performance.

3 See pp. 69–70 for the full description.

4 The proposal was made by Dr Henry John Gauntlett; see Scholes (ed.) *Mirror of Music*, vol. 2, p. 583.

5 Pictured in Herbage, *Messiah*, p. 62.

6 See p. 44.

7 See p. 58.

8 See p. 98 for the work's performance: further Saxe Wyndham, *August Manns*, p. 151. The parts were loaned by W. H. Cummings.

9 *The Musical Times*, 38/652 (June 1897), p. 387.

10 *Musical Instruments and Memorials of Musicians being the Catalogue of the International Loan Exhibition*, Crystal Palace, London (Crystal Palace Handbooks: Office of the *Musical News*), 1900.

11 The extensive Handelian representation was largely drawn from the collection of Col. Shaw Hellier. It included a complete set of orchestral instruments, full scores and parts used by the private orchestra maintained in the time of Handel by Sir Samuel Hellier (*The Musical Times*, 41/690 (August 1900), p. 527).

12 See the groundplan on Plate 6. The Rockhills entrance was to the north end adjacent to the Queen's Apartments.
13 Situated on Anerley Hill, next to the south water tower. It was the only building to survive the fire.
14 Ernst Pauer (1826–1905). As well as his wide range of teaching, which included the RAM and the RCM, he edited much early music, notably twelve volumes of *Alte Musik* for Breitkopf und Härtel.
15 W. C. Berwick Sayers, *Samuel Coleridge Taylor, His Life and Letters*, London (Augener), 1927, pp. 173–4.
16 *The Musical Times*, vol. 22, no. 463, September 1881, p. 459.
17 See J. F. Bridge, *A Westminster Pilgrim*, London (Novello), n.d., p. 83.
18 Graves, *The Life of Sir George Grove*, p. 292.
19 *The Musical Times*, 14/315 (May 1869), p. 77.
20 See Appendix 5 for listings of musical works advertised for performance in the Theatre; supplementary information is provided in Kurt Ganzl, *British Music Theatre*, 2 vols., London (Macmillan), 1986.
21 Noted in *The Musical Times*, 14/319 (September 1869), p. 204.
22 Auction Catalogue, 1911.
23 The longest-running of these works was Balfe's *The Bohemian Girl*, which recurs in later years.
24 As part of the Toc. H. celebration; see Scholes (ed.), *Mirror of Music*, p. 237.
25 Rosa, who first appeared at the Palace as a violinist in 1866 (see p. 88), returned from the USA to create his own opera company specializing in new productions of classic works.
26 *The Illustrated London News*, 53, 26 December 1868, p. 632.
27 Saxe Wyndham, *August Manns*, p. 78.

12 THE GREAT POPULAR FESTIVALS

1 Gladstone's Education Bill of 1870 was the work of W. E. Forster 'an ardent churchman, though of Quaker origin' (G. M. Trevelyan, *English Social History*, p. 580). It was of crucial importance in providing the first state schools funded through the education board of the local authority (hence Board Schools), which thus became responsible for the maintenance of standards, the beginning of the slow systemization of the national education provision. See H. C. Barnard, *A History of English Education from 1760*, London (University of London Press), 1961.
2 These were called, respectively, British Schools (from the British and Foreign School Society, of nonconformist origin), and National Schools, because founded by the (Anglican) National Society: both were known as Voluntary Schools (see H. C. Barnard, *History of English Education*, London (University of London Press) and Trevelyan, *English Social History*, pp. 580–1. For the history of the (generally much older) charity schools, see M. G. Jones, *The Charity Schools Movement*, London, 1938. For evidence of parish music and performance by

charity scholars, see Scholes (ed.), *Mirror of Music*, vol. 2, pp. 533–53.

3 See note 32 for the history.

4 See comment by Scholes, *Mirror of Music*, vol. 2, p. 534.

5 C. F. Pohl, *Mozart and Haydn in London*, Vienna, 1867, vol. 2, 'Haydn in London', p. 212.

6 Berlioz judged instrumental design at the Great Exhibition; for his description of the St Paul's experience see A. W. Ganz, *Berlioz in London*, London (Quality Press), 1950, pp. 99–102.

7 See *Grove's Dictionary*, 1904–24, vol. 1, p. 505.

8 This was the biggest meeting to have taken place at the Crystal Palace by that date. Various press reports were included with the programme of the meeting in a publication by Novello bearing the title *Meeting of the Metropolitan Charity School Children* (Wednesday 4 August 1858).

9 Ibid., p. 11.

10 Ibid., p. 6.

11 Ibid., p. 10

12 Ibid., p. 8. See also pp. 33 and 244, n. 58, for the role of Distin's drum in the Handel Festival 1857.

13 Ibid., p. 7.

14 Ibid., p. 8. The conductor was George Bates (1802–81), and the organist George Cooper (1820–76), both prominent London organists, the latter subsequently of the Chapel Royal.

15 The meeting of the 'National and Endowed Schools' seems to have been an affiliation for purposes of musical performance of the national schools (see p. 257, n. 2) and the grammar schools, the latter being the principal recipients of endowments other than through the church (see Trevelyan, *English Social History*, pp. 364–5). These schools therefore occupied a very different social stratum from the charity schools.

16 George William Martin (1828–81) was a noted trainer of school choirs, and took over the Charity School Children performances in 1860; he edited the *Journal of Part Music* in 1862.

17 John Hullah (1812–84). See further F. Hullah, *The Life of John Hullah*, London (Longman), 1886. E. J. Hopkins (1818–1901), English organist and composer, was the organist of the Temple Church, London, from 1843 to 1898. He was a founding member of both the College of Organists and the Musical Association (prior to their royal affiliation).

18 The meeting on 8 June 1865 was regarded by *The Musical Times* as 'the best yet given', through Hullah's 'careful teaching and training' of 4,000 children and 1,000 adults; the audience was of 20,000.(12/ 269, July 1865, p. 101).

19 Hullah had wished to study the methods of Josef Mainzer in Paris in 1839, but, since they had been discontinued, attended G. L. Bocquillon Wilhem's school. He was invited to teach the methods at the newly founded Battersea training institution from 1840, having impressed the first secretary to the Privy Council Committee for the supervision of

national education, John Kay Shuttleworth, further to the 1839 Education Act. He was commissioned to translate Mainzer's *Manuel Musical* into English. He taught at King's College in 1844–74, becoming the first government inspector in music (further to the Forster Act) in 1872. (See B. Rainbow, *The Land without Music*, p. 121–38.) The disagreement with Curwen came to a head in Curwen's paper, *The Present Crisis of Music in Schools: A Reply to Mr Hullah*, London (Curwen), 1873.

20 John Curwen (1816–80). See further J. S. Curwen, *Memorials of John Curwen*, London (Curwen), 1882.

21 Sarah Anna Glover (1786–1867): her *Scheme* was published in 1835, with a second edition in 1850.

22 Reference is made in Curwen, *Memorials*, p. 86, to the *sol fa* edition of Mozart's Twelfth Service being learnt by the *Sol Fa* Association as early as 1861. The pervasive influence of the movement cannot be overestimated as Curwen's comment in *c.* 1865 shows: 'Our movement is rooted in the great voluntary movements of the kingdom. The great Temperance movement, the grand and merciful ragged school movement, and all the youngest and most vigorous movements for singing in Schools, Homes and Congregations cannot do without us' (ibid., p. 218).

23 Curwen, ibid., p. 55.

24 Curwen, ibid., p. 140.

25 See Scholes (ed.), *Mirror of Music*, vol. 2, p. 637.

26 This observation seems to confirm other indicators that, after the fashionable popularity that surrounded the opening, the Palace still possessed a populist image with the artistically cultivated (Curwen, *Memorials*, p. 91).

27 Quoted by Ian Bartlett in 'An Historical View of Tonic Sol Fa', *The Music Teacher*, 55/5, May 1976, pp. 9–11; this article includes an evaluation of the different *sol fa* methods.

28 John Stainer (1840–1901), reforming organist of St Paul's Cathedral, composer, scholar, educationalist: he was Hullah's successor as Inspector of Music in the Elementary Schools of England for the privy council (*Grove's Dictionary*, 2nd edn, vol. 4, p. 670.)

29 See: John Curwen, *Tonic Sol Fa in the Church of England*, London (Curwen), *c.* 1888.

30 Sarll was the leading choir trainer of the movement in earlier years, capable of filling the Exeter Hall with his pupils for inspiring annual meetings. Joseph Proudman, who was also organizer and Secretary of the movement, took the *Sol Fa* Choir on a memorable visit to Paris in 1867 and was particularly associated with the Crystal Palace meetings. (See Curwen, *Memorials*, various entries.)

31 The Sunday School Movement was founded in 1780 by Robert Raikes (1736–1811), the result of a steady development through the later eighteenth century. (See J. Belcher, *Robert Raikes: His Sunday School and his Friends*.) The Sunday School Union (later National Sunday School

Union) was founded in 1803, and subsequently developed many associated organizations. Already *c*.1800 the later importance of music is anticipated in Sunday School Melodies, containing more than 250 hymns, published in Nottingham, which remained in print till at least 1936 (10th edn). See also *Sunday School Songs*, London 1813; *The Sunday School Hymnary*, 1905.

32 Carey Bonner (1859–1938), a Baptist minister and musician. He edited *The Sunday School Hymnary* (1905, National Sunday School Union) and the revised edition of *The Baptist Hymnal* (1935, Psalms and Hymns Trust) as well as composing many hymns, choruses and small pieces for the movement. Henry Walford Davies (1869–1941), composer, organist, educationalist and broadcaster: as well as directing music at St Georges's Chapel, Windsor, he also pioneered the radio series 'Music and the Ordinary Listener' from 1926.

33 T. W. Beale, *The Light of Other Days*, London (Richard Bentley and Son), p. 350

34 Ibid.

35 *The Musical Times*, 15/354 (August 1872), p. 561. *The Musical Times* reported the event more extensively than *The Musical World* which, though welcoming it initially, became doubtful of the value of a national rather than regional event. Its report of 13 April 1872 details the concessionary rates given by the railway companies from the principal cities (for example, Aberdeen 27s. 6d., Liverpool, 10s, Portsmouth 5s.).

36 Beale *Light of Other Days*, p. 349

37 *The Musical Times*, 15/ 354 (August 1872), p. 562.

38 Ibid., p. 561.

39 Beale, *Light of Other Days*, p. 350.

40 *The Musical Times*, 15/ 354, p. 562.

41 Ibid.

42 For reference to the long connection between the Royal Artillery at Woolwich Garrison and the Crystal Palace see H. G. Farmer, *Memoirs of the Royal Artillery Band. Its Origin, History and Progress*, London (Boosey), 1904, various entries.

43 *The Musical Times*, 16/ 366 (August 1873), p. 176.

44 *The Musical Times*, 17/ 390 (August 1875), p. 171.

45 *The Musical Times*, 17/ 393 (November 1875), p. 266.

46 An unusual exception is in the massed concerts of the National Union of School Orchestras, which took place for several years after 1905, as a result of the initiative of Murdoch and Co in providing musical instruments at special rates for children. A concert, conducted by Allen Gill, is reported in *The Musical Times* (51/810, p. 532, August 1910), which commented 'it is safe to say that never before has there been assembled together under one roof such an extraordinary number of violinists'. Two orchestras took part: an Intermediate Orchestra of 2,500 elemen-

tary players and an 'Advanced' Orchestra of 2000 players. See also Scholes (ed.), *Mirror of Music*, vol. 1, p. 362.

47 See Appendix 5 for a list of the winning bands in 1860–3 and 1900–36.

48 For discussion of the brass band movement see: Arthur R. Taylor: *Brass Bands*, London (Granada), 1979; Cyril Bainbridge, *Brass Triumphant*, London (Frederick Muller),1980; T. L. Cooper, *Brass Bands of Yorkshire*, Clapham (Via Lancaster) (The Dalesman Publishing Company), 1974; J. F. Russell and J. H. Elliott, *The Brass Band Movement*, London (Dent), 1936; Trevor Herbert, ed., *The Brass Band Movement in the 19th and 20th centuries*, Milton Keynes and Philadelphia (Open University Press), 1991.

49 Listed in Taylor, *Brass Bands*, p. 51. The Palace programmes advertise 'two Campanology Contests'.

50 Writers differ on the financial arrangements for travel to the 1860 contest. Taylor states that the bands travelled entirely free of charge (*Brass Bands*, pp. 51–2), Bainbridge that they travelled from, for example, Leeds to London for 4s. 6d. (*Brass Triumphant*, p. 39).

51 Taylor, *Brass Bands*, p. 53.

52 Charles Godfrey, sen. (1790–1863): the Godfrey family had strong later connections with the Palace. His three sons included Charles Godfrey, jnr (1839–1919) and Daniel Godfrey,sen. (1831–1903), who was a conductor with the Palace band in the 1870s to 1880s. The latter's son Daniel, jnr (1868–1939) appears also as conductor in the early 1890s. He was later to conduct the Bournemouth Symphony Orchestra, having moved in 1893 to Bournemouth to organize the band.

53 See Taylor, *Brass Bands*, p. 56 for details of the financial aspect.

54 *The Guardian*, 26 July 1861.

55 In the view of Taylor, *Brass Bands*, p. 59.

56 See Taylor, p. 97.

57 For a list of the set pieces for the National Championships at the Crystal Palace, 1900–36 see Appendix 5.

58 Iles's own term (see Russell and Elliott, *Brass Band Movement*, p. 174).

59 Bainbridge, p. 46.

60 Taylor, *Brass Bands*, p. 100.

61 *The Musical Times*, 77/1124 (October 1936), p. 895.

62 Taylor, *Brass Bands*, pp. 144–5. However, Bliss thought more generally that 'some bands were inclined to concentrate on technical brilliance and neglect the more artistic side of their playing' (*The Musical Times*, 77/1124 (Oct. 1936, p. 936)

63 *The British Bandsman*, 1812, 5 Dec.1936, p. 11.

64 The tightrope displays of Blondin (the pseudonym of Jean François Gravelet, 1824–97) were a regular attraction at the Palace from 1861. The location of his feats of balancing was the Centre Transept, where he turned somersaults on a high wire placed parallel with the Great Handel Orchestra at a height of 70' and a length of 256' north to south

(as described in an advertisement of Palace entertainments): an illustration appears in: Beaver, *Crystal Palace*, p. 113.

65 *The Musical Times*, 17/ 393 (Nov. 1875, p. 277).

66 Blanche Cole (Mrs Sidney Naylor), soprano (1851–88).

67 *The Musical Times*, 51/ 807 (May 1910), p. 309.

68 The temperance movement was the major movement of social reform in many countries in the nineteenth century, especially Britain and the USA. In Britain its achievements were already being surveyed in 1853 in the pamphlet *The Temperance Movement; its Rise, Progress and Results*, London, 1853. It manifested itself in many organizations chiefly of non-conformist kind (though see also Trevelyan's listing of membership of the Church of England Temperance Society by 1909 in *English Social History*, p. 570). The National Temperance Society was founded in 1843 (later National Temperance League?) and the United Kingdom Band of Hope in 1855. The latter had a strong musical tradition, as in its song collection of *c.* 1878, *The Crystal Spring Songs. New and Choice Pieces for Band of Hope Meetings, Festivals and Anniversaries*, London (UK Band of Hope, Tweedie and Co), 1978. The Independent Order of Grand Templars appears to have been an offshoot of the International Order of Good Templars (founded Utica, NY, 1851), the first international temperance organization.

69 In addition to his instructional publications in *sol fa*, listed in *Grove's Dictionary*, fifth edn, vol. 5, p. 103, Curwen produced numerous other collections of material in both *sol fa* and staff notation, which are advertised in the programmes of the many popular meetings which used them: they do not appear to have been publicly listed.

70 See Robert Sandall and Arch R. Wiggins, *The History of the Salvation Army*, London (Nelson), 5 vols., 1947–68 (vols. 1–3 by Sandall, vols. 4–5 by Wiggins).

71 William Booth (1829–1912) took the title of 'General' of the Army and was its father figure; other members of his family prominent in the movement were: his wife Catherine (1829–90); their daughter Evangeline Booth (1862–1926) who worked in the temperance movement in America, and son Herbert Booth (1862–1926), who took the leading role in developing the music, first in the extensive provision for the 1890 meeting, the success of which was due to him. In this year was published his *Songs of Peace and War*, with original music, London (Salvation Army Printers and Publishers), 1890.

72 Brindley Boon, *Sing a Happy Song* (A History of Salvation Army Vocal Music), London (Salvation Army Publications and Supplies), 1978, p. 74.

73 Wiggins, *History of the Salvation Army*, vol. 4, p. 238.

74 Ibid., p. 307.

75 Ibid.

76 Brindley Boon, *Play the Music, Play*, London (1976), p. 196.

77 Wiggins, *History of the Salvation Army*, vol. 4, p. 238. At the conclusion

the Household Troops played Herbert Booth's 'Promoted to Glory' in memory of Catherine Booth (see Boon, *Play the Music, Play*, p. 196).

78 Ibid., p. 197.

79 The Chalk Farm Band under Punchard was the outstanding Salvation Army band of the period, later touring in Holland. George Bernard Shaw adversely compared general standards in symphony orchestras with theirs, commenting that 'in point of discipline, alertness and conscientiousness, all the bands are first-rate ... [because] the men are playing not for money but for the glory of God' (see Wiggins, *History of the Salvation Army*, vol. 5, p. 207).

80 Ibid., vol. 4, pp 240–302.

81 Boon, *Play the Music, Play*, p. 197.

82 Ibid.

83 Reported in *The Salvationist*, 29 November 1986, p. 14.

84 Charles Harriss (1862–1929): Canadian composer, impressario and organist, who, first in Canada, pioneered gala performances with the aim of stimulating ' music, commerce and patriotism throughout the Empire' (*Grove's Dictionary*, fifth edition, 1975, vol. 8, p. 257).

85 The British Empire Exhibition at Wembley in 1924–5 was designed to display the natural resources of the various countries within the Empire and the activities, industries and societies of their population. The Wembley stadium was built as part of the exhibition complex. The permanent relocation there of the Football Association Cup Final, which had been held at the Crystal Palace before the First World War (on the site of the south-west fountain basin – the site of the present International Athletics Stadium) is another example of the declining attraction of the Palace after the war. Later exhibition venues at Earl's Court and Olympia (1928) further eroded the Palace's function.

86 The co-operative movement dates from 1844 (see Trevelyan, *English Social History*, p. 546), well before the foundation of the Independent Labour Party and the Fabian Society. It developed a complex national organization in protection of workers' interests against those of retailers. The Crystal Palace was especially associated with its most important local organization, The Royal Arsenal Co-operative Society, Woolwich, whose meetings it hosted in the 1920s and 30s.

87 Advertised as 'Part of the Brotherhoods, Sisterhoods and Kindred Societies' (37, Norfolk St, W.C.) fellowship movements grew with the reform of education and the development of internationalist ideas in the early twentieth century, as expressed, for example, in the publication *Brotherhood: a magazine of faith, optimism and forward thinking for the reconstruction of souls and bodies into health and for the peaceful evolution of a juster and happier social order*, Welwyn Garden City (The Alpha Society), 1897–1932. The National Brotherhood Council, with the National Council of the Adult School Union, produced in 1909 *The Fellowship Handbook*, London (Headley Brown).

Bibliography

Arditi, L. *My Reminiscences*, compiled and edited with introduction and notes by Baroness von Zedlitz

Bache, C. *Brother Musicians*, London (Methuen), 1901

Bainbridge, C. *Brass Triumphant*, London (Frederick Muller), 1980

Barnett, J. F. *Musical Reminiscences and Impressions*, London (Hodder and Stoughton), 1906

Bartlett, I. J. 'An Historical View of Sol Fa', *Music Teacher*, 55/5, May 1976, pp. 9–11

Beale, T. W. *The Light of Other Days*, London (Bentley and Son), 1890

Beaver, P. *The Crystal Palace*, Chichester (Philimore), 1986

Beecham, T. *A Mingled Chime: Leaves from an Autobiography*, London, 1973

Berwick-Sayers, W. C. *Samuel Coleridge Taylor, Musician. His Life and Letters*, London (Augener), 1901

Bird, A. *Paxton's Palace*, London (Cassell), 1976

Bispham, D. *A Quaker Singer's Recollections*, New York (Macmillan), 1920

Bonten, A. *A Memoir* (privately printed) n.d.

Bowley, R. K. *An Account of the Arrangements for the Opening of the Crystal Palace at Sydenham* (MS), London, Royal College of Music

The Sacred Harmonic Society. A Thirty-Five Years' Retrospective, London (Sacred Harmonic Society), 1867

Brian, H. ed. M. MacDonald, *Havergal Brian on Music: Selections from his Journalism*, vol. 1, London (Toccata Press), 1986

Bridge, J. F. *A Westminster Pilgrim*, London (Novello) n.d.

Brown, J. and Stratton, S. *British Music Biography*, Birmingham (Stratton), 1897

Carse, A. *The Life of Jullien*, Cambridge (Heffer), 1951

Chadwick, G. F. *The Works of Joseph Paxton*, London (Architectural Press), 1981

Clapham, J. *Antonin Dvořák, Musician and Craftsman*, London (Faber and Faber), 1966

Colles, H. C. *Walford Davies* (Oxford University Press), 1942

The Crystal Palace, Sydenham [Auction Catalogue], London (Hudson and Kearns, printers), 1911

Crystal Palace; Musical Instruments and Memorials. London (Crystal Palace), 1900

Curwen, J. S. *Memorials of John Curwen*, London (Curwen), 1882
Davison, J. W. *From Mendelssohn to Wagner. Being the Memoirs of J. W. Davison*, London (Reeves), 1912
Edwards, F. G. 'Mr August Manns', *The Musical Times*, vol. 39, March, 1898, pp. 135–7
Edwards, F. G. 'Schubert's Music in England', *The Musical Times*, vol. 38 no. 648, February, 1897, pp. 81–4
Ehrlich, C. *The Music Profession in Britain Since the Eighteenth Century*, Oxford University Press, 1985
Elgar, E. *A Future for English Music and Other Essays*, London (Dennis Dobson), 1966
Forbes, E. *Mario and Grisi*, London (Gollancz), 1985
Foster, M. B. *The History of the Philharmonic Society of London 1813–1912*, London (The Bodley Head), 1912
Ganz, A. W. *Berlioz in London*, London (Quality Press), 1950
Ganzl, K. *British Musical Theatre*, 2 vols., London (Macmillan), 1986
Goode, C. T. *To the Crystal Palace*, Bracknell (Forge Books), 1984
Graves, C. L. *The Life of Sir George Grove*, London (Macmillan), 1903
The Great Exhibition, 1851: Official Descriptive and Illustrative Catalogue, 3 vols. and suppl., London (Spicer Bros, W. Clowes and Sons), 1851
Grove, G. *Beethoven and his Nine symphonies*, London (Novello), 1895
Grove's *Dictionary of Music and Musicians*, first edn, ed. G. Grove, *Grove's Dictionary of Music and Musicians*, second edn, ed. J. A. F. Maitland, London (Macmillan), 1904–22
Haweis, H. R. *Music and Morals*, London (Bogue), 1881
Hellborn, K. von. *Franz Schubert*, Vienna (Gerold) 1865: translated Coleridge, *The Life of Franz Schubert*, London (Longmans, Green), 1868
Herbage, J. *The Story of Handel's Messiah*, London (Max Parrish), 1948
Herbert, T. ed., Bands: *The Brass Band Movement in the 19th–20th Centuries* (Popular Music in Britain), Buckingham and Bristol, PA (Open University Press), 1991
Hollins, A. *A Blind Musician Looks Back*, London (Blackwood), 1936
Howes, F. *The English Musical Renaissance*, London (Oxford University Press), 1966
Hullah, J. *The Life of John Hullah by his Wife*, London (Longmans), 1886
Hurd, M. *Vincent Novello and Company*, London (Granada), 1981
Jacobs, A. *Arthur Sullivan: A Victorian Musician*, Oxford (Oxford University Press), 1986
Jones, M. G. *The Charity School Movement*, London (Cambridge University Press), 1938
Kennedy, M. *Portrait of Elgar*, Oxford (Oxford University Press), 1987
The Halle Tradition: A Century of Music, Manchester (Manchester University Press), 1960
Klein, H. *Thirty Years of Musical Life in London*, 1870–1900, London (Heinemann), 1903
Mackenzie, A. C. *A Musician's Narrative*, London (Cassell), 1927

Mackerness, J. L. *A Social History of Music*, London (Routledge, Kegan Paul), 1964

McDermott, E. *Routledge's Guide to the Crystal Palace and Park*, London (Routledge), 1854

Maine, B. *Elgar, His Life and Works*, London (Bell), 1933

Maitland, J. A. F. *A Doorkeeper of Music*, London (John Murray), 1929

Maitland, J. A. F. *English Music in the 19thC*, London (Grant Richards), 1902

Nettel, R. *The Orchestra in England: A Social History*, London (Cape), 1948

Northrop-Moore, J. *Edward Elgar, A Creative Life*, Oxford (Oxford University Press), 1984

Osborne, C. *The Music Monster*, London (Quartet), 1984

Phillips, S. *The Crystal Palace and Park*, London (Bradbury and Evans), 1854

Pohl, C. F. *Mozart and Haydn in London*, 2 vols, Vienna, 1867

Rainbow, B. *The Land without Music. Musical Education in England 1800–1860 and its continental antecedents*, London (Novello), 1967

Raynor, H. A. *Social History of Music since 1815*, London (Barrie and Jenkins), 1976

Reed C. *The Music Monster*, London (Quartet), 1984

Reed, W. H. *Elgar as I knew him*, London (Gollanz), 1936

Reeves, G. *Palace of the People* (Bromley Library Services), 1986

Russell, D. *Popular Music in England, 1840–1914: A Social History*, Manchester (Manchester University Press), 1987

Russell, J. F. and Elliot J. R. *The Brass Band Movement*, London (Dent), 1936

Sandall, R. *The History of the Salvation Army*, London (Nelson), 5 vols., 1947–1968 (vols. 1–3). See also under Wiggins A. R.

Santley, C. *Student and Singer*, London (Arnold), 1892
  Reminiscences of my Life, London (Pitman), 1909

Saxe Wyndham, H. *August Manns and the Saturday Concerts*, London/New York (Walter Scott), 1908

Scholes, P. A. *The Mirror of Music, 1844–1944*, London (Novello/Oxford University Press), 2 vols., 1947
  The Oxford Companion to Music, Oxford University Press, 1938

Shaw, G. B. *Shaw's Music*, ed. Dan H. Lawrence (The Bodley Head Bernard Shaw), London (The Bodley Head), 1981

Shinn, F. *Catalogue of the Principal Instrumental and Choral Works performed at the Saturday Concerts* (October 1855–May 1895), London, Crystal Palace (Evans) 1896: published with Shinn, F. *Forty Seasons of Saturday Concerts at the Crystal Palace: A Retrospect and an Appeal*, Sydenham

Smyth, E. *The Memoirs of Ethel Smyth*, abridged and introduced by R. Crichton, Harmondsworth (Viking), 1987

Soldene, E. *My Theatrical and Musical Recollections*, London (Downey), 1897

Stanford, C. V. *Interludes, Records and Reflections*, London (Cassell), 1922
  Studies and Memories, London (Constable), 1908

Pages from an Unwritten Diary, London (Constable), 1914
Sullivan, H. and N. Flower, *Sir Arthur Sullivan*, London (Cassell) n.d.
Taylor, A. B. *Brass Bands*, London (Granada), 1979
Thistlethwaite, N. *The Making of the Victorian Organ* (Cambridge Musical Texts and Monographs), 1990
Trevelyan, G. M. *English Social History*, London (Longmans Green), 1942
Walker, E. 'An Orchestra of the Past' in *Free Thought and the Musician and Other Essays*, London (Oxford University Press), n.d.
 Music In England, London (Oxford University Press), 1936
Warwick, A. R. *The Phoenix Suburb*, London (Blue Boar Press), 1972
Weber, W. *Music and the Middle Classes*, London (Croom Helm), 1975
 The Rise of Musical Classics in 18th-Century England, Oxford (Clarendon), 1992
Wiggins, A. R. *The History of the Salvation Army*, 5 vols. (vols. 4 and 5), London (Nelson), 1947–1968. See also under Sandall
Wolfson, J. *Sullivan and the Scott Russells*, Chichester (Pack Publishing), 1984
Wood, H. *My Life of Music*, London (Gollancz), 1938
Young, K. *Music's Great Days in the Spas and Watering Places*, London (Macmillan), 1948

Periodicals

The Illustrated London News
Macmillans Magazine
Musical Opinion
The Musical Standard
The Musical Times
The Musical World
Pall Mall Gazette
Punch
The Saturday Review
The Sunday Times
The Times

Index

Of the numerous composers and performers associated with the Crystal Palace, only the most prominent, or those with special connections with it, are indexed here. For detailed reference to composers see Part 3, chapter 6, pp. 95–116; and to performers Part 3, chapter 6, pp. 86–95. Names listed in the appendixes and notes are not reproduced here unless they also appear in the main text.